JAPANESE BLUE COLLAR

THE CHANGING TRADITION

JAPANESE
BLUE
COLLAR

THE CHANGING TRADITION

ROBERT E. COLE

UNIVERSITY OF CALIFORNIA PRESS
BERKELEY LOS ANGELES LONDON 1971

University of California Press
Berkeley and Los Angeles, California
University of California Press, Ltd.
London, England
Copyright © 1971, by The Regents of the University of California
Library of Congress Catalog Card Number: 77-107656
International Standard Book Number 0-520-01681-5
Printed in the United States of America

To my patient parents

PREFACE

In a study of this nature, it becomes almost impossible to assign priorities of indebtedness. Without any one of many links combined with a series of chance occurrences this research would not have been completed. The series of events leading to my entry into two Japanese companies required the cooperation and encouragement of a great many people. I would particularly like to mention the financial support given by the Keio-Illinois project sponsored by the Ford Foundation; the assistance of the Institute of Labor and Industrial Relations at the University of Illinois under Directors Martin Wagner and Melvin Rothbaum, and the typing of the manuscript under the supervision of Anice Duncan; the help given me by the members of the Institute of Management and Labour Studies at Keio University under former Managing Director Minemura Teruo and Associate Director Kawada Hisashi, and the cooperation of the Japan Institute of Labour and its staff under President Nakayama Ichirō, former Managing Director Kaite Shingo and Senior Researcher Shirai Taishirō.[1] I am indebted to the Center for Japanese Studies and the Institute of Labor and Industrial Relations at the University of Michigan for providing financial support for the summer of 1968, at which time extensive revisions were made in the manuscript.

Of utmost importance to my research plans were the actions of the managements of both firms studied. They not only permitted me to enter the plants but their cooperation with my research was critical to its success.

1. Japanese names are written with the family names first as is the custom in Japan.

I owe a special debt to Okamoto Hideaki of Tokyo Metropolitan University, who tolerated my endless questions and was a source of great intellectual stimulation. On the American side, Professors Bernard Karsh and Solomon Levine encouraged this research, made its realization possible, and gave me the benefit of their experience and insights into Japanese society.

Were I to limit my statement of indebtedness to one party, it would have to be to the Japanese workers who willingly accepted me and gave of their time and knowledge to teach an ignorant foreigner about a very different world from the one to which he was accustomed. I thank them for making the time spent together lead not only to the completion of a research project but to a meaningful human experience that shall remain indelibly impressed upon my memory.

My wife Ingrid endured, sometimes laughing sometimes crying, four eventful years. Somehow during these four years she found time to bear two children and give me the encouragement and advice I needed.

R.E.C.

CONTENTS

TABLES

Industrial man develops new patterns of relations different from those of tribal members and chieftain, serf and lord of the manor, craftsman and merchant prince, or even worker and capitalist. These relations are more varied and more complex than in preexisting societies. Industrial man leads a new kind of life and, in the course of it, becomes a new kind of person. He views himself and others, society, and the universe in new ways. The old ideologies and the old theories lose their meaning.

> Clark Kerr *et al.*
> Industrialism and Industrial Man

Men make their own history, but they do not make it just as they please; they do not make it under circumstances chosen by themselves, but under circumstances directly encountered, given, and transmitted from the past. The tradition of all the dead generations weighs like a nightmare on the brain of the living.

> Karl Marx
> The Eighteenth Brumaire of Louis Bonaparte

All developed countries exemplify a more or less viable symbiosis between their traditional social structures and the consequences of industrialization.

> Reinhard Bendix
> Nation-Building and Citizenship

INTRODUCTION

A British poet sees the paternalistic employer-employee relationship in Japan as idyllic in its harmony. A Western businessman complains about unfair competition from cheap Japanese labor. An American congressman includes Japanese workers among the nameless "Asian hordes." An American labor official denounces Japanese workers and their major union organizations as "communistic." A Western European Socialist condemns Japanese labor organizations as ineffectual company unions and deplores the exploitation of the workers. An American journalist writes that Japanese workers are happily secure in their knowledge that they will never be fired. A Western scholar sees Japanese workers driven by some mystical Oriental need to work hard out of a sense of shame, duty, and group loyalty. A Swedish industrialist is impressed by the diligence of Japanese blue-collar workers. A West German economist points to the low per capita productivity of Japanese workers.

These are some of the contrasting Western images of the Japanese blue-collar worker. Despite their diversity, most of them have the same sources: sensational newspaper accounts or conversations with Japanese management personnel.[1]

1. Western social scientists inevitably rely upon the works of Ruth Benedict and James Abegglen as their sources on the Japanese worker. Yet Benedict's penetrating work is primarily a prewar study that does not consider the momentous changes of the postwar period, and it makes no special reference to workers. Abegglen's book is a study of the Japanese factory but relies almost entirely on management sources. See Ruth Benedict, *The Chrysanthemum and the Sword* (Boston: Houghton Mifflin, 1946) and James Abegglen, *The Japanese Factory* (Glencoe: Free Press, 1958).

SIGNS OF THE TIMES

The popular image of Japan as the land of geishas, rickshaws, cheap toys, and cherry blossoms is giving way to a more sophisticated understanding. The isolated, overpopulated Japan of the early nineteenth century has today become the third-largest steel producer in the world, exceeded only by the United States and the Soviet Union, one fact among many which has compelled a restructuring of images and stirs our imagination. Yet, despite the increasing understanding, Western knowledge of the Japanese blue-collar worker remains remarkably superficial. Since blue-collar labor has been indispensable to the success of Japanese industrialization, that industrialization process cannot be understood without an understanding of the Japanese blue-collar worker. It was in an effort to achieve such understanding that the present research was undertaken. The research is based on case studies of blue-collar workers in two Japanese companies: a diecast firm and an auto parts company.

Despite rapid economic growth, a high level of industrialization, and an increasingly modern employment structure, Japanese per capita national income remains low. The high population density and the low per capita productivity of many sectors keep Japan's per capita income low. She ranked twenty-first among the nations of the world in 1966 ($818) and moved to the sixteenth position in 1969 ($1,289).[2] Despite impressive increases in real wages almost every year in the past decade, heavy inflationary pressures have introduced a growing element of instability into the livelihood of the worker. Consumer prices rose an average of 7.4 percent annually from 1960 to 1968. The rate of increase in consumer prices from 1960 to 1966 was roughly four times that of the United States and twice those of Britain and Germany.[3] The burden of taxation, which is not taken into

2. This figure is based on the official exchange rate of 360 yen to the dollar. This rate can only be used as a rough guide, however, because the purchasing power of the yen for consumer goods and services is considerably higher than the official exchange rate would indicate.

3. Office of the Prime Minister, *Survey of Family Budgets for Calendar 1965* (Tokyo: The Office, Bureau of Statistics, 1966).

consideration when real wages are computed, doubled between 1960 and 1967. Workers in general, and especially those in small and medium-sized firms, find themselves in a difficult economic and social position.

Housing is a chronic problem, particularly for urban blue-collar workers. Many of them live in small, one-room apartments. In Tokyo, for example, where one out of every ten Japanese lives, 29 percent of the households faced "housing difficulties" in 1963 according to a government agency. Households were classified as facing difficulties if they were confined to less space per person than 2.5 mats (45 square feet), if they were housed together with another household, or if they were housed in buildings other than dwellings. When these households are added to those defined by the agency as "exceedingly cramped," they total 757,000; this means that 35 percent of all the families in Tokyo are inadequately housed. In Japan the middle- and upper-income groups have greater access to inexpensive company and public housing. As a result, large numbers of moderate- and low-income families are concentrated in comparatively low-grade private rental houses or in high-rent rooms.[4]

The inadequacy of housing reflects the failure of social spending to keep pace with the high rate of economic growth. The ratio of social overhead capital stock to the gross national product (in real terms) fell from 1.02 in the fiscal year 1955 to .87 in 1965.[5] This has meant an increase in what the Japanese call "public hazards": air and river pollution, urban overcrowding, inadequate sewers, and congested traffic. Blue-collar workers, concentrated in urban centers and lacking the financial resources to buy themselves out, suffer the brunt of the deteriorating living environment.

Japan's economy is still basically a production-oriented economy of scarcity, and the corresponding psychology is deeply imprinted on the minds of the Japanese. This psychology is reflected in worker-employer relations and serves

4. Economic Planning Agency, *Economic Survey of Japan* (1964–65) (Tokyo: The Japan Times, 1966), pp. 99–105. In six leading prefectures, 23.4 percent of the households faced housing difficulty in 1963.

5. *Ibid.* (1967–68), pp. 141–143.

as a major support for traditional values and structures. Management uses these values to justify holding down wages. Although the signs of an emerging mass-consumption society are becoming more evident, those values and practices which emphasize scarcity persist. Japan's dearth of natural resources has forced the people to raise themselves from poverty by their own collective will and little else. Reminders of this struggle are everywhere: ricefields reclaimed from precarious mountainsides; kimonos cut without wasting the slightest bit of cloth; the ceaseless rush of urban commuters.

Still, the changes are evident. Television spreads the vision of what is possible, and aspirations rise. The term "rising aspirations" may not yet apply to blue-collar workers in some countries but it certainly does in Japan. The standard of living steadily increases, and some economists now anticipate wage levels approaching those of France and Italy. Real wages in all Japanese industries rose 42.8 percent from 1955 to 1961 and 35 percent from 1960 to 1967.[6] The high rate of economic growth is the key factor in Japan's development from a production-oriented society of scarcity to a consumption-oriented society of abundance. The May Day "We Want Food" demonstrations of the early postwar period have been replaced by marches of well-dressed workers holding a child in one hand and a new camera in the other. On May Day 1966, one male worker expressed something of the new tone with a placard reading, "May Day is swinging, baby, when I walk with you." [7] Blue-collar workers, like other Japanese, are eating better, living better, and enjoying more leisure. Statistics on the numbers of household appliances become outdated almost as soon as they are published.[8] The

6. Minobe Ryokichi, "People's Living after Economic Growth," *Contemporary Japan*, Vol. 28, No. 3 (May 1966), p. 534. Japan Institute of Labour, *Japan Labor Bulletin*, Vol. 6, No. 12 (December 1967), p. 1.

7. *Shiawase da na. Boku wa kimi to aruite iru toki ga suki.* I have tried to capture the feelings and intentions of workers' words and make them understandable to a Western audience rather than relying on literal translations. At times, this may risk imparting a consciousness to Japanese workers not present in Japanese culture.

8. Surveys of the distribution of household appliances in nonagricultural households in 1960 reported that the only major appliance owned by over 70 percent of the households was the radio. By 1969, there was added

psychology of scarcity as a management ploy is becoming less successful in restraining worker demands for higher wages. While management appeals for worker-management cooperation to make its goods competitive in both foreign and domestic markets, the unions increasingly call for the "European wage."

Japan, with a real economic growth rate averaging 10 percent annually during the past ten years, has reached the level of the top-ranking industrial nations. In terms of productivity as measured by gross national product, Japan now ranks third in the world, having surpassed England, France, and West Germany between the years 1965 and 1968. This enormous growth has brought about great changes in the employment structure. Employment in agriculture has dropped dramatically from 40 percent of the total working population in 1955 to less than 20 percent in 1967. Young men and women have deserted the farms and crowded into the bursting cities in search of a better life in the factories, offices, and stores. The striking urbanization of Japan is evident in the growing proportion of the population living in cities; it rose from 10 percent in 1889, to 38 percent in 1950, to 68 percent in 1965.[9]

Table 1 provides an occupational breakdown of paid employees in the nonagricultural Japanese labor force of 27,830,000. We may make a rough estimate of the total number of blue-collar workers by adding up the entries under the last five headings: workers in mining and quarrying, workers in transportation and communication, craftsmen and production process workers, laborers, and service workers. According to this estimate, blue-collar workers total 15,400,000—55.3 percent of all paid nonagricultural employees or 32.4 percent of the total Japanese labor force of 47,870,000.[10] If we look only

to the list sewing machines, television sets, electric washing machines, electric refrigerators, fans, kerosene stoves, and electric cleaners. *Economic Survey of Japan* (1968–1969), p. 133.

9. Institute of Population Problems, *Jinkō Mondai ni Tsuite no Omona Sūji* (Principal Figures on the Population Question) (Tokyo: Ministry of Health and Welfare, No. 15), (May 1968).

10. These percentages would be even higher if self-employed and unpaid family members were included. The craftsman and production process

at manufacturing, the key productive sector in an industrial economy, in 1964, blue-collar workers made up 78.6 percent of all employees, with the remainder being white-collar employees.[11]

TABLE 1

Paid Employees in Nonagricultural Industries
By Occupation
(Average for 1965)

Occupation	Number of workers (in millions)	Percent of total
Professional and technical workers	2.02	7.3
Managers and officials	1.16	4.2
Clerical and related workers	6.29	22.6
Sales workers	2.38	8.6
Farmers, lumbermen, and fishermen	.59	2.1
Workers in mining and quarrying	.20	.7
Workers in transportation and communication	1.84	6.6
Craftsmen and production process workers	8.82	31.7
Laborers	2.22	8.0
Service workers	2.32	8.3
TOTAL	27.84	100.1 [a]

SOURCE: Office of the Prime Minister, Rōdōryoku Chōsa Hōkoku (Annual Report on the Labor Force Survey), (Tokyo: The Office, 1966), pp. 76–77.
[a] Differs from 100 percent because of rounding.

Because of their increasing numbers, blue-collar workers have become an important group, one to be courted by politicians and by firms serving the growing domestic market. As the patterns of employment change, parochial values and traditional society begin to loosen.

category alone includes an additional 2,250,000 self-employed and almost 1,000,000 unpaid family workers. The unusually large number of self-employed workers and unpaid family members testifies to the key role played by smaller firms. For comparative purposes, it may be noted that blue-collar workers totaled about 36 percent of all employed persons in the United States in 1968.

11. Ministry of Labor, Chingin Kōzō Kihon Chōsa (Wage Structure Basic Survey), (Tokyo: The Ministry, 1964).

INDUSTRIALIZATION AND TRADITION

Throughout the world the relationship of industrialization to traditional values and social structures has concerned both social scientists and policy makers in recent years. This interest in social process has accompanied the increased economic development of the "Third World." Let us first try to reach a working definition of "tradition," a word used ambiguously and indiscriminately by many writers on the subject.[12] For some, it is simply a synonym for values and behavior that existed in "the past"—whether five or five hundred years ago—and have been carried over to the present. Others have sought refuge in simplified classifications such as "tradition" versus "modernity." Accompanying attributes of each type are specified, and the two polar opposites are seen as mutually exclusive. Such an approach ignores the dialectic that actually operates between these generalized pairs to produce change. Depending on a person's political philosophy, the word "tradition" may evoke positive or negative connotations. Generally, in the West the radical view has seen tradition as exploitative, while the conservative view has seen it as protective. In Japan, also, political considerations have molded the concept of tradition. Most Japanese intellectuals equate tradition in social, political or economic behavior with feudalism; tradition, in this view, is something bad that must be rooted out to build a modern society. These intellectuals criticize Western scholars for their emphasis on the positive aspects of traditional values and practice in modern Japan. Western scholars have, in fact, been interested in the strength of tradition as part of the explanation for Japan's success in industrialization and for the absence of strong revolutionary currents. Often, however, this bias has led them to gloss over the link between Japanese industrial success and the rise of fascism. For the Japanese, the two are inextricably

12. For a treatment of the myths associated with the concept of tradition see Joseph Gusfield, "Tradition and Modernity: Misplaced Polarities in the Study of Social Change," The American Journal of Sociology, Vol. 72, No. 4 (January 1967), pp. 351–362.

related and therefore Japanese industrialization cannot be considered a "success." Rather, Japanese intellectuals believe that emphasis on the "smoothing" role of tradition leads Western scholars to overlook the conflict, exploitation, suffering, and dislocation that occurred during Japanese industrialization.

In the following pages tradition is understood as the legacy of preindustrial values or patterns of behavior (social structure) found in industrial society. It is important to separate values and behavior patterns because it is possible for only one to provide the link between past and present. This study will examine the extent to which traditional forces persist through the more advanced levels of industrialization and will give particular attention to the role of tradition in governing the behavior of contemporary blue-collar workers. It will be important to distinguish tradition-based ideology from tradition-based behavior. Objectively, the persistence of preindustrial values or social structure is neither good nor bad but poses empirical questions about the role these patterns play in advanced industrial society.

In examining the role of tradition, this study should provide some data for assessing the validity of the much discussed convergence theory. This theory, which has found expression in a variety of popular versions, was formally introduced to industrial and labor relations research through the work of Clark Kerr and his associates.[13] Kerr suggests that the technology common to industrializing societies generates increasingly uniform patterns of bureaucracy and rationality and growing individualism. The inexorable result is that industrial societies become more alike than different, and unique national identities play a more and more restricted role in determining behavioral patterns. According to Kerr, tradition is inimical to the requirements of an industrial so-

13. Clark Kerr *et al., Industrialism and Industrial Man* (Cambridge: Harvard University Press, 1960). The essence of the convergence theory may be seen in the earlier work of Thorstein Veblen. He advanced the view that machine technology had a coercive character and generated a materialistic matter-of-fact skepticism in the population. Thorstein Veblen, *The Theory of Business Enterprise* (New York: Scribner's, 1915), pp. 302–373.

ciety. This perspective is closely related to the sociologists' usage of the pattern variables set forth by Talcott Parsons. Social roles in industrial societies are seen as syntheses of the following attributes: affective neutrality (norms calling for the non-expression of feeling), specificity (expressly limited obligations), universalism (obligations irrespective of the social status of the other), achievement (concern with performance), and self-orientation (norms calling for satisfaction of self-interests). These role attributes reduce the scope of the alternative criteria of affectivity, diffuseness, particularism, ascription, and collectivity-orientations that predominate in traditional societies.[14]

According to another view advanced by Reinhard Bendix and others, tradition and modernity coexist in industrial societies.[15] Tradition, according to this view, is not a fixed element characteristic to nonindustrial societies; nor can its course be logged and its future charted as a simple response to the "logic of industrialization." Rather, the meaning of tradition can only be understood in terms of its historical context. To determine the scope of tradition in an industrial society such as Japan requires an examination of the preindustrial social structure and value system as well as the historical availability of a stock of transnational social and technological knowledge.

An understanding of worker behavior and attitudes is important for evaluating the convergence theory. Convergence in the sense of growing similarities among industrial nations does not in itself confirm convergence theory. Convergence theory is based on the premise that these growing similarities arise out of the pressures created by common technologies. There are, however, alternative explanations for convergence. One such explanation, for example, attributes the growing similarities to the diffusion of cultural practices made possible by the great expansion of international com-

14. See Talcott Parsons, *The Social System* (New York: Free Press, 1951), pp. 51–67.
15. See Reinhard Bendix, "Tradition and Modernity Reconsidered," *Comparative Studies in Society and History*, Vol. 9, No. 3 (April 1967), pp. 292–346.

munication networks. These conflicting explanations under-
line the importance of specifying the causal factors leading
to convergence. Consequently, whenever convergence between Japanese and Western factory practices was apparent,
I tried to examine its sources.

The way in which rewards are distributed in factories
provides an important means of evaluating the convergence
theory. If a worker is promoted or given a wage increase because of his high productivity, then the operative criteria are:
affective neutrality, functional specificity, universalism and
achievement. If he is rewarded because he is the superior's
nephew or an Irishman like he, then the operative criteria
may involve affectivity, functional diffuseness, ascription, and
particularism. Between these two extremes, however, are a
number of bases for distributing rewards that reflect "mixed
criteria." For example, promotion on the basis of the ascriptive quality of age may, in fact, also be based on the training
and experience one accumulates with age, thereby reflecting
achievement criteria. It has been commonly thought, and is
specifically postulated in the convergence theory, that achievement and universalistic orientations, with their emphasis on
rewarding merit regardless of status, become dominant in
successfully industrialized societies. The Bendix position,
however, suggests that traditional practices and ideology may
be interwoven with achievement and universalistic orientations. The applicability of these contrasting predictions will
be examined in the light of how the reward system operated
in the two firms studied.

Westerners know a great deal more about Japanese unions and company policies than they do about Japanese workers.[16] We know about the existence of "paternalism" in the
Japanese firm but understand little of what paternalism means
on the level of interpersonal relationships in the plant. The
Western view of Japanese company paternalism is based upon

16. For a treatment of Japanese trade unions, see Solomon B. Levine,
Industrial Relations in Postwar Japan (Urbana: University of Illinois Press,
1958) and Alice Cook, *Introduction to Japanese Trade Unionism* (New York
State School of Industrial and Labor Relations, Ithaca: Cornell University,
1966). For an analysis of company policy and ideology see Abegglen, *op. cit.*
and M. Y. Yoshino, *Japan's Managerial System* (Cambridge: The MIT
Press, 1968).

notions about hierarchy, traditional authority patterns and group loyalties. One consideration of this study, however, will be the extent to which paternalism may be attributed to specific labor-market situations.

As an object lesson with specific application to developing countries, the Japanese experience is probably of limited value, for at least two obvious reasons. First, the historical period during which Japan industrialized had unique characteristics which can never be repeated for the benefit of presently industrializing countries. Second, the unusual racial homogeneity and sense of nationhood among the Japanese is rarely found in developing nations.

This study was designed to present an accurate picture of the blue-collar worker's world and behavior. It is above all an empirical study, which seeks to observe and interpret the everyday activities and thoughts of those workers. This cannot but increase our knowledge of the possible range of human thought, inventiveness, and institutional arrangements.

CULTURAL UNIQUENESS

The average Japanese is delighted when Westerners refer to Japanese society and its institutions as "unique." This has been the customary interpretation of many Western social scientists, particularly cultural anthropologists and historians, who until recently have been the most prominent of Japan's interpreters in the West.[17] The work of Ruth Benedict is probably the most representative of this view, with its stereotype of the putative Japanese tradition.[18] The conclusions one draws from this point of view are diametrically opposed to those of the convergence theorists. Together, the two interpretations constitute the Scylla and Charybdis between which the researcher must navigate if he is to achieve a balanced understanding of the Japanese worker today.

More recently, social scientists have gained new insights

17. Abegglen's *The Japanese Factory* is typical of this approach. Tominaga Ken'ichi has presented a biting critique of such efforts in "Some Sociological Comments on Observations of Japanese Society by Western Social Scientists," paper presented at the University of Michigan, Center for Japanese Studies, Ann Arbor, November 1968.
18. Benedict, *op. cit.*

into industrial relations systems by viewing their features not as unique but as functional equivalents, variations, and exaggerations of tendencies common to all industrial societies. By functional equivalents we mean that differing behavioral patterns and institutional arrangements may have common functional outcomes. This approach is basic to comparative social science.[19] It represents an attempt to bridge the gap between convergence theory and explanations based on historical uniqueness. But in Japan the view persists that Japanese industrial relations, like other Japanese cultural institutions, are unique. This sense of cultural uniqueness derives from centuries of isolation and from the unusual racial homogeneity of the Japanese; it was fortified by prewar and wartime nationalistic propaganda. Although the World War II defeat and the postwar reforms did much to remove the grounds for such a view, the view itself has persisted. It is particularly strong among management people and, to a lesser extent, among scholars in the social sciences. Even Japanese Marxist scholars often claim to have evoked a unique Marxism adapted to Japanese socio-economic conditions.

It is hoped that future researchers into the relationship between Japanese tradition and contemporary industrial relations will find in this study a bench mark, an empirical graph of the role of tradition in Japan today. Because such bench marks have been lacking in the past, researchers often report social change in relation to an allegedly traditional set of social practices that have never in fact been confirmed.

THE FIRM AS CORPORATE GROUP

Many researchers have compared the Japanese firm to the family unit, an analogy which has also been promoted by Japanese management.[20] Too often taken literally, this analogy diverts the observer from the actual relationships within the Japanese firm. A more accurate analogy, and one without the affective connotations of "family," would be to the semi-

19. Reinhard Bendix, "Concepts and Generalization in Comparative Sociological Studies," *American Sociological Review*, Vol. 28, No. 4 (August 1963), pp. 532–539.

20. For example, see Robert Ballon, *Japan's Life-Time Salary System*, Bulletin No. 11, Sophia University Socio-Economic Institute, Tokyo, 1966.

closed corporate group. The corporate-group analogy stresses boundaries, the exclusiveness of the firm; the importance of the place where one belongs rather than what one is and does. An unusually strong unity prevails in the firm, both internally and vis-à-vis the outside world.[21] This feeling of unity means that consciousness of occupation—job characteristics that are transferable among employers—is rather weakly developed in Japan.

One of the first things I found remarkable about the diecast workers was that they associated only among themselves during the lunch recess, despite the plant's location in a crowded factory area. They knew none of the workers in the factory across the narrow street although for years they had been having baseball catches side by side at noon. Ezra Vogel points to the same phenomenon when he writes:

> The basic cleavages in Japanese society have not been between different social classes but between one corporate group (composed of people at different social positions) and other corporate groups. The strong commitment of an individual to his group has not been conducive to the smooth integration of groups in the wider society, but it has been conducive to a very high degree of solidarity and conformity within any single group.[22]

As the number of Japanese employees increases with economic growth, the business firm assumes ever greater importance as a social unit. The strength of these corporate

21. An article by the social anthropologist Nakane Chie, which attracted much attention among Japanese interested in industrial relations, was especially helpful in clarifying my thoughts on this subject. Nakane Chie, "Nihon-teki Shakai Kōzō no Hakken: Tan'itsu Shakai no Riron" (An Approach to the Social Structure of Japan: Theory of a Unitary Society), *Chūō Kōron* (Central Review), Vol. 79, No. 5 (May 1964), pp. 48–85. An adapted English version has since been published: Nakane Chie, "Towards a Theory of Japanese Social Structure: An Unilateral Society," *The Economic Weekly* (Bombay), Vol. 17 (February 1965). The original article has since become the basis for Nakane Chie's widely discussed book, *Tate Shakai no Ningen Kankei: Tan'itsu Shakai no Riron* (Human Relations in a Vertical Society: Theory of a Unitary Society) (Tokyo: Kōdansha, 1967; English translation: Berkeley and Los Angeles: University of California Press, 1970).

22. Ezra Vogel, "Kinship Structure, Migration to the City, and Modernization," in Ronald Dore (ed.), *Aspects of Social Change in Modern Japan* (Princeton: Princeton University Press, 1967), p. 108.

groups has, no doubt, discouraged the smooth integration of the wider society, as Ezra Vogel suggests. But for the individual the corporate group has served as an important linking mechanism in Japanese society. The individual can rely on his experiences in one corporate group to tell him what to expect in seeking and gaining entrance to other corporate groups. The corporate group, characterized by exclusiveness and loyalty, is a common structural element of Japanese institutions—a mode of integration for the individual that contributes both to developing his identity and his socialization.[23]

Historically speaking, the business firm is a relatively new innovation in Japan. The exclusiveness of social groups is not. We can clearly identify this group spirit as a characteristic of Japanese social structure at least as far back as the sixteenth century, which saw the full flowering of feudalism in Japan. At that time, the politically decentralized government allowed the absolute rule of local magnates over their subjects. The followers of these local rulers were closely clustered around them in compact territorial units. The *daimyo* wielded absolute power over his vassals and in turn guaranteed them their fiefs.[24] But Japanese group consciousness goes back to the even more distant past. Strong clan-like social organization seems to have been a persistent feature throughout Japan's history. It is for this reason, John Hall suggests, that the leader-follower relation has so often been expressed in terms of paternalism and familism.[25]

Unlike some Japanese scholars—Nakane Chie for example—I do not think it is sufficient to emphasize Japan's retention of its "vertical tradition." [26] Much of this book is devoted to comparing Japan's corporate commitments with those of other industrial societies and to exploring the kinds

23. The ideas in this paragraph are an elaboration and a selective adaptation to Japan of theories presented in S. N. Eisenstadt, *From Generation to Generation* (New York: Free Press, 1956) and in H. H. Gerth and C. Wright Mills, *Character and Social Structure: The Psychology of Social Institutions* (New York: Harcourt, Brace, 1953).

24. John Hall, "Feudalism in Japan: A Reassessment," *Comparative Studies in Society and History*, Vol. 5, No. 1 (October 1962), p. 44.

25. *Ibid.*, p. 50.

26. Nakane Chie, *op. cit.*

of economic and cultural variables that strengthen or weaken Japanese corporate group consciousness. The need for security is universal among workers. Different societies develop different institutional arrangements in their efforts to satisfy that need. This, then, is a book about the kinds of institutional and interpersonal commitments Japanese workers have and their consequences.

CHAPTER I

THE FRAMEWORK OF NATIONAL POWER, LEGISLATION, AND THE ECONOMY

Industrialization produces a complex of interrelations among managers, workers, and government agencies.[1] This industrial relations system is conditioned by the distribution of power in the larger society and by the prestige, position, and access to power of the various groups within the industrial relations system itself. The relations among these groups are further constrained by the nature of the market in which they operate. In Japan, to a great extent, the nature of the market is in turn determined by what is called the "dual economic structure." To provide a general framework for the materials presented in the following chapters, Chapter I will deal with the questions of blue-collar access to power, labor legislation, and the nature of market constraints as embodied in the dual economic structure.

POLITICAL POWER AND THE WORKERS

The critical turning point in the access of Japanese blue-collar workers to political power on the national level came with the defeat of Japan in World War II. In the prewar

1. The framework used in this chapter relies on the theoretical orientation presented by John Dunlop in his book, *Industrial Relations Systems* (New York: Henry Holt, 1958). His approach, however, has been modified to suit the purposes of this research.

period, blue-collar workers had no direct access to political power. During the "liberal period" of the 1920s some ameliorative labor legislation was passed, which indicates that the workers had developed some indirect access to political power, but in terms of practical effects blue-collar workers remained largely subject to the arbitrary will of employers in a paternalistic order. Moreover, those signs of growth in the labor movement which saw the formation and development of The Friendly Society (Yūaikai) in 1912 gradually disappeared as the Society disintegrated under heavy government and management pressure into an impotent splintering of left-wing radical organizations.

Following World War II, with the employer class in almost complete disarray, the Supreme Commander for the Allied Powers (SCAP) provided the initiative for the enactment of legislation that would further the rights of workers and encourage the formation of labor unions. Insofar as the Occupation policies were designed to "democratize" Japan, they indirectly gave blue-collar workers access to power on the national level. For the first time in Japanese history political power was being consciously used to bring about social justice with the interests of the working class rather than the ruling class as the objective. Among the most notable legislation imposed by SCAP in this period was the Trade Union Law (1945) and the Labor Standards Law (1947). The Trade Union Law, partially modeled after the American Wagner Act, guaranteed the rights to organize, to bargain collectively, and to strike, and provided corrections for anti-union discrimination. The Labor Standards Law, embodying the principal conventions of the International Labor Organization, established minimum working conditions for both union and nonunion workers.

Union membership soared; by June 1948 there were some 6,500,000 union members. After initial fluctuations, union membership stabilized at between 33 and 36 percent of the total Japanese work force. From the beginning, the postwar labor unions reflected many of the political divisions that had existed in the prewar period. Two major federations emerged: the General Federation of Labor (Sōdōmei) represented right-wing socialist unionism, and the Congress of Industrial Unions (Sanbetsu) represented left-wing socialist unionism. Sanbetsu came increasingly under Communist domination. In 1950 a large part of the Sōdōmei membership combined with some elements of the disintegrating Sanbetsu to form the General Council of Japanese Trade Unions (Sōhyō). Sōhyō remains today the largest labor union federation in Japan, with 4,250,000 members. It provides the major financial and organizational support for the Social Democratic Party of Japan (Shakaitō). (The Social Democratic party is referred to below as the Socialist party.) Right-wing socialist elements, however, left Sōhyō in 1954 and in 1964 combined with the remaining Sōdōmei group to form the General Confederation of Japanese Labor Organizations (Dōmei). The withdrawal reflected right-wing Socialist criticism of what was termed Sōhyō's ultra-left orientation and its emphasis on political rather than economic priorities.[2]

Dōmei, with almost 2,000,000 members, mostly in the private sector, is the major support for the moderate Democratic Socialist Party (Minshatō). The other major labor organization is the Federation of Independent Unions (Chūritsurōren), with 1,000,000 members, which tends to align itself with Sōhyō.

The postwar Socialist Party (JSP) was launched in 1945 and included all the divergent factions that had been split into different parties during the prewar era.[3] In the same year the first legal Japanese Communist party (Kyōsantō) was successfully established. As the workers' party, the So-

2. In recent years, there appeared to be a trend in which Sōhyō was minimizing its extensive political activities in favor of securing economic gains. But the international situation, particularly the Vietnam war, and internal considerations seem to have arrested any such major changes, at least for the time being.

3. The sources for this account of the development of the Socialist Party are: Robert Scalapino and Masumi Junnosuke, *Parties and Politics in Contemporary Japan* (Berkeley and Los Angeles: University of California Press, 1962) and Allan B. Cole, et al., *Socialist Parties in Postwar Japan* (New Haven: Yale University Press, 1966). For a comprehensive work on the social democratic movement in prewar Japan, see George Totten, *The Social Democratic Movement in Prewar Japan* (New Haven: Yale University Press, 1966).

cialist party became important in Japanese postwar politics. It achieved a brief taste of power in the coalition governments of 1947–1948, but for variety of reasons the coalition was a failure. Scalapino and Masumi point out that "the major reforms of the American Occupation were engineered while Japanese conservatives held all major offices, whereas the advent of the Japanese Socialists to high office coincided with the Occupation's shift from reform to rehabilitation. Thus, as the conservatives had been forced to execute radical reforms, the Socialists were forced to effect retreat, retrenchment, and austerity."

The Socialist party has consistently been a minority party in the postwar period, never supported by more than one-third of the voting electorate. They polled 27.9 percent of the popular vote and won 140 of the 469 seats in the all important lower house in the 1967 election. The commanding dominance of the conservative Liberal-Democratic Party (LDP) led Scalapino and Masumi in their study of the subject to refer to the Japanese "one-and-one-half party system." [4] Sōhyō, the left-wing union federation, has not only been the major support of the Socialist Party but has exercised considerable control within the party. Although there is a wide divergence among left- and right-wing factions, the Socialist party has for the most part maintained a Marxist viewpoint tempered with neutralism. The stagnation of the Socialist party in recent years is commonly attributed to its excessive reliance on the unions for electoral support and its consequent failure to build up an independent party membership and structure. A second factor is the high priority the Socialists assign to ideology and their failure to develop programs to deal with the bread-and-butter issues that concern voters.

The Communist Party (JCP) has been a rather negligible factor in voter behavior since the Party reached its peak with 10 percent of the vote in 1949. In 1967, the JCP polled 4.8 percent of the popular vote and secured five seats in the lower house.

The Democratic Socialist Party (DSP) was founded in

4. Scalapino and Masumi, *op. cit.*, p. 37.

1960 by right-wing splinter groups in the Socialist party. Its roots in the postwar period, however, can be traced back to 1947 from which time there was a series of expulsions, splits, and mergers among left- and right-wing Socialist factions. Supported by the Dōmei labor federation, the DSP unequivocally endorses parliamentarism and takes a position resembling British Fabianism while rejecting Marxism. They polled 7.4 percent of the popular vote and secured thirty seats in the lower house election of 1967. Those who saw the emergence of this party as a middle ground in Japanese politics whereby a combination of workers and other elements in the "middle strata" would be successful in achieving political power so far have been disappointed. The DSP has not yet challenged the JSP for leadership of the anti-conservative forces in the population, nor does it seem likely to do so in the future.

If anything, it has been the rapidly rising Sōka Gakkai (Value Creating Study Society), an offshoot of the Nichiren Buddhist sect, that has posed a threat to the Socialist Party. With some 4,000,000 committed households, their political arm, Komeitō (Clean Government Party), received 5.4 percent of the popular vote and took twenty-five seats in 1967 in their first contest for seats in the lower house. In the important Tokyo municipal elections of 1969, Komeitō replaced the Socialists as the second largest party after the LDP. Komeitō has great appeal to those alienated from the present party system and from existing social and economic arrangements. Some see in it a potential revival of Japanese fascism.

The Liberal-Democratic party has not been known for its consideration of blue-collar worker interests. This is not really surprising since their main electoral support comes from other groups. In the 1967 election, they received 48.8 percent of the popular vote and took 277 seats. It was the first time they had polled less than 50 percent of the popular vote. While the major legislative reforms of the immediate postwar period remain intact, there has been regression in a number of areas. Restrictive labor legislation increased toward the end of the Occupation and afterwards. The government's main thrust has been against the Marxist-oriented Sōhyō labor federation. In the Diet, bitter opposition between the Socialists and the Liberal-Democrats has not permitted the interests of blue-collar workers to be advanced through compromise, though this public conflict has at times served as a smoke-screen for informal cooperation.

On the other hand, the Liberal-Democrats' preoccupation with economic growth has certainly paid off handsomely in a growing national prosperity that has raised the living standards of blue-collar workers. The conservatives hope that continued prosperity will lessen the appeal of militant Marxism among the general public as well as among left-wing leaders, in order to effect a reconciliation between the Socialists and the Liberal-Democrats on the LDP's own terms. They have coopted the welfare platform of the Socialists in a stated desire to develop a welfare state on a par with Western countries. Their success in building an increasingly effective social security system has obviously benefited blue-collar workers. In recent years, however, financial deficits in these programs have led the LDP to increase the amounts of individual contributions to social security and in general to make many of the programs more restrictive.

The Socialists, with their emphasis on Marxist ideology rather than pragmatic solutions, certainly bear some of the responsibility for their party's intransigent opposition to the Liberal-Democrats and for the resultant failure to advance worker interests through compromise. There can be no doubt, however, that the existence of a strong Socialist party, representing almost one-third of the electorate and backed by the militant Sōhyō federation, has been one of the major bulwarks in maintaining postwar democracy in Japan. As such, they have acted to prevent excessive back-sliding by the conservatives. Public sentiment mobilized by the Socialist party, Sōhyō, and sympathetic intellectuals, combined with obstruction tactics in the Diet, has made the Liberal-Democrats tread softly in their attempts to dilute postwar reforms. Certainly, this has been in the interests of blue-collar workers, giving them some measure of control over national politics, to an extent that did not exist in the prewar period. But this has been at best a negative power—the power to say no, and not always successfully at that.

The outcome of the 1967 lower house election and of subsequent local elections, particularly in urban areas, presages the future dissolution of the one-and-one-half party system. The apparent trend is not toward a simple balance between Socialists and Liberal-Democrats. Rather it is toward a gradual reduction in the relative power of the LDP, the emergence of a multi-party system, and the possibility of a coalition government. The trend was further strengthened in the 1969 lower house election when the Liberal Democratic party dropped from 48.8 percent of the popular vote to 47.6, and the Socialists dropped from 27.9 percent to 21.4, while Komeitō jumped from 5.4 percent to 10.9, the Democratic Socialists rose slightly from 7.4 percent to 7.7, and the Communist Party moved from 4.8 percent to 6.8 of the popular vote.

SOCIAL SECURITY SYSTEM

In industrial societies, one important reflection of the way blue-collar power is wielded in the national arena is the nature of social security programs. When a blue-collar worker reports that from his total monthly income of 46,406 yen, 2,040 yen is deducted for health insurance and welfare pension and 319 yen for unemployment insurance, it is important to know just what kind of protection is provided and who pays for it.[5]

The first social insurance program established in Japan was the Workers' Health Insurance Law in 1922. This was

5. Sources for this brief overview of social security programs include: Takahashi Takeshi, "Social Security in Japan," *The Changing Patterns of Industrial Relations* (Tokyo: Japan Institute of Labour, 1965); Japan International Social Security Association, *Study of Social Security Schemes in Japan* (Tokyo: The Association, 1965); The Social Insurance Agency, *Outline of the Social Insurance in Japan* (Tokyo: The Agency, 1966); Ministry of Health and Welfare, *Social Welfare Service in Japan* (Tokyo: The Ministry, 1965); Japan Institute of Labour, "Medical Care Program in Japan," *Japan Labor Bulletin*, Vol. 4, No. 4 (April 1965); "Pension Plans in Japan," *ibid.*, Vol. 4, No. 8 (August 1965); Japan Federation of Employer Associations, "Amendment of the Welfare Pension Insurance Law," *JFEA News*, June 1965; "Management Outlays for Employee Welfare in Japan," *ibid.*, September 1965; "Trend of the Retirement System in Japan," *ibid.*, September 1965.

designed primarily for low-income factory and mine workers. It was not until soon after World War II, however, that the present system was given a firm foundation. It was Article 25 of the new Japanese Constitution of 1946 which specified the state's responsibility for the promotion and improvement of social welfare, social security, and public health. Social security has become one of the essential public services in postwar Japan with the reorganization of previously existing systems and the establishment of a number of new programs: Workmen's Accident Compensation Law, 1947; Unemployment Insurance Law, 1947; Livelihood Protection Law (public welfare), 1950; National Pension Law, 1959; and Inhabitants' Health Insurance Law, 1961.

The development of these various new programs has by no means been steady, nor have they all reached the levels attained by Western industrial nations. Some, such as the health insurance program, are impressive in their scope and coverage, while others such as old age pensions as yet give scant protection to blue-collar workers. In 1964, government expenditures for social insurance were divided as follows: 68.7 percent for medical insurance, 11.8 percent for unemployment insurance, 13.8 percent for pension insurance, and 5.7 percent for workmen's accident compensation.[6] The percentage of the gross national product devoted to social security in Japan (5.8 percent in 1963) is considerably below the average for countries of the European Economic Community (14.7 percent in 1963). Japan, however, ranks only slightly below the United States, where social security expenditures amounted to 6.5 percent of the gross national product in 1963.[7]

Any assessment of the effectiveness of social security programs for blue-collar workers must also evaluate their impact on income redistribution. This involves consideration of the programs' financing. In 1963, insured persons paid 26.2

6. Secretariat of Social Security Council, Annual Report of Social Security Statistics, 1964 (Tokyo: The Council, 1965).

7. Felix Paukert, "Social Security and Income Redistribution: A Comparative Study," International Labour Review, Vol. 98, No. 5 (November 1968), p. 430.

percent of social security receipts in Japan. This compares with an average of 22.7 percent in the European Economic Community.[8] The entire cost of social security programs for workers, however, may be still higher since the cost of contributions from employers and the state is, to some extent, passed on to the general public. Unfortunately, economists have great difficulty in measuring these factors, and no detailed comparative analysis appears to be available.

Despite their comparatively low international standing, there can be no question that Japanese blue-collar workers are far better protected by the postwar social security system than they were in the prewar period. Social security has contributed greatly to stabilizing the livelihood of blue-collar workers.

In many companies, particularly in large firms, the underdeveloped state of social security programs is balanced by the extensive welfare programs carried out under the auspices of the company. Table 2 reports the findings of the 1966 survey of 715 large firms by the Japan Federation of Employers' Associations.[9] Fringe benefits are shown as a percentage of average monthly earnings (annual wages including mid-year and year-end bonuses divided by 12). When the extensive invisible subsidy for company housing is included, it can be seen that voluntary welfare costs far surpass those required by law. Comparisons with past surveys indicate that fringe benefits have been increasing faster than have monthly earnings in recent years.

Medical Care

Medical care among blue-collar workers is, for the most part, obtained through health insurance. There is, however, free medical assistance for needy individuals and families and public health services for the treatment of certain diseases such as tuberculosis and mental illness. The health insurance system in Japan can be divided broadly into two types according to membership: compulsory insurance for employees and

8. *Ibid.*, p. 441.
9. Japan Federation of Employers' Associations, "Fringe Benefits in Today's Japan," *JFEA News*, No. 32 (March 1968), pp. 6–8.

TABLE 2

Average Portion of Monthly Wages Per Employee Paid For Various Types of Welfare Programs (1966)

	Amount paid (in yen)	Percentage of total wages
1. Social Security Contributions Total	3,382	6.1
Health insurance	1,675	3.0
Welfare pension insurance	999	1.8
Unemployment insurance	391	0.7
Workmen's compensation insurance	306	0.6
2. Voluntary Welfare Costs Total	4,316	7.8 [a]
Housing [b]	1,701	3.1
Medicine and sanitary services	435	0.8
Payment in kind [c]	1,399	2.5
Mutual aid	220	0.4
Cultural and recreational services	391	0.7
Others	170	0.3
3. Retirement Allowance Total	2,838	5.1
TOTAL (1 + 2 + 3)	10,536 [d]	19.0 [e]
Monthly Wages	55,431	100.0

[a] Based on comparisons with past Labor Ministry surveys, we may estimate the comparable figures for smaller firms (with 100–499 employees) to be 7.0. Ministry of Labor, *Year Book of Labor Statistics,* 1964 (Tokyo: The Ministry, 1965), pp. 260–267.
[b] Housing costs include construction, depreciation, and maintenance costs.
[c] Payment in kind includes free meals, discount sales of commodities, clothing, commutation subsidy, nursing, cash congratulatory gifts to employees, etc.
[d] If the invisible subsidy for company house rent (the difference between rent collected and current market rent) is included, this figure rises to at least 20,536 yen. It is estimated that 40 percent of the total number of married employees in manufacturing live in company apartments or houses and 50 percent of the unmarried live in their dormitories.
[e] If the invisible subsidy for rent is included, this figure rises to about 38 percent.

voluntary insurance for inhabitants. The voluntary plan may be seen as a residual category of government-sponsored insurance for citizens who are not covered through compulsory employee insurance.

For employees there are two major programs. First, in firms with five or more employees, there is the government-administered health insurance program, which covers the ma-

jority of Japanese employees (10,864,000 employees and
11,204,000 dependents insured as of March 1964). Secondly,
there is the program by which, with the consent of more than
half of the employees, a health insurance society may be
established by a single employer or jointly by several employers who together employ more than 300 people. This requires the approval and is under the supervision of the Ministry of Health and Welfare. There are about 1,200 health
insurance societies established at company or plant level
(6,565,000 employees and 8,535,000 dependents insured).
These health insurance societies, established primarily in the
large companies, are a concession to traditional paternalistic
practices among large-scale employers. They are a continuation of a prewar practice by which company mutual aid societies were allowed to run their own health service by contracting out from the health insurance program administered
by the government. In keeping with the pattern of a "dual
economic structure," which will be described below, the
health insurance societies in large-scale firms tend to pay
higher benefits for dependents of the insured and to require
a lower rate of employee contribution than does the government-administered program. Thus, the average blue-collar
member of the government program pays 3.15 percent of his
monthly salary for his health insurance, with the employer
contributing an equal sum, while those blue-collar workers
at firms with their own health insurance societies contribute
on the average only 2.73 percent of their monthly wages, and
the employer on the average contributes the equivalent of
3.96 percent. Moreover, large firms will often subsidize the
medical expenses of employees' family members. These differences constitute one factor in the strong commitment of
employees in large firms to their company. Generally speaking, the blue-collar workers who belong to the government-
administered programs as opposed to the health insurance
societies work in firms with lower wages and poorer working
conditions.

Medical benefits in the employee insurance programs
are granted to the insured at a nominal charge with no limitation on the benefit period. Thus, a blue-collar worker can

receive medical treatment by paying 200 yen at the start of the service and 60 yen a day for hospitalization without any other charge.[10] Family members of the insured worker must pay half of their medical expenses.

Workers employed in firms with fewer than five employees are at a disadvantage since they must rely on the inhabitant insurance, which does not compensate for loss of earnings due to sickness or maternity. Both they and their families must pay 30 percent of all their medical expenses. An additional weak point of the system is that unemployed persons are outside the scope of any health insurance program, although they may apply for medical care under the public welfare program. In short, the blue-collar employee at a major enterprise has far better medical coverage than one at a small firm or than an unemployed worker.

In addition to contributing to medical benefits under health insurance, large Japanese companies sometimes continue to pay the wages of a long-time employee should illness make it impossible for him to work. At larger companies, the unions often bargain on this matter, and it is not uncommon that wages are paid for as long as two years after an employee is unable to report for work. Workers also can usually borrow from company mutual aid societies during their illness. Mutual aid societies are set up with workers contributing a fixed monthly sum such as 50 yen and the company providing perhaps double the worker's contribution. Depending on length of service, workers can then make loans at low interest rates, payable within a fixed period.[11]

Old Age Pensions

The present system of public pensions is based essentially on the 1954 Workers' Welfare Pension Insurance Law under which most employees in the private sector are covered (17,872,744 as of March 1965). There is a special plan for

10. These totals represent an increased rate resulting from a 1967 amendment. For those with an income of 24,000 yen or less, the respective fees are 100 yen and 30 yen.

11. In addition to granting loans, the mutual aid society may also make payments at times of death, marriage, birth, retirement, sickness, injury, and accident.

employees in the public sector; the same is true with respect to medical insurance.

Pensions cost only .5 percent of the national income.[12] As of March 1965 the average benefit level was 3,586 yen a month. At the same time, the average level of earned wages in all industries was 39,360 yen a month.[13] This means that the pension amounted to only 9 percent of the monthly wage level. In fact, the average level of old age pension payments was far below the average level of public welfare payments, and with public welfare the beneficiary is not required to make any contributions. For a blue-collar worker to receive an old age pension, he must have contributed for at least twenty years. Moreover, the worker is not eligible to receive his monthly pension until he reaches age sixty and has lost the status of insured employee. If he chooses to continue working, he is not eligible again until age sixty-five. If he again chooses to keep on working, he loses 20 percent of his benefits throughout the duration of his employment.

The ineffectiveness of the pension system is indicated by the low number of retired employees actually receiving pensions (133,023 as of March 1965, at a time when there were 6,200,000 people aged sixty-five and over). Those sixty-five and over make up 6.3 percent of the total population and this is expected to rise to 7.1 percent by 1970. Clearly, the present average benefit level of 3,586 yen a month is inadequate to stabilize workers' livelihoods after the normal retirement age of fifty-five.

Through a 1965 amendment to the law, the government is seeking to raise the benefit level to an average of 10,000 yen a month for an employee whose contribution has been based on an average salary of 25,000 yen a month. This is to be achieved, in part, by raising the premium rate from the 3.5 percent which male employees have had to pay from their standard monthly wages (3 percent for insured females) to

12. This excludes war veterans' pensions.
13. This total is for all firms employing more than 30 workers and includes overtime, bonuses, and allowances. Ministry of Labor, *Rōdō Haku-sho 1965* (White Paper on Labor: 1965) (Tokyo: The Ministry, 1965), p. 342.

5.5 percent (3.9 percent for insured females). Employers contribute an equal amount. The 10,000 yen a month pension will not take effect until the employee has contributed for a twenty-year qualifying period. Moreover, there is no guarantee that with rising living costs the 10,000 yen a month pension will have much value twenty years from now. Although the government has said that it is important to keep the benefit level in line with rising living costs it has not indicated how it plans to go about doing this in any systematic fashion. Another recent change permits companies to establish their own pension plans. As with the health insurance societies, this involves a contracting out of the government pension plan in a way that seems to reinforce the "dual economic structure" described below.

Pressures to improve the pension system have come from a number of sources: (1) there has been a rapid increase in the working class population; (2) the number of older people has continually increased in proportion to the total population and will continue to do so at an accelerated pace; (3) while life expectancy has been lengthened, the compulsory retirement age in most firms is fifty-five; (4) the disruption of World War II did not permit many people now approaching retirement to prepare for their retirement; and (5) there has been a rapid transition from the extended family system to the nuclear family system with the number of three-generation households rapidly decreasing, so that it becomes more difficult for aged people to depend on their children for support.

The widespread existence of company-paid lump sum retirement allowances outside the social security system is a reflection of the underdeveloped state of the statutory pension in Japan. This system, to a great extent, has taken the place of social security as a means of guaranteeing the livelihood of the retired. This is particularly true among employees of larger firms; smaller firms are less likely to have retirement benefits and when they do they pay lower benefits.[14]

14. In 1964 a government survey reported that at the retirement age of fifty-five, middle school graduates in firms employing over one thousand employees received on the average 3,316,606 yen, while firms with 100 to

Unemployment Benefits

Following World War II amid spiraling inflation and social unrest, there arose the problem of what to do with the unprecedented number of jobless persons. At an earlier stage of Japan's industrialization it could be assumed that the jobless would be reabsorbed into the countryside. But this assumption was now questionable given the enormity of the problem and the limits of rural productivity. To meet the problem the unemployment insurance law was enacted on December 1, 1947.

The unemployment insurance now in force is primarily based on the principle of compulsory enrollment.[15] Workers at firms which employ five or more are compulsorily enrolled. At firms with less than five employees, workers may be voluntarily insured. Only 10 percent of the firms in this latter category have taken advantage of this provision. There are also cases where small firms enroll and do not fulfill their obligations to pay their own and their employees' contributions.

To qualify for benefits, an employee must have been insured six months or more during the year preceding the date of separation from employment. Having satisfied this condition, the unemployed worker must report to the Public Employment Security Office in his district, apply for a new job, and obtain certification of his unemployment so that he can receive benefits. Unemployment benefits are paid for 90 to 270 days, according to the individual's length of employment before becoming unemployed. The benefits are granted after a waiting period of seven days with the restriction that the recipient must not refuse to take a new job without proper reasons.

Generally speaking, the benefits amount to 60 percent of the claimant's daily wages just before separation from employment. There are also small supplements for dependents.

199 employees paid on the average 1,911,499 yen. Kurozumi Akira, *Teinensei Taishokukin Taishoku Nenkin* (Retirement System: Lump Sum Retirement Allowance and Retirement Pension), (Tokyo: Rōdō Junposha, 1966), p. 407.

15. This excludes firms engaged in agriculture, forestry, fishery, education, research, and investigation. There are also special programs for seamen and casual workers.

Payments are limited to a maximum of 860 yen a day or 25,800 yen a month. Employers and employees make equal contributions: each worker has .7 percent of his wages deducted for employee contribution, and the employer thus pays 1.4 percent of his total wage bill per month into the program.

Unemployment in the nation fell from 500,000 in 1960 to 370,000 in 1964; employment in these years rose from 45,110,000 to 47,100,000.[16] The decrease in unemployment came about primarily in urban areas, with rural unemployment remaining at about 120,000. Of the total of 17,772,900 covered employees, 1,900,000 claims were filed during 1964. Despite a growing labor shortage, the number of recipients has increased in recent years. Two basic factors that account for this are the increased use of unemployment benefits by seasonal workers and the growing number of female recipients. Many women recipients retire from employment because of marriage or pregnancy but seek to collect unemployment benefits, even though they are not really seeking new jobs. New legislation pending in the Diet seeks to broaden the system to cover workers in small-scale enterprises, to limit the benefits available to seasonal workers, and to prevent illegal claims.[17]

Workmen's Accident Compensation

The Workmen's Accident Compensation Insurance Law of 1947 was an historic step forward in guaranteeing the livelihood of working people. Firms compulsorily covered under this insurance are those engaged in manufacturing, mining, and transportation which regularly employ five or more workers.[18] In addition, there is a category of voluntarily covered firms; that is, they are covered when the employer's

16. Ministry of Labor, *Year Book of Labor Statistics, 1965* (Tokyo: The Ministry, 1966), pp. 6–7. The concept of unemployed refers to the totally unemployed who actively sought work but were unable to find it during the survey week of December 20–26. The totals do not cover the category of underemployed or underutilized labor.

17. Editorial in *Asahi Evening News* (Tokyo), March 18, 1967.

18. Smaller specialized groups also are covered under the compulsory provision.

request for admission is granted by the government. If more than half of the employees in a firm not automatically covered desire coverage, their employer must apply for admission into the program. The government proposed in 1967 that all establishments employing between one and five workers automatically be included in the program.

The program is financed solely from employers' contributions. Benefits are provided for injury, sickness, invalidism, and death resulting from employment. The benefits are calculated on the basis of average wage. As of March 1964, there were some 19,500,000 insured employees, and the benefits granted in fiscal 1964 were 43,509,680,000 yen.

There are six types of benefits: medical care benefit, absence from work benefit, disability benefit, survivors' benefit, funeral expense benefit, and long-term disability benefits. Medical care is given to the worker with an injury or disease resulting from employment until he is cured or dies of the injury or disease. The treatment is essentially free for the recipient and is given at specially designated industrial accident hospitals. The absence from work benefit pays 60 percent of the worker's average wage.

LABOR STANDARDS LAW

The impact on the lives of individual blue-collar workers of decisions made at the national level is seen further by an examination of Japanese labor legislation.[19] During the postwar rush to democratization, the Labor Standards Law was passed in 1947. Based essentially on International Labor Organization conventions, it was by no means the first such legislation in Japanese history designed to affect the treatment of workers. It was epoch-making, however, in its attempt to realize social justice and a democratic adjustment in the employer-employee relationship. These goals were to be achieved by setting the basic minimum standards for work-

19. For a complete English translation of Japanese labor laws see Ministry of Labor, *Japan Labour Laws*, 1968 (Tokyo: Institute of Labor Policy, 1968). For several commentaries on the legislation see, *The Changing Patterns of Industrial Relations*, under the heading "Changing Role of Government in Industrial Relations."

ing conditions upon which employers and workers would be expected to conclude their contracts. The scope of the Labor Standards Law in private enterprise is very broad. With few exceptions, the law covers all employees in the private sector regardless of size of enterprise and applies to the public sector as well.

The Labor Standards Law directly regulates the content and form of work rules (*shugyō kisoku*) in Japanese factories. Conditions set in individual labor contracts and collective bargaining agreements are held invalid if they are inferior to the standards set by provisions of the Labor Standards Law. The provisions of the Labor Standards Law are written directly into company work rules to make it easier to determine whether the conditions in labor contracts satisfy the law. The law is also intended to make the terms and conditions of employment clearly known to workers. The employer is obligated to make clear to employees their wages, hours, and other working conditions. Should the practice of the employer differ from these contract specifications, the worker may cancel the contract without notice.

Japanese collective bargaining agreements between employers and unions do not ordinarily contain detailed regulations on working conditions. When those matters are covered in the collective agreement, they usually serve to raise standards above the minimum set by the law. In the same way, an individual worker may also conclude terms of employment in his labor contract that are superior to the legal minimum, or the company may adopt work rules above this minimum.

Experience in many countries has shown that a model labor standards law may not be realized in practice. A great deal depends on the provisions for enforcement, the diligence of government officials in securing compliance, the cooperation of employers, and the willingness of workers to exercise their rights. To secure effective enforcement of the provisions of the Japanese Labor Standards Law there is an administrative office in charge of inspection (Labor Standards Bureau in the Ministry of Labor). Under the law an employer is obligated to keep certain records, and report on required matters. It is the employer's duty to disseminate laws and regulations, to report to the inspection organization, and to consult the wishes of the majority of his employees when making work rules. There are penal provisions for violations of the Labor Standards Law.

Actual compliance with the Labor Standards Law varies considerably with the size of the enterprise. In big corporations, the standards usually are far above the minimum requirements set by the Labor Standards Law. But in the smaller firms, where enforcement is more difficult, workers less conscious of their rights, and employers more inclined to feel that compliance would endanger the firms' survival chances, compliance is often poor. In recent years, however, the tightening labor market and the rising educational level of workers have led to an increasing compliance even in the smaller firms.[20] With the growing labor shortage, employees, particularly younger workers, can afford to be more discriminating and to hold employers to the legal standard. From the worker's standpoint, what is necessary for increasing compliance is not only the legal right to refuse the employer's contract but the practical possibility of securing another job. Viewed from the other side, the tightening labor market encourages employers to comply with the law and raise their standards if they are to get and hold competent workers. In addition, the rising educational level of Japanese blue-collar workers results in their being more conscious of their rights. The increasing standard of living makes workers less tolerant of inferior working conditions and low wages. A number of surveys in recent years have sought to account for the high rate of job-changing among younger workers. They have reported that a major reason for leaving jobs has been worker dissatisfaction over the discrepancy between promised and actual working conditions.

Working Hours, Overtime, and Vacations

Chapter IV of the Labor Standards Law deals with working hours, recess, holidays, and annual vacations with

20. See Inoue Akira, "Shugyō Kisoku no Jittai to Sono Mondaiten," (Actual Conditions of Work Rules and Problems), *Kikan Rōdōhō* (Labor Law Agency), Vol. 13, No. 48 (Summer 1963).

pay. The law specifies that the hours of work shall not exceed eight hours a day and forty-eight hours a week, exclusive of rest time. No firm may stipulate a work week in excess of this standard, though firms may set higher standards.

The Labor Standards Law does allow for a relaxing of the statutory forty-eight-hour week. Specifically, Article 36 permits regular overtime and holiday work when the majority of employees or their union make a written agreement with the employer and submit the agreement to the appropriate government agency. This article makes no limitation on the amount of overtime and holiday work. In short, the statutory forty-eight-hour week, particularly in small and medium-sized firms, is nothing more than a standard for the calculation of wages.[21]

The total number of hours worked per regular employee has fluctuated according to rates of economic growth. They reached a peak in the high growth year of 1960, in which an average of 207 hours a month (51 hours a week) were worked per regular employee in all manufacturing firms employing thirty or more. This average fell to 191.8 hours a month (47.9 hours a week) in 1965 and then rose to 193.6 hours a month (48.4 hours a week) in 1967.[22] The trend since 1960 indicates a steady decline in scheduled hours, reflecting reductions in the standard work weeks of many companies. Labor unions, in particular, have taken up the shorter work week as a bargaining issue. The trend with respect to overtime is harder to interpret. After 1960, there was a gradual decline through the economic slowdown of 1965; in 1966 and 1967, however, once again there was a sharp increase in overtime worked. Managerial incentive to cut down on overtime increases as wages rise and overtime rates cost the employer proportionately more (usually based on the legal standard of a 25 percent premium). On the other hand, the developing labor shortage in recent years, combined with continuing

21. For this section a useful discussion and analysis appeared in Japan Institute of Labor, "Hours of Work and Trade Unions in Japan," *Japan Labor Bulletin*, Vol. 4, No. 11 (November 1965).

22. *Year Book of Labor Statistics*, 1964, p. 204. *Ibid.*, 1965, p. 200. *Ibid.*, 1967, pp. 218–219. The totals for blue-collar workers alone are only slightly higher than the average for all regular employees.

high rates of economic growth, has contributed to the up-surge in the amount of overtime worked.

The Labor Standards Law specifies that employers shall grant six days annual vacation with pay to workers who have been employed continuously for a year and were present over 80 percent of the working days.[23] Employers are required to grant an increased annual vacation with pay at the rate of one additional day for each continued year of employment. The law, however, permits employers to limit the total to twenty days annual vacation with pay. In practice, workers in most companies do not lump together their allotted vacation days but scatter them throughout the year. Should a company have in force a labor contract that grants longer vacations than those required by law, the company may, in agreement with worker representatives, buy back those days in excess of the legally required minimum.[24] When workers choose not to take their allotted vacations, this is seen as demonstrating their loyalty to the company. Such practices, however, are increasingly limited to older workers, with younger workers more willing to take full advantage of their rights under the law.

Minimum Wage Law

Japan's minimum wage law, adopted in 1959, has not proved very effective since it depends on voluntary employers' agreements approved by the Labor Standards Offices. In 1968, the minimum wage system was revised. The employers' agreements are to be replaced within two years by decisions of the prefectural Labor Standards Offices in consultation with central or regional minimum wage councils. These wage councils will be composed of an equal number of members representing workers, employers, and the public interest. It is not yet clear how the new system will operate, but it would seem to make possible a more effective minimum wage policy in the future.

23. In addition, all employees receive twelve paid public holidays a year.

24. The specific authorization for this is through the Labor Standards Office Notification No. 3650, 1948.

THE DUAL ECONOMIC STRUCTURE

So far this chapter has sketched the nature of blue-collar access to national political power, the social security programs, the Labor Standards Law, and the Minimum Wage Law. Another critical constraint upon the industrial relations system as it operates in any given company involves what the Japanese refer to as their dual economic structure.

This term contrasts the large-scale firms which pay relatively high wages and have good working conditions to the mass of small and medium-sized enterprises, often family owned, which subsidize the major enterprises by their low wages, long hours, and poor working conditions. These smaller firms are often under the control, in effect if not formally, of the major firms. The large firms, in contrast to the small ones, are highly unionized, highly capitalized, and have specialized managerial, sales, and personnel organizations. As defined in the Basic Law on Small and Medium-Sized Enterprises, a small or medium-sized firm in the manufacturing sector is one which is capitalized under 50,000,000 yen or employs less than 300 workers. In 1966, the 7,177,000 employees in small and medium-sized firms accounted for 69.7 percent of all employment in manufacturing and about 50 percent of the total production.

This dual structure has enormous consequences for employees in both large and small firms. There are great differences in living standards and life styles as a consequence. For example, workers in small and medium-sized firms have less job security and often must reckon with the possibility of bankruptcy. The rate of bankruptcy is high, with a large number of small firms commonly used as economic buffers by the major firms.[25] For another example, the incidence of deaths and injuries from occupational causes for small and medium-sized enterprises (30 to 299 employees) is approximately three times that of the large enterprises (300 or more employees). The discrepancy in death and injury rates rises to

25. Economic Planning Agency, *Economic Survey of Japan* (1964–65) (Tokyo: The Japan Times, 1966), pp. 39–41.

four times when comparing firms with over 300 employees to firms with 10 to 29.[26] One may hypothesize that the job security of those in large firms and the insecurity of those in small firms should lead to significantly different conceptions of self among the employees in the two sectors. This seems especially likely because Japanese culture reportedly places a high premium on predictability.[27] Moreover, the firm tends to circumscribe the interests and activities of its members. It shapes the self by foreclosing most of the opportunities that might encourage the growth of alternative bases for personality development. Such a situation is most applicable to large-scale firms that recruit young middle school graduates for lifetime employment and have live-in facilities.[28]

The dual structure cuts across the blue-collar/white-collar classification to a great extent; the blue-collar workers in major corporations view themselves, and are viewed, as members of an elite which includes the salaried employees in these firms. At the other end of the spectrum are the salaried employees and blue-collar workers in often less productive small and medium-sized firms. The difference in life styles between employees in the two sectors is reflected in such personal matters as selection of marriage partners. For example, it would be inappropriate if a male worker in a small subcontract firm were matched with an employee in a big company. Different aspirations, it is felt, would perhaps mean a mismatch. The function of the arranged marriage or semi-arranged marriage in contemporary Japan is to match families with similar backgrounds and status.

The different standard of living resulting from employment in one sector rather than the other can be seen in government statistics on wage levels according to size of firm. In 1964 wages in firms employing from 10 to 29 workers were 73 percent of wages in firms employing more than 1,000

26. Year Book of Labor Statistics, 1966, p. 249.
27. Ruth Benedict, The Chrysanthemum and the Sword (Boston: Houghton Mifflin, 1946), pp. 26–28.
28. For an extreme case, see Erving Goffman, Asylums (New York: Doubleday, 1961).

workers.[29] Moreover, the semi-annual bonuses and retirement allowances are much higher in the larger firms. As described above, welfare benefits are also sharply differentiated according to the dual structure.

Because of the dual economic structure with its enormous social consequences, the Japanese tend to see themselves as faced with a unique problem. But every industrial economy has its advanced and backward sectors, with the backward sector to some extent supporting and subsidizing the advanced sector.[30] There are, of course, variations in the types of dual economy, and the Japanese version is characterized by its pervasiveness, by the nation's acute consciousness of the system, and by the commanding grip of the larger "parent" companies over the smaller firms. A common practice of large companies facing poor business conditions, for example, is to delay payment to their subcontract firms. This sometimes results in serious financial difficulty, delayed or reduced wages, and even bankruptcy for the subcontract firms.

Recently, the dual structure in Japan has showed signs of breaking down. Increasingly, employment has been shifting to larger firms and from light industry to the heavy industries like chemicals and steel. A look at the composition of the labor force in manufacturing shows that in 1956, 16 percent of the workers were in firms employing one to nine workers; this had decreased to 9 percent in 1965. Similarly, in 1956, 30 percent of the labor force in manufacturing were in firms employing 500 or over; by 1965, this had increased to 37 percent. Those employed in heavy industries increased from 51 percent of all manufacturing employees in 1956 to 60 percent in 1965.[31] In addition, a shortage of young man-

29. Economic Planning Agency, *op. cit.*, p. 96. For an international comparison of wages and value added by size of firm see Tsujimura Kōtarō, "The Employment Structure and Labor Shares," *Postwar Economic Growth in Japan*, Komiya Ryūtarō (ed.), (Berkeley and Los Angeles: University of California Press, 1966), p. 113.

30. Benjamin Higgins, "The Dualistic Theory of Underdeveloped Areas," *Leading Issues in Development Economics*, Gerald Meier (ed.), (New York: Oxford University Press, 1964), p. 61.

31. *Japan Labor Bulletin*, Vol. 6, No. 8 (August 1966), p. 6.

power has forced smaller firms to pay higher wages and improve working conditions to get their share of productive labor. This has had the effect of narrowing the great wage differentials that have existed in the dual economy. Wages in small and medium-sized firms employing 10 to 99 persons rose from 59 percent of those in large-scale firms in 1954 to 80 percent in 1964. Among workers aged 20 to 24 years, the gap between wages in small and large firms has been almost closed.[32]

These kinds of changes are all productive of a more egalitarian society, as differences in life styles and opportunities are diminished. Yet, the problems resulting from the dual economy are by no means solved. This is indicated by the continuing high rate of bankruptcy among small-scale firms, with the disruptive consequences this has for employees and employers.[33]

32. Economic Planning Agency, *op. cit.*, pp. 47, 96. The trend toward closing the wage gap between large and small firms which occurred between 1959 and 1965 was, however, somewhat reversed between 1966 and 1968.

33. A general discussion of economic dualism in Japan appears in the work of Seymour Broadbridge, *Industrial Dualism in Japan* (Chicago: Aldine Publishing Company, 1966). A detailed discussion of the future of the dual economy appears in the work of Itō Takkichi, "The High Growth of the Japanese Economy and the Problems of Small Enterprises," *The Developing Economies*, Vol. 1, No. 2 (July–December 1963), pp. 3–34.

CHAPTER II

THE SETTING

I spent three months working as a machine expediter at the Takei Diecast Company in their Tokyo plant. My aim was to accept, so far as was possible, the same working conditions as other blue-collar workers. This meant working a six-day, 51-hour week, asking for no special privileges, being paid a reasonable wage, socializing with the other workers after work, and living in a Japanese-style apartment in a lower middle class/working class neighborhood near the factory. It was at the Tokyo diecast plant that the major portion of the research for this book was conducted. In order to compare plants of different sizes and in different locations, I also worked for two weeks at the new suburban plant of the diecast company and then for one month on the clutch assembly line of the Gujo Auto Parts Company.[1] The Tokyo diecast research was not limited to three months; the friendships and contacts made while working were further developed during the following eleven months. This was also true to a lesser extent in the suburban diecast plant and in the auto parts plant. In addition to the research material I gathered on the job and in meeting workers in the evenings on an informal basis, I conducted formal interviews with fifteen workers in the press and maintenance sections at the Tokyo diecast plant and with fifteen workers on the clutch assembly line and machining sections at the auto parts factory. While

1. While working at the suburban diecast plant, an opportunity arose for work at the auto parts firm. Rather than risk losing this chance, I left the job at the diecast company sooner than I had intended.

working, I kept a daily diary that provided the basic data for this research.

Access to the two companies was difficult to arrange. Before being accepted, I was refused at five other companies. These refusals by no means represented wasted effort, as they reveal a great deal about Japanese society. The difficulty a foreigner has in gaining access to employment for research purposes stems, above all, from the failure of Japanese scholars to do these kinds of studies.[2] Except among Japanese scholars trained in Western research methods, the participation observation method is unknown in Japan.

The lack of participation observation studies by scholars is a commentary on Japanese social structure with its compartmentalization into semi-closed corporate groups. Japan is still to a great extent a vertical society, and horizontal movement between different corporate groups is looked upon with suspicion and avoided when possible. Company officials tend to be secretive and to view the stranger with hostility. There is an assumption that he is up to no good, perhaps motivated by the desire to steal industrial secrets or injure the company's reputation.

I obtained my jobs with the two companies I worked for by different routes, through management in the diecast plant and through the union in the auto parts plant. In both, management was cautious and skeptical, setting a three-month limit to my employment at the Tokyo diecast plant and a one-month limit at the auto parts plant. Wages were paid to me on the basis of my temporary status; thus they were considerably below the average monthly wages of regular workers. My take-home pay in the diecast plant averaged about $60 a month, and in the auto plant the pay was $80 for the month.

2. Significantly, the classic study in Japanese on the life and working conditions of Japanese blue-collar workers was not done by a scholar but by a social-minded journalist. Yokoyama Gennosuke, *Nippon no Kasō Shakai* (Japan's Lower Class Society), (Tokyo: Iwanami Shoten, 1948). Originally published in 1898.

WORKING IN THE FACTORY

At the Takei Diecast Company my basic duty as a machine expediter was to service the press operators with new castings. Items such as auto and camera parts produced in the diecasting section were trimmed of excess metal by the press machines. The press operator job may be classified as semi-skilled. In the Tokyo plant, the average age of the press operators was 28, and they averaged 4.5 years employment with the company. The fact that I was about the same age as most of the operators was an advantage in my research. This made it easier to establish social relations with the workers. We had something in common, and there was a certain curiosity about how a foreigner of the same age was living out his life.

The machine expediter job was ideal for carrying out my research. First, it gave me mobility not only in the press section but throughout the plant. My duties required that I move around the plant a good deal, and I was able to talk to many of the other workers. Second, the duties were simple to learn, so that I could soon devote my energies to the research. Third, the duties of a machine expediter sometimes required that I work in an isolated second-floor room which I could also use for working on my notes, as well as for private discussions. Fourth, the work load was uneven; an hour of hard work could be followed by an hour in which there was relatively little to do. Fortunately, enforcement of the company rules about talking on the job and walking around the factory was lax, so I could spend these periods talking to other workers as they worked. I took my breaks at the welder shop, which was near the press section and was a key communication point for the workers, who were continually coming from all over the factory to bring in pieces to be welded. While they waited, they talked with the congenial welder about the latest happenings in the shop or about last Sunday's clam fishing.

My job at the Gujo Auto Parts plant was to make the

initial assembly on the clutch. It was far less suited to carrying out my research. The assembly line job gives the worker almost no chance to move around the plant. He is restricted to the line, where a six-man crew turns out an unending series of clutches, 45 every hour. Moreover, company discipline was stricter than at the diecast plant, so it was more difficult to leave my machine or to wander around the factory unnoticed to talk with workers. It was also hard to take notes inconspicuously. On the other hand, many of these difficulties were not present on the night shift, on which I worked half of the time while at Gujo.

It is common in participation observation studies in the West for the researcher not to inform workers of his real status but to try simply to blend into the work group. In Japan, because of the firm's nature as a semi-closed corporate group and because inter-firm worker mobility is less common than in the West, it takes a long time for new workers to be fully accepted by their fellow employees. It could take years for a Japanese researcher to be accepted by his fellow workers to the extent that he could freely ask questions and get satisfactory answers.

There was no question, however, of a six-foot-two, mustached hairy Westerner's blending into the work group.[3] Yet this was not entirely to my disadvantage. The workers understood that an outsider, uninvolved in their society and the plant status system, had no sinister motives and, more particularly, no power over them. I think that many were able to accept and talk to a stranger in a frank and honest way that would have been impossible among themselves. In my three months at the Tokyo diecast plant, I was accepted to an extent that would probably have taken a Japanese researcher several years. As an admitted researcher, I was able to ask numerous questions that from an ordinary new man would have made workers suspicious. Were a Japanese researcher to admit to his real role, he might be suspect as a

3. Language was a problem, especially in the early stages, as working class Japanese is not what I was taught in American universities. Prior to entering the factory, I had studied Japanese intensively at an American university for nine months and had then lived for eleven months in Tokyo.

management spy, but there was no question of management's picking a semi-literate foreigner as a spy.[4]

Fortunately, I could legitimately present myself to the workers as a student researcher, with the accent on student. The researcher's problem is to obtain the confidence of his subjects and to understand their point of view, while maintaining his critical distance. By presenting myself simply as a student interested in social relations in Japanese factories, I allayed many of the workers' natural suspicions. This was especially important in a society in which people are accustomed to thinking in terms of status hierarchies.

In general, the workers' reception of me was far better than either management or I had anticipated. Of course, there were unanticipated problems such as machines that had not been built for a tall foreigner or the foreman I was unable to understand because all of his teeth had been pulled out the day before I started work. But these belong to the category of minor nuisances, and indeed, because of their humor, they often helped to build a rapport with the workers.

My reception by different types of workers was revealing. Commentators often see the ability to accept the stranger as an attribute of modernization.[5] In the Tokyo diecast plant, where the majority of workers were second-generation urban dwellers or had lived in an urban center like Tokyo for at least ten years, my reception was friendly, and it was relatively easy to establish good rapport with the workers. In the auto plant, where the majority were young rural recruits, the

4. Georg Simmel, in his classic study on the role of the stranger, has pointed to the combination of nearness and distance in relationship to others that characterizes the phenomenon of the stranger. He specifically notes the objectivity of the stranger, while indicating that it is based not on passivity but on a special kind of participation that balances indifference and involvement, distance and nearness. One consequence of this relationship is that the stranger often receives the most surprising confidences that would be withheld from a more closely related person. Georg Simmel, "Notes on the Stranger," The Sociology of Georg Simmel, translated and edited by Kurt H. Wolff (Glencoe: Free Press, 1950), pp. 402–408.

5. See Fred Waisanen and Alfredo Mendez D., "Some Correlates of Functional Literacy," paper presented to the Inter-American Congress in Psychology, Miami, 1964. A similar understanding of modernization is discussed in Daniel Lerner, The Passing of Traditional Society (Glencoe: Free Press, 1962).

reaction was much more cautious, and it was harder to establish social relationships with the workers. Many of them came from isolated areas where conservative parochial views prevailed, and they found it very difficult to communicate with a foreigner.

My reception at the Tokyo plant, while favorable from the very first day, was undoubtedly more polite than genuine for the first few weeks. It was some time before the workers' natural doubts were quieted. As one worker, who became one of my best informants, said over a cup of coffee some five months later,

> If I had been the employer, I would never have let you in. When you first came, there was a wall between you and the men, though superficially you were accepted easily. We knew you were a researcher, but felt we didn't know you as a human being, and this made us reluctant to talk to you freely at first. Economically and because of management pressure, things are tough for us now, and we don't like to talk to a stranger about such matters; in general we don't like to share our personal affairs with strangers. I envy your role as a third party observer who doesn't have to live with the consequences of what is happening the way we do.

The comment about envying my role was a rather common one; it seemed that many of the workers identified vicariously with the researcher. Worker enthusiasm for gathering information for me seems, in part, to have been generated by this identification. Workers would often go out of their way to point out things in the shop that they thought might interest me.

For the first two weeks, conversations centered on me and America. This is not in accordance with the principle that the observer should not influence or become a part of the situation he is observing, but I believed that I should satisfy their curiosity as fully as possible in the hope that the novelty would soon wear off. This is exactly what happened, especially in the press section. After two weeks, questions about myself and America fell off rapidly. Soon I could sit in on conversations about such sensitive matters as gripes against foremen and union policy without the subject being changed when I sat down and without feeling the content was being altered by my presence. During the period when the workers did ask a great deal about me, however, a useful technique was to return their questions. When they asked about my hobbies or what I thought about Vietnam, I would simply ask them the same thing. It is not always possible or desirable to minimize the researcher's effect on his subjects. It may be unavoidable that the subjects will react to him, so the researcher must try to apply their reactions to meet research objectives.

While I was working at the diecast company, there was a serious conflict between the management and the union and also within the union itself. The conflict centered around the management's attempt to increase productivity and rationalize operations while tightening its control over the workers. The workers split roughly into three camps: those who emphasized cooperation with the company as a solution to the company's financial problems and because it was in their own long-term self-interest, those who accepted cooperation with management but emphasized the protection of the workers' interests, and those who saw a basic difference of interest between the company and the workers. These divisions affected their attitudes toward me. Despite my protestations that I was not there to judge, I was often regarded by leaders of the factions in the union and by management people as a third-party observer who must be won over to their side. This exposed me to valuable information, though it often came in the form of propaganda from all sides. Since everyone knew that as a participant-observer I was there for only a limited time and was entirely without power, it is highly unlikely that my presence affected the course of developments. The cooperation I received from the leader of the dominant left-socialist faction in the union seems to have been motivated not only by his naturally friendly nature, but by his hope that somehow my recording and analysis of events could serve to salvage something good from the destruction of the union.

The Communist faction in the diecast plant presented a special problem. At first, the leaders of this faction were the most cautious and suspicious in the plant. This did not appear to be motivated by any anti-Ameircan feeling directed toward me personally, though the Communists often carried "Go Home Yankee" signs at demonstrations and were strongly critical of the American role in the Vietnam War. They had a strong organization at the plant operating primarily through their youth organization, Minseidō.[6] For the first month, they were rather reluctant to talk about their organization. Early in the second month, I invited one of the Communist leaders out after work and made it clear that I had not come to judge or censure the Communist role in the union. If the workers wanted a Communist union that was their business, I told him. My concern was with the reasons for such a choice and the sources of strength of the Communists in the shop. Moreover, I said that my only obligation toward management was to show them a copy of what I would write before publication and to consider any suggestions they had. I told him that I would like to set the same condition with the union. These explanations and my good will were apparently sufficient to gain his confidence. Through informal conversations over the course of several months, I learned who the Communist supporters were. By the time I left Japan, the Minseidō members were inviting me to their social gatherings and speaking to me freely about their organization. My only request directly refused was for permission to sit in on one of their formal meetings. But, individual members responded freely to questions about their reasons for joining Minseidō, the size of the group's membership and its activities.

PARTICIPATION OBSERVATION AS A RESEARCH METHOD

Participation observation as a research method is primarily suited to exploratory studies. By definition, it is intensive rather than extensive. Since participation observation usually gets done as a case study, it shares many of the drawbacks of that method and these should be kept in mind in reading this study. First, generalization to the society or the

6. The official title of the youth organization is the Democratic Young Communist League (Minshushugi Seinen Kyōsanshugisha Dōmei).

industrial sector or even a given industry is not reliable. Firms and the employees interviewed are not chosen on the basis of a scientific sample, so it is hard to know how to interpret the results to obtain any broad insights. Second, the very nature of the case study tends to accentuate the unique characteristics of the selected firm.[7] Third, the case study lends itself to the researcher's seeing what he wants to see, to the confirmation of his own views and expectations.

In addition, the problem of interpretation and analysis of data is especially hard for the foreign researcher. He is likely, consciously or unconsciously, to be making comparisons with his native country. This can be dangerous where there is no systematic basis for comparison. I have sought to make comparisons with the American situation only when relevant comparative data was available.

It is impossible to eliminate one's values as influences on the selection and analysis of research materials. This is true of all sociological research, but especially so with participation observation, in which one is apt to become particularly close to and identify with the research subjects. The best one can do is to try to minimize the influence of one's own values when possible and, insofar as one is aware of them, try to make those values explicit. With this admonition in mind, I would like to make it clear that I am sympathetic to the postwar democratization in Japan, including the rise of labor unions, though I am skeptical as to how deeply the spirit of democratization has taken root among employees and employers. Further, many times I found myself identifying with the diecast workers. This was useful to the extent that the object of my research was to present the factory as seen by its workers. The danger, of course, is that such identification might invalidate the researcher's objective judgment. Whether this has occurred will be for the reader to decide. Within the space available, as much as possible of the raw data has been presented so that the reader will be in a position to reach some of his own conclusions.

There are, of course, some very real advantages to par-

7. A participation observation study could, be designed that would eliminate this drawback by putting many observers in the field on the basis of a scientific sampling.

ticipation observation. It makes possible an investigation in depth, something particularly valuable in exploratory studies which we begin knowing little about the subject. It helps us avoid the superficialities of survey research methods. The researcher can explore the relationships between workers' attitudes, verbal statements, and their behavior, in a way not possible with formal interviewing techniques.[8] It is not uncommon for workers to say one thing to interviewers and to act quite differently on the shop floor. But, when the researcher is on the shop floor eight-and-a-half hours a day, six days a week, constantly listening to what workers say and observing how they act, he becomes aware of discrepancies. He can make a more accurate analysis than if he were to rely on statistically reliable survey data. Moreover, workers on the job make spontaneous remarks that can lead the researcher to entirely new and productive considerations. Such remarks would be less likely to occur if the researcher sat in an office having one-hour interviews with nervous workers. Similarly, a researcher on the job is in a position to recognize the significance of certain behavior and attitudes that an outsider would overlook.

In short, one of the real virtues of the participation observation method, particularly for a foreign researcher, is that it makes him aware of the important questions that should be asked. It also gives the researcher a chance to pre-test questions and reject irrelevant ones. This is especially useful when the participation observation period is to be followed by formal interviewing. Furthermore, with the participation observation method the researcher can deal with sensitive subjects, such as worker restriction of production, that would be unapproachable using conventional research methods.

In order to make reliable generalizations that would apply to more than just the workers in the two firms, I constantly checked my interpretations with Japanese scholars

8. There is no reason why survey research data and participation observation data cannot be used to supplement each other. A recent study of the perceptual differences between American and Japanese workers is: Arthur Whitehill, Jr. and Takezawa Shin'ichi, *The Other Worker* (Honolulu: East-West Center Press, 1968). Professor Whitehill was kind enough to make a manuscript available to me before publication.

and labor practitioners. In addition, the various statistics of the two firms were checked against the available national statistics. Particularly helpful was the great amount of industrial relations research done by Japanese scholars in recent years. By comparing my observations with these sources, I hoped that the two firms could be set in perspective within modern industrial Japan and that their unique characteristics could be identified and made explicit.

The excitement of participation observation as a research method comes from being literally immersed in the research materials. It is the excitement that comes from recording everything, even the most commonplace information, never knowing what might turn out to be useful. It is the excitement of comparing the myriad data gathered in the factory to some of the wider theoretical frameworks that have been proposed to deal with Japan, Japanese workers, industrial work, industrialization, and social change. It is the excitement of producing data that suggest confirmation or modification of these theories.

The participant-observer in an alien culture is often not aware of what the behavioral options of the actors may be and why some options are open and not others. To carry out such a study, then, is in many ways more difficult than in his native culture. But as a stranger, he also brings to his subject the fresh viewpoint of the uninvolved, or what the Swedish poet Gunnar Ekelof called "newly washed eyes." He is struck by behavior and attitudes that participants or native observers take for granted. The excitement of a participation observation study in an alien culture is, in its largest sense, the essential excitement of sociology itself or of any science; it is the excitement of discovery.

TAKEI DIECAST

Mounted on a tin roof above a maze of one- and two-story structures is a large sign. A combination of Chinese characters and Japanese script spells out Takei Diecasting Joint Stock Company. Below, the tin roof and tin sidings covering the steel frame of the building seem shabby and give the appearance of having been put up for temporary use. The area is one of many in Tokyo that mix small-scale manufacturing and residences. This one covers about two square miles bordering on a polluted river whose stench spreads over the area during the summer months. In the area are small diecasting firms with anywhere from one to thirteen diecast machines, small machine shops, a TV cabinet maker, and several other medium-sized firms. Employment in these firms ranges from just the immediate family in the smallest to perhaps 300 in the largest.

It was in this same location that Takei Diecast began its operations in 1918 just as World War I was ending. Seven businessmen of various backgrounds got together and contributed a modest sum of money to establish the company. Their small company turned out diecast goods of zinc and tinplated lead. All the foundry equipment was hand-operated. The fledgling company, while not making much money, showed signs of promise until the great earthquake of 1923 struck Tokyo and all but destroyed the facilities. As a result, the company went bankrupt.

Undaunted, the group reassembled and started the company again the following year. This time, Takei Masataka, age twenty, who had impressed the investors with his ideas about running the company, assumed the job of factory manager. Not much is known about his past, except that he had come from a farm family in Toyama prefecture and was a graduate of the prewar elementary school. He was one of the original employees of the company and began accumulating and increasing his share of the company stocks while he worked as an employee.

The company prospered and, with the growing capital fund, bought hydraulic pressure and vacuum pressure diecast machines from Germany in 1928. Production gradually shifted to supplying the growing war industries; by the late 1930s the company was yielding great profits and two new factories were built. It became a limited partnership and took its present name of Takei Diecasting. Takei Masataka became president in 1938, and the Takei family slowly increased its control over the company. In 1945, employment reached a peak of 2,000 workers, and the company was turning out aluminum alloy goods at the rate of sixty tons a month. As the allied bombings increased in intensity, the plants burned down one by one. Takei Masataka died and the company was officially dissolved in 1947.

Again the company demonstrated its survival power as relatives, friends, and the immediate family soon set it in operation once again. Using the preserved equipment, the owners collected sixteen of the peak number of 2,000 employees and started production on the original Tokyo plant site. The former president Takei's son, Koji, was made president. But he was only nineteen, and real power was vested in others, particularly his two uncles, one of whom served as managing director and the other on the board of directors. Koji's younger brother also was a director, and his mother worked as auditor and accountant; she exercised considerable informal power. Gradually, the company began to grow again as the Japanese economy itself began to recover. Orders spurted upward with the outbreak of the Korean War. By 1952 the firm had eighty employees, nine diecast machines, and fifteen machine tools.

There had never been a union at Takei. Before the war there had been a "harmonious relations association" but it had had no power to make demands on management. The Takeis had used it to encourage higher production and to get a sounding of worker views. Prior to formation of the union, the paternalistic spirit had been strong at Takei. The strong familial feeling between employees and employer was gradually eroded by the growing impersonality of the expanding firm and by the increasing dissatisfaction of workers with their low wages.

In 1950 a friendship society was organized with the encouragement of management; the company contributed 5,000 yen a month toward its support. In December 1952 a dispute arose among workers in the friendship society sparked by those who wanted to separate employee representation from management control. At this point the term "union" was not used, for most workers had no intention of founding a union. While the key figure in the organizational effort was a Communist, the majority of workers who took the lead in the shop were long-time employees who were fearful of building a union, which they equated with general strikes and Communist Party organization.[9] They believed that the term "union" might antagonize the management and provide an excuse for its intervention. Meetings and discussions among the workers continued until March 1953, when the matter came to a climax in a workshop meeting. A decision was made to exclude the section chiefs from the new organization; thus, the form of the new organization as a union was determined.

Despite resistance by the Takei family, 88 of the 114 employees joined the new union. Although many of the section chiefs had been critical of the friendship society, they were still sufficiently linked with the company to want the new employee organization to be based on close cooperation with management. Without the section chiefs, the new union was able to develop into an autonomous employee organization. But some workers and management personnel felt that this decision may also have led to an excessive militancy on the part of the new union.[10]

The company officials, although deeply upset by the turn of events, reluctantly recognized the union and agreed to some of its demands. In the next eight years, there were numerous confrontations between the union and the company over wages and bonuses. The union often resorted to slow-downs and short strikes to win its demands and was rather successful during this period. The company's profits were high and it could afford to meet the union's demands.

Throughout its history, the union has remained an independent enterprise union, choosing not to affiliate with one of the large national federations.[11] Nonetheless, the majority

9. Throughout this book the term Communist refers to dues-paying members of the Communist party as well as workers who, though not members, publicly identify with Party policies.

10. The source of this union history is a book written by a union official on the tenth anniversary of the union. The company management accepts it as an objective account.

11. In the majority of Japanese labor unions, the focus of union power is at the enterprise even if the union is a member of an industrial or national federation. This is the source of the term "enterprise unionism."

of the union leadership has usually been sympathetic to Sōhyō, the largest union federation, which supports the Socialist Party.

In the mid-fifties, a Takei managing director visited the United States under the auspices of the Japan Productivity Center and was impressed to find American companies casting large-scale items.[12] He saw this as the wave of the future. Filled with enthusiasm, he convinced the Takeis to borrow money from a large machine manufacturer and from the banks. As a result, in 1959 they built, at the expense of 7,000,-000,000 yen, a new suburban plant with diecast machines capable of producing aluminum castings up to 75 pounds.[13] This proved to be the most momentous decision in the life of the company and its workers. If things went well, the Takeis could expect to maintain control of a greatly expanded prosperous company. But things did not go as expected; times were bad, orders were slow, and profits were down. The Takeis were unable to pay the interest on their loans. They had increasing trouble with the union between 1957 and 1962. The union held two strikes a year over wages and bonuses. They blamed what they termed the company's bad management for the company debts. Because of its poor financial situation, the company tried to hold down wage increases and bonuses.

This culminated in a tumultuous strike in 1962, when

in 1966, 24 percent of Japan's ten million union members belonged to enterprise unions that, like the Takei union, did not affiliate with national federations.

12. The Japan Productivity Center is one of several organizations that have been seeking to expose Japanese executives to modern technology and management theory. It is estimated that the Japan Productivity Center sent as many as 454 teams consisting of 4,665 people to the United States between 1955 and 1963. See Noda Kazuo, "Postwar Japanese Executives," Postwar Economic Growth in Japan, Komiya Ryūtarō (ed.), (Berkeley and Los Angeles: University of California Press, 1966), p. 238.

13. The new plant's location is in line with the move of heavy industry out of Tokyo in the search for cheaper land, expanded facilities, and less congested transportation. Tokyo diecast companies, which used to dominate Japanese diecast production, account for less and less of the total production (31 percent in 1956). Tōkyō ni okeru Daikasuto Sangyō no Jittai Bunseki (Analysis of the Actual Conditions of the Diecast Industry in Tokyo), (Tokyo: Tokyo City Economic Bureau, 1960).

the company announced that it could not grant any wage
increases. It was a year in which blue-collar workers in manufacturing firms with 100 to 499 employees received nominal
wage increases averaging 8.6 percent nationally.[14] Most of
the workers at the Tokyo plant went on strike. Red flags
hung from all the entrances. Union pickets blocked the drive-
ways, preventing trucks from making any pick-ups for three
weeks.[15] A settlement was finally reached in which the workers were to return to work immediately with wage hikes to
be discussed later. But after the return to work, there was a
decrease in orders, as former customers looked elsewhere or
continued their temporary arrangements. Debts mounted and
the company tottered on the brink of bankruptcy. The machine manufacturer demanded payment on its loan to the
Takei company. When Takei was unable to pay, the machine manufacturer sent in a whole new front-line management staff. Yamagishi-san, a tough-minded management
official at the machine manufacturing company, was named
general affairs manager and came to hold the reins of power.
The machine manufacturing firm itself had the reputation
of taking a hard line on labor relations. The new management insisted on a "peace stabilization contract" (antei
kyōtei), which was to run three years. Its provisions were: no
strikes by the workers, fixed wage hikes over the next three
years, fixed bonuses, no dismissals by the company, and union
agreement to cooperate on "rationalization" measures.[16] The
far left-wing faction of the union violently opposed such a
contract, and many quit in protest when the workers voted
to accept it.

14. Ministry of Labor, Rōdō Hakusho 1963 (White Paper on Labor
1963) (Tokyo: Labor Laws Institute, 1963), p. 334.

15. This is an unusually long work stoppage in a country where work
stoppages are usually measured in hours rather than days. In 1965, for example, there were only 920 work stoppages of more than one day in the
manufacturing sector and of those only 37 lasted 21 days or more. Ministry
of Labor, Year Book of Labor Statistics, 1964 (Tokyo: The Ministry, 1965),
p. 311.

16. To the Japanese, the term "rationalization" means far more than
changes in plant technology. It includes all attempts to modernize the firm
and improve its competitive position; this may mean discharging workers
and reorganizing work to cut costs. In the Takei case, the discharging of
workers was specifically prohibited.

The following five years saw a gradual reduction in employment at the Tokyo plant from its peak of 272 in 1959 to 65 in April 1967. At the same time, employment in the new suburban plant reached a peak of 340 in 1966 and then leveled off to 324 by April 1967. At the time I worked in the Tokyo plant in late 1965, it employed 185 workers, 145 of them blue-collar; and the suburban plant and headquarters employed 328 workers, about 220 of them blue-collar. Of the 202 employees who left the Tokyo plant between 1959 and 1967, most quit, but about 55 transferred to the new suburban plant and remained there. The rest of the labor force at the suburban plant was made up of local residents, newly graduated middle school and high school boys recruited from distant rural areas, and a group of about fifty former coal miners who lost their jobs when their mines were shut down. The workers transferred from the Tokyo plant to the suburban plant were carefully screened by the company and most were promoted in a short time to supervisory positions. Those who did not get promoted usually quit.

In 1965, a new union, more sympathetic to management, was successfully organized at the suburban plant. At the same time, the Communists for the first time emerged as a majority on the executive board of the Tokyo plant union. The two events were integrally related. The takeover by the Communists was but an ironic symbol of the destruction of the original Takei diecast union. By April 1967, the Tokyo union was reduced to an impotent 21 members.

TAKEI DIECAST IN PERSPECTIVE

There are about 1,000 diecast companies in Japan. Most are "papa-mama" firms which, as the name indicates, depend to a great extent on family labor. Few of them have over 100 employees. In addition to these 1,000 firms, there are large companies like auto manufacturers which have their own diecast operations. It is an industry of intense competition, long hours, relatively poor working conditions, and low wages. Takei is one of the larger, more modern companies in the industry.

As an operational unit, Takei is primarily a subcontrac-

tor both for the large machine manufacturer which controls
it and for other firms such as auto and camera companies.
The employees at the large machine manufacturer are estimated by Takei management to earn, on the average, 15 percent higher wages than employees at Takei (fringe and welfare benefits included). They also have far higher retirement
pay and shorter hours. The machine manufacturing firm was
a member of one of the powerful prewar industrial zaibatsu
(combines), which also included a bank, a chemical company, a steel maker, etc. These industrial combines have not
been re-established on the prewar basis, but they have
grouped together again and now maintain informal cooperation on a variety of matters such as investment and manpower needs. For example, when Takei needed workers for
its new suburban plant, it got them from one of the other
members of the combine that had a surplus of employees.

Takei, in turn, has its own still smaller subcontractors
which do 80 percent of the finishing work on its castings; this
consists of hand-filing them.[17] These rural subcontractors are
used by Takei because it can pay the workers less to do the
job than if it were done in Tokyo, where the labor costs are
much higher. There are three of these subcontract firms with
an average of 27 employees apiece. Prior to 1965 there were
eleven separate companies, some with as few as three workers. The company found this troublesome, and as a part of
its modernization program, forced these small firms to merge
into three companies by refusing to give orders to firms with
fewer than twenty workers. These companies are not formally
owned by Takei and take orders from other diecast companies as well. They employ farm housewives, mostly in their
forties, who work full time on a piece-rate system. The work
pace is intense, they have no union, and their wages are perhaps 20 to 30 percent below those at Takei. But, their wages
are an important supplement to their farm incomes.

Even though it has its own subcontractors, Takei can
still be classified as one of the mass of small and medium-
sized firms that constitute the overwhelming majority of firms
in Japan, which are dependent on major companies. Unlike

17. The remaining 20 percent Takei sends directly to its customers.

the very small firms, however, Takei has a large and diversi-
fied line of products. In medium-sized firms such as Takei,
industry-wide competition for workers and sales is intense.
Consequently, industry-wide standards tend to determine
labor and product standards. At the other extreme, there are
the major corporations whose oligopolistic market permits
them to set their own standards. By virtue of the competition
in the medium-sized firms like Takei, there is an emphasis on
efficiency and worker skills that is less apparent in the very
small firms. In Takei, selection of workers is based more on
the direct assessment of a worker's ability in an open labor
market than on his connections and family relations, as is
often the case at small firms, or on his educational qualifications, a common prerequisite for selection in the major corporations. In medium-sized firms such as Takei, with their
emphasis on efficiency, the wage system and the whole reward structure are likely to be geared more to the direct reward of worker's abilities rather than to maintaining worker's
living standards, as in smaller firms, or to rewarding age and
length of service, as in the major firms.[18]

In some respects, Takei is not a typical firm, and this
should be kept in mind in evaluating this study. It is one of
the larger, more modern firms in the diecasting industry. On
the other hand, it has not had the rapid growth of Japan's
new industries like autos and electronics. At the time this
study was made, both the diecast industry and the country
generally were experiencing a decline in the rate of economic
growth; this undoubtedly affected worker behavior and attitudes. Moreover, inflationary pressures were especially strong
at this time. In 1965 the increase in the cost of living actually
surpassed wage increases and resulted in a decline in real
income of .3 percent in the nation from the preceding

18. Okamoto Hideaki of Tokyo Metropolitan University has suggested a provocative typology of Japanese firms which includes four types:
livelihood-earning household, limited workshop, specialized factory, and
oligopoly concern. Takei Diecast would fall into the specialized factory type.
For the characteristics of the different types and the consequences of the
differences, see Okamoto Hideaki, "Industrial Relations in Small and
Medium-Sized Enterprises in Japan: A Sociological Perspective," *Japan Labor
Bulletin*, Vol. 6, No. 7 (July 1967).

calendar year. In addition, since many of the Tokyo plant workers had recently quit or transferred to the new suburban plant, the nature of the sample I encountered at the Tokyo plant was bound to be affected.[19] The uncertainty of the company's future strongly conditioned worker attitudes and behavior. Takei also was conspicuous for the relatively strong union that had been built at the Tokyo plant. This is a phenomenon not common to the small and medium sector, where firms often have no union or unions that are clearly subordinate to a dominating though perhaps paternalistic employer.

On the other hand, the process of a union's formation out of an employee cooperative society was a rather typical one among the many small and medium-sized firms that became unionized after the Korean War. In addition, the strength and success of the union in its early years is not unusual because of the plant's location. Unions have been able to take advantage of the concentration of industry in urban areas to build strong organizations. Communist Party organization also was known to be strong in the Takei plant area, as it is in many of the industrial areas of Tokyo.

Similarly, the process by which Takei, a family-owned firm, came under the control of a major corporation and the consequences of that control follows patterns that are common among small and medium-sized firms. The building of a new plant and its impact on the workers and the union also repeat a process that is common in Japanese industry. This includes the decline of the old factory, the destruction of the old union, the dislocation of people's lives, and such accommodations to these changes as the building of a new union more sympathetic to management. The company's efforts to modernize its operations and the worker and union reactions are also processes that are typical in present-day industrial Japan.

19. It is difficult to judge what kinds of workers quit or transferred and what kinds remained, for many variables must be considered: age, marital status, political orientation, housing situation, desire to get ahead, need for a secure and predictable future, alternative jobs, etc.

GUJO AUTO PARTS

The second plant in which this research was conducted was the Gujo Auto Parts Company. It shows marked differences from the Tokyo diecast plant. Gujo Auto Parts is located in a rural area three hours from Tokyo by train, near a town of 60,000 people. The spacious modern plant has all the facilities normally associated with large-scale enterprises in Japan. These include company dormitories housing 680 unmarried employees of whom 500 are blue-collar, recreation halls, baseball fields, large cafeterias, and training facilities for workers. The auto parts firm supplies parts to a large auto company which, in turn, is a division of a still larger firm in the metal industry. Until 1954 the Gujo Auto Parts Company was part of the auto firm, but it was decided at that time to set it up as an independent company. It still supplies 90 percent of its parts to the same auto company and can be viewed as its subcontractor. As is often the case with such subsidiaries, most managers of the Gujo firm have been recruited from the parent auto firm.

Since it was set up as an independent company in 1954, Gujo has shown remarkable growth parallel with the growth of the entire Japanese auto industry.[20] Modern automatic machinery made both in Japan and West Germany has been installed. The company has registered a tenfold increase in total annual sales within the last ten years. The labor force has grown from 800 employees in 1953 to 3,000 in 1967. In 1966, during the time this research was conducted, of the 2,600 employees, 1,600 were blue-collar workers and 580 were white-collar and technical workers.

The company has had stable labor relations since 1954. At that time a militant left-wing union, which had organized all the divisions of the metal firm, including the auto com-

20. In the production of motor vehicles (passenger cars, trucks, and buses), Japan now ranks second in the world after the United States. Employment in the industry has increased from 129,000 in 1955 to 415,000 in 1965. It is estimated that about 60 percent of the labor force in the major auto makers is between 15 and 29 years old.

pany, went on a long strike. With the encouragement of management, a new union more sympathetic to the company was successfully organized during the strike. This union, which is now affiliated with the moderate Dōmei federation, replaced the old union. The Gujo management personnel speak proudly of their record of cooperation with the new union.

THE TWO WORKER TYPES

In any highly developed industrial society such as Japan, there is a highly structured and varied labor force. Yet observers often seem to have an uncontrollable urge to speak of *the* Japanese worker or *the* Japanese factory. While generalization is a proper goal, it frequently outruns available knowledge.

Undoubtedly the auto parts workers had a great deal in common with the Tokyo diecast workers. They shared the same cultural heritage, common exposure to the now omnipresent television, a respect for authority, and a sense of participating in a tight web of reciprocal obligations. In both firms, there were signs that this web holds the workers less tightly as traditional patterns of authority weaken and worker dependence on the firm decreases.

Still, the differences between the labor forces were striking, reflecting to a great extent dissimilar life experiences. Moreover, the auto parts workers and the Tokyo diecast workers were but two of a large number of worker types. The researcher's object, of course, is to isolate the significant and more representative types. The urban-rural and the small plant-large plant differentiations of the two worker types in the firms studied suggest that a comparison of these two would be useful in understanding a broad segment of Japanese workers. The characteristics noted below were not common to all the workers in each plant but represented the prevailing behavior and attitudes in both plants.

The Tokyo diecast workers might be characterized as sophisticated urban workers. They were knowledgeable about factory life and their union. They were often critical of both the company and the union and showed a strong streak of cynicism toward the world around them. Their attitude and behavior suggested a certain independence and self-assurance that was absent among the auto parts workers. This was reflected in the unwillingness of the diecast workers to identify uncritically with the company. They were reluctant to permit the company to become involved in their personal affairs. Their desire for independence could also be seen in the high value they placed on securing a skill. Skills that could be transferred to other companies put them in a better bargaining position with their company. Most of the Tokyo diecast workers were articulate about a wide range of matters ranging from factory issues to the nature of the industrial society in which they lived. They were both responsive to and capable of using abstract concepts.

Many of the diecast workers were avid readers, and the subjects often included social and political matters. Their television preferences also included a strong dose of news, news analysis, and documentary programs. Politics was often a subject of conversation in the shop. Most of the diecast workers identified themselves as members of the working class. But, despite the contentions of faction leaders, they usually did not make any great distinctions among the three working-class parties. There was a rather free and open exchange of political ideas. The one exception was the small minority supporting the Liberal-Democratic Party, who felt their position too unpopular to discuss publicly in the shop.

By contrast, the auto parts workers were primarily rural recruits. They generally knew very little about the factory apart from their own work. For many, holding a job in the factory meant that they could stay home from the fields on Sundays or go out occasionally dressed in a suit and tie; these became symbols of their emancipation from the hard, unrewarding life on the farm.

Most of the auto parts workers had little knowledge of or interest in the union. They were inclined to accept union and company judgment on matters that concerned them. They tended to identify uncritically with the fortunes of their company and lacked the independence so characteristic of the Tokyo diecast workers. For example, few attached great importance to acquiring a skill as did the Tokyo diecast workers. They were more willing to put their future in the hands of the company. The auto parts workers had difficulty either understanding or expressing themselves on matters other than those of a concrete nature.

Unlike the Tokyo diecast workers, they tended to read little except detective magazines and the sports pages of the newspaper. Sports were a major topic of conversation in the shop. Their television viewing was confined to similar subjects. Few of the auto parts workers saw themselves as members of the working class. Indeed, they had difficulty understanding the concept of class and often denied the existence of social classes. They had relatively little interest in politics and it was seldom a topic of conversation in the shop.[21]

One indication of the marked differences between the two labor forces could be seen in their respective attitudes and behavior with regard to working hours. Article 26 of the Takei work rules stated that the company had the right to order employees to work overtime if required by business conditions. The Tokyo diecast workers had never accepted this rule. They emphasized the individual worker's right to accept or reject overtime. For example, unless orders were slow the usual pattern was that the press workers were expected to work overtime, but one or two of the nine press workers often chose not to work, and no explanations to the foreman were offered or expected. Sometimes, the foreman would make personal requests to the workers that everyone work overtime, because the section was behind in its work. The workers then usually responded favorably, viewing it as an obligation to the foreman.

21. In neither company was sex a persistent topic of conversation. It was, however, by no means absent. One welder at the diecast factory, for example, often held his fellow workers spellbound as he recounted the skills of Peking women he had met during his military service. Generally speaking, male blue-collar workers behaved quite chivalrously toward their female fellow employees. This contrasted with their often raucous behavior after work at cabarets where sexual innuendo dominated their conversation with the hostesses. This turnabout of behavior reflects the concern of workers with developing harmonious social relations in the corporate world of the firm and their need to be free of restraints when dealing with an anonymous public.

On one occasion, the press foreman requested that in the future more overtime be worked "for the sake of the company." He further suggested that he post a fixed schedule for overtime, asking only a limited number of the press operators to work overtime each day. The foreman explained later that, while he tried to give everyone the same amount of overtime in the name of equality, he was trying to introduce more flexibility into the arrangement. The worker reaction to these proposals, although expressed in a friendly fashion, was firm opposition. To the suggestion that they work more overtime "for the sake of the company," they spontaneously replied, "We work to protect our standard of living and not for the benefit of the company." In strong terms, the workers defended the individual worker's right to choose whether or not to work overtime. They were also careful to avoid a situation in which the company could play off one worker against another. This reaction was typical of the experienced Tokyo worker, who will stand up for his rights and is not about to accept what he regards as any nonsense from the company. In this particular instance, the workers were successful in opposing the new plan.

The situation at the suburban diecast plant and at the auto parts company was quite different. The overtime set by the foreman was, in effect, regarded as compulsory by the workers. They could not conceive of refusing to work overtime unless they had a specific excuse for that day, such as a dental appointment. "Even when the company requests Sunday work," one worker explained, "it is half compulsory."

This difference in attitude toward overtime was one factor that prompted the diecast management to announce that the company would no longer recruit Tokyo workers but would seek more cooperative rural middle school graduates in the future. In its organizing at the suburban diecast plant, one argument the new opposition union used to condemn the Tokyo workers and their union was that the Tokyo union had sought only to protect the selfish interests of individual workers on the matter of overtime. They argued that a union should look at overtime in terms of its benefit to the company and all the workers. This is an example of the sharp difference between the individualism of the Tokyo diecast workers and the corporate orientation of the suburban plant workers. The Tokyo union supported a worker's right to decide on overtime in terms of his own self-interest. The suburban union interpreted this as selfishness and maintained that all employees working for higher production would bring increased wages and employment security for the workers.

Overtime constituted 30 percent of the total wages of the Tokyo diecast workers. They were quite clearly dependent on overtime to maintain their standard of living.[22] Management took the paternalistic view that since this was the case they would offer overtime even when the work requirements did not justify it. They saw it as a favor to the workers. The workers saw it differently; they seemed to regard overtime more as a right. That is, management had an obligation to offer the workers overtime, but the workers had a right to refuse it. Even when there was work to do during overtime, as there usually was, the work pace slackened noticeably. When the 4 P.M. buzzer rang signaling the start of overtime, the workers usually reacted by lighting a cigarette. The breaks became longer during overtime. Essentially, the workers saw overtime not as a time for work but as a time for earning a couple of hundred more yen.

It is quite different in a larger firm like the auto parts plant. There overtime made up only 10 to 15 percent of employee wages, so the workers were not as dependent on it. In the auto parts company, overtime was more closely geared to the production needs of the firm. Management believed that too much overtime was not good, because "workers get tired from it and production drops." It was not generally viewed as a favor to the workers by management nor as a right by the workers. No noticeable slackening of work pace occurred during overtime.

BACKGROUND FACTORS IN THE TWO TYPES

The kinds of differences noted above reflect the Japanese dual economy and grow out of the differing character-

22. In a more advanced industrial society like the United States, overtime is probably seen by industrial workers more as a means of financing an additional appliance or of saving for leisure activity than as a necessary prop to the maintenance of their standard of living.

istics of the respective work forces. The Tokyo diecast workers, employed in one of the many small and medium-sized firms with an uncertain future, were compelled to assume independent attitudes and behavior to protect their interests as they perceived them. They could not rely on the firm to provide a secure future and were thus unwilling to identify uncritically with it. The absence of the wide range of welfare benefits, such as housing and recreation facilities granted by larger firms, also forced the workers to be on their own. Yet, various comments by the diecast workers suggested that many would gladly have traded their independence for a secure future in a major corporation.

Many employees in small and medium-sized firms with an uncertain future do not feel compelled to take such an independent stance. On the contrary, this sector has many non-unionized workers and often exhibits very traditional social relations between employers and employees. Such social bonds, reflected in a strong company paternalism, preclude a sense of independence on the part of employees. The smaller the firm the more likely this is to be the case. In looking for additional factors to explain the differences between the two workers types, militant union leadership and a Tokyo location were probably also important in determining the independent and critical stance of the Tokyo diecast workers.

The average male blue-collar worker in manufacturing during 1965 received 31,900 yen before taxes in monthly wages.[23] This is somewhat below the average wage of 34,416 yen paid to Takei employees in the same year. These totals include overtime but not the semi-annual bonuses, which at Takei averaged about 70,000 yen a year. At Takei, in contrast to many of the larger firms, there were no sharp wage differentials between blue-collar and white-collar employees. There was a slight difference between the entering wages for high school graduates and those for middle school graduates, but most blue-collar workers at Takei, unlike those in many

23. *Year Book of Labor Statistics*, 1965, p. 121. The Takei average wage is compared to the average wage of male workers because there are few female workers in diecast firms. The intense heat, other poor working conditions, the high degree of skill required of diemakers and the physical endurance required of diecasters are key factors in explaining this situation. Most of the female employees at Takei were office workers.

big firms, were high school graduates. Taking into consideration the higher educational level of the workers at Takei, the
Takei wages were about average in the manufacturing industry. Among workers of the same age, the Takei wages were
well above the average, since the average age at Takei was
only 27.5, compared to 32.6 for the average male in manufacturing.

Average monthly wages at the Gujo company were
about equal to those at the diecast firm, but given the youth
of its labor force, its wages may be considered higher, because
Japanese workers are commonly paid according to their age
and length of service. In effect, the twenty-four-year-old with
four years of service at the auto parts company was making
as much as the twenty-six-year-old with five years of service
at the diecast plant. In short, among workers of the same age
and length of service, wages were somewhat higher in the
Gujo company. Moreover, the semi-annual bonuses and welfare benefits were considerably higher at the auto parts company.

In particular, the auto workers' access to company dormitories at the nominal cost of 350 yen a month contrasted
with the high rents paid by most of the diecast workers at the
Tokyo plant. The auto parts workers could also eat three
meals a day at the company cafeteria for 3,600 yen a month,
whereas Takei workers had no access to subsidized meals.
These differences indicate the critical importance of a worker's location in the dual economic structure in determining
his living standards and life style. The average unmarried
Takei worker lived in a four-and-a-half mat room (81 square
feet) and paid from 15 to 25 percent of his monthly wages
for rent. Even after marriage and the birth of a child, a
worker often continued to live in the same sized apartment.
An example was the thirty-year-old married leader of the socialist faction in the Takei plant union. He paid 5,500 yen
of his 33,000 yen monthly take-home pay for rent and considered this cheap. Kitchen, toilet, and washing facilities were
shared with four other families on the same floor. The apartment, slightly larger than a standard American double bed,
was half filled by the clutter of objects on all sides of the

room. When the bedding was out at night, there was no un-filled space in the apartment.

Although such workers would like very much to find larger quarters, the costs are often prohibitive. Ideally, they would like to build their own homes. However, the cost of land accounts for 60 percent of total house construction costs in urban and suburban areas in Japan. The soaring costs of real estate constitutes one of the major obstacles to the advance of the Japanese worker's standard of living.[24] Rent for a two-room apartment in Tokyo was at least 12,000 yen in 1965, about a third of the average worker's monthly income. Only workers in their middle thirties or older had wages high enough to be able to afford such rents. Moreover, rents in big cities have increased by about 10 percent annually in recent years. Government housing (kōei jūtaku danchi) would be a cheaper alternative, but most workers' incomes are not high enough to make them eligible to apply, except for those units most distant from Tokyo. The cheap city and prefectural housing is in such demand and the supply so short that workers often must wait several years, and even then there is no guarantee that their patience will be rewarded.

In effect, the diecast workers earned much less than the auto parts workers. Because they had heavier obligations in the form of housing costs, and the overall high cost of living in Tokyo, the diecast workers felt their standard of living to be threatened in a way that the auto parts workers did not. This contributed to their discontent and bred a cynicism in a society where the bounty of the consumer's life is increasingly featured on the television screen.

Furthermore, living in urban rental housing, the diecast workers had more access to the outside community than did the auto parts workers, who lived mainly in company dormitories and family farm households. The diecast workers were exposed to a wider range of ideas and conflicting views. The lengthier work-histories of the diecast workers meant that

24. Fujita Yoshitaka, *Wages and Labor Situation in Today's Japan* (Tokyo: Japan Federation of Employers' Associations, 1965). The land price index for major urban areas in Japan based on 100 in March 1955 rose to 1,038 in 1965, and to 1,165 by March 1969.

they had many friends outside the company, another source of intellectual ferment for them. Eighty percent of the blue-collar workers at the Tokyo diecast plant had previous non-farm work experience; this was true of only 35 percent of the blue-collar workers at the auto parts company. Having lived for long periods of time among the diverse currents of urban life, the diecast workers possessed a worldliness and cynicism not apparent among the rural recruits in the auto parts firm and this made them more reluctant to fully commit themselves either to the company or to their union.

The level of education among the workers in the two firms was quite different. In 1965, 80 percent of the blue-collar workers at the Tokyo diecast plant were either high school graduates, prewar higher elementary school graduates (eight years), or technical high school graduates, the remainder being primary school or prewar elementary school graduates (six years). At the auto firm, only 20 percent of the blue-collar workers were in the first category, with the large majority being middle school graduates. Furthermore, most of the diecast workers had graduated from urban schools, which are superior to the rural schools attended by the auto parts workers. Education, too, contributed to the differences in sophistication, independence, and political consciousness between the two types of workers.

The differences between the two labor forces were also the result of the difference in average age between the two firms. The Tokyo diecast workers were generally older (average age 27.5) than the auto parts workers (average age 24). This accounted for some increased sophistication and worldliness. Unlike the auto parts workers, the diecast workers were often married or thinking of marriage and thus were more inclined to think seriously about the future and their own prospects. The older age of the diecast workers meant that many of them remembered the hard times of the early postwar period, and this contributed to their class consciousness.

The picture presented here conflicts with the popular view that it is the newly recruited rural workers who provide the troops for politically oriented social movements. Such a view assumes that the newly recruited industrial workers are torn loose from the traditional communal solidarity of the village. As a result, they are considered alienated from both village and urban society and ready converts to politically conscious movements. But as this chapter has made clear, the diecast workers, not the auto parts workers, were the more politically conscious and active. This was because the diecast workers had been thoroughly socialized into urban society and urban means of organization and protest.

The essential differences between these two work forces fall into four categories. These are urban/rural, high school/ middle school, large firm/small firm, and older worker/ younger worker. The characteristics of the labor force of any Japanese firm in terms of these four dichotomous categories are a key factor in understanding the quality of labor-management relations that develops in that firm. The subsequent chapters deal with the articulation of these differences and their consequences.

One may speculate whether the diecast workers or the auto parts workers represent the Japanese blue-collar workers of the future. In view of the growing urban character of the labor force, the rising educational level among workers, and the aging of the Japanese labor force, the diecast workers, with their urban sophistication, cynicism, and militancy, would seem to be the more representative. The increasing shift of employees to large firms, however, suggests that the auto parts workers, with their rising living standards and their confidence in a secure and predictable work career, are also representative. The future industrial worker, then, is likely to be a mixture of these two diverse types. All else being equal, one may anticipate an increased militancy among Japanese workers in their demands upon management, but it will be a militancy tempered by pragmatism rather than a militancy based solely on left-wing ideology. In any case, the future is likely to show a reduction in worker subservience based on uncritical acceptance of company goals.

CHAPTER III

REWARDS: WAGES AND THE WORKER

Monetary compensation, employment security, and promotion are the three pillars supporting the complex of industrial relations rules and are the three basic rewards offered to blue-collar workers.

These three reward systems are intended to accomplish diverse objectives. They may be designed to stimulate work motivation; to reward past work and loyalty; to increase union loyalty (if the union has a say in forming these rules); to differentiate among categories of employees; and to maintain, increase, or decrease the number of employees. The task of this chapter and the next is to describe the system of compensation, employment security, and promotion. We will examine how they achieve their purpose or create tensions leading to change, and the actual changes. We will show who is paid what, who becomes a regular employee, who is promoted, who is assigned the best job, and who may work overtime.

Throughout, where statistics or the concept include white- and blue-collar workers, I have used the word *employee*. The word *worker* is used for blue-collar workers only.

MODERNIZATION AND THE WAGE STRUCTURE

The wage-rate structure of Japanese firms, as measured by the formal criteria of the Western economist and sociologist, suggests that of an industrially underdeveloped nation. The most striking indication of underdevelopment is the existence of wages determined by a worker's length of service, age, and educational level. This is in contrast to the Western expectation of explicit wage-rate structures for job classifications or occupations which are created during economic development.[1] Company housing and housing allowances are also associated with early stages of industrialization.[2] In 1964, 5,500,000 Japanese employees of a total of 11,300,000 in the manufacturing sector benefited from company housing or housing allowances (46 percent of all employees in the manufacturing sector).[3] Family allowances, a common practice in the early stages of industrialization, also exist in Japan.[4] The extensive welfare benefits paid by Japanese firms for transportation, canteen and other food services, medical, purchasing, and cultural and recreational facilities are associated with industrially underdeveloped nations.[5] The Japanese practice of paying semi-annual bonuses, which account for nearly 25 percent of all regular wages, has no counterpart in other industrially advanced nations. Worker training within the firm ordinarily is most pronounced in the early stages of industrialization when there is a shortage of skilled workers.[6] On-the-job training is still a distinctive feature of industrial relations despite Japan's sophisticated educational system. The practice of permanent employment is a part of the Japanese wage-rate structure. Usually such immobility is considered incompatible with modern industrial requirements.[7]

Despite the seemingly anachronistic reward systems, Japan's recent history provides a remarkable case of rapid industrialization. Its rapid growth during the postwar period is especially impressive. We can, therefore, assume that a "backward" wage-rate structure has not inhibited economic growth.

1. John Dunlop, *Industrial Relations Systems* (New York: Henry Holt, 1958), p. 365.
2. *Ibid.*, pp. 357–358.
3. Ministry of Labor, *Year Book of Labor Statistics, 1964,* (Tokyo, The Ministry, 1965), pp. 246–247.
4. John Dunlop, *op. cit.,* p. 374.
5. *Ibid.*, pp. 357–358.
6. *Ibid.*, pp. 351–352.
7. Clark Kerr *et al., Industrialism and Industrial Man* (Cambridge: Harvard University Press, 1960), pp. 17–18.

In fact, Japan's economic success must in some measure be attributed to this highly functional wage-rate structure.

There are two explanations for this apparent contradiction between the "backward" wage-rate structure and Japan's striking economic growth. The first explanation is that the Japanese wage-rate structure as a transitional mechanism has had positive consequences for industrialization, but that with continued economic growth it will have to be transformed into a "modern" wage-rate structure. This is interpreted by cultural lag: the wage-rate structure is seen as a reflection of past responses to problems of early industrialization and that in time this structure will have to be brought up to present-day realities. For this explanation one may garner much evidence. In particular, the changes occurring in Japanese enterprises suggest great tensions and strains have been built up in the existing wage-rate structure. A number of observers believe a wage-rate structure similar to that of other industrially advanced countries will emerge.[8] A variant of this position holds that until now Japan could afford the luxury of an inefficient wage-rate structure, but that with increasing competition and rising wages, Japanese companies will be forced to develop a more rational structure. These views are in harmony with the convergence hypothesis discussed in the introduction.

A second explanation sees the Japanese wage-rate structure not as backward as many Westerners think; the existence of formal complex written wage rules is an indication of a highly sophisticated industrial relations system. The durability of the Japanese system suggests that Western observers may have paid too much attention to different institutional arrangements without examining similar functional outcomes, for there are functional equivalents in industrialized societies that tolerate different institutional arrangements.

Which of the two explanations is the more plausible? The case study material presented here gives both explanations a claim to validity.[9] As elements of the wage-rate struc-

8. See Nakayama Ichirō, "The Modernization of Industrial Relations in Japan," *The Changing Patterns of Industrial Relations* (Tokyo: The Japan Institute of Labor, 1965), pp. 85–96.

9. A real problem for social scientists dealing with this question con-

ture become dysfunctional with the achievement of new levels of economic growth, changes will occur. Indeed, as an historical practice caught up in the process of industrialization all wage-rate structures are in constant flux; this certainly is characteristic of Japan.

Japanese management looks to Western and to its own experiences in search of alternative approaches. Nevertheless, certain cultural values and practices endure and permit only so much change as is necessary to keep them in tune with modern requirements.[10] Japanese managers show great ingenuity in manipulating these practices for their desired ends. They consciously develop new functions for existing practices like the proverbial pouring of new wine into old bottles.

JAPANESE WAGE-RATE STRUCTURES

The wage system in Japan is called *nenkō joretsu chingin*; the term explains the dominant role played by length of service and age in wage determination. This wage system is part of a still larger system called *nenkō seido,* which denotes both the system of promotion and employment tenure. Table 3 shows the distribution of the average monthly wage of 34,415 yen at the diecast company in 1965.

The basic wage is the most important element (56 percent), and is a common feature of Japanese wage-rate structures. In the manufacturing sector the basic wage averages 86.3 percent of the monthly contract wages (excluding overtime, shift differentials, and holiday work).[11] Generally, the basic wage consists of the starting wage plus annual increments (*teiki shokyu*) and a portion of the yearly "base up" (*besu appu*). The unskilled blue-collar worker receives the

cerns the selection of data. Proponents of both views have no difficulty in gathering data to support their position. What is necessary are objective standards for selection of data.

10. This leads to disagreements among observers which are analogous to the controversy over whether the glass of water is half full or half empty. There are linguistic problems in labeling behavior patterns and values that are undergoing social change to which social scientists have not yet seriously addressed themselves.

11. Figure is for regular employees in firms with thirty or more employees. *Year Book of Labor Statistics,* 1965, pp. 171–172. An examination of the wages of production workers *only* shows roughly the same percentage being accounted for by the basic wage.

TABLE 3

Wage-Rate Structure at Takei Diecast Company in 1965

	Yen	Percent
Standard Wage		
Basic wage (kihonkyū)	19,340	56
Work allowance (shokunōteate) [a]	1,350	4
Welfare allowance (fukushiteate) [b]	1,400	4
Supervisory position allowance (yakuzukiteate)	80	–
Casting allowance (chūzōteate)	230	–
Family allowance (kazokuteate) [c]	570	2
Supplementary Wage		
Overtime (zangyō)	5,660	16
Second shift allowance (ni kōtaiteate)	2,330	7
Third shift allowance (san kōtaiteate) [d]	140	–
Holiday work (kyūjitsu shukkin)	380	1
Yearly paid holidays (nenji yūkyū kyūkai)	1,320	4
Injury disability guarantee (rōsaihoshō)	55	–
Attendance allowance (seikinteate)	390	1
Housing allowance (jūtakuteate) [e]	1,170	3
TOTAL	34,415 [f]	98

[a] Paid for daily attendance.
[b] Equivalent to worker contribution for health insurance and old age pension.
[c] In the early postwar inflation, family allowance was important in stabilizing worker livelihoods, but in recent years has declined in importance.
[d] Only the diecast section of the new suburban plant was on a three shift system.
[e] The housing allowance, although administered by the company, is considered negotiable by the Takei Union. This is the case in most Japanese unions.
[f] In addition, Takei paid 737 yen commuting allowance per employee.

starting wage on entering the firm after graduating from middle or high school. It is determined by market factors. In the past, the starting wage in Japanese factories was close to the monetary earning ability of the agricultural labor force from which industrial manpower has been supplied. The annual increments to the starting wage, the second element in the basic wage, are determined, in order of their importance, by length of service, age, and rating assessment of superiors. The emphasis on length of service in the firm obviously puts experienced workers, who enter the firm later, at a disadvantage.

Takei makes rating assessments of workers twice a year.

The foreman makes the initial assessment which is passed on to the supervisor and section chief for their comments. Foremen reported that they based their ratings on: diligence, seriousness, lack of absence and lateness, productive performance, and cooperation with fellow workers. They believed upper management sometimes altered their assessments by weighing union activity, political affiliation, and loyalty to the company. The assessment is not open to worker scrutiny or a matter for worker grievance. Differences in pay among workers resulting from these assessments are not large, but may add up over the years.

Differences in annual increments may seem small to outside observers and unlikely to serve as incentives, but they are important. Takei workers discussed and compared their annual increments with great intensity. The annual increments are a reflection of daily competition among workers in terms of production and winning the favor of superiors. Workers have quit in both the diecast and auto parts company when they learned that other workers of the same age and with the same length of service received slightly higher increments.

The third element of the basic wage is the yearly "base up." Japanese unions negotiate for the lump sum of the total wage cost of the firm which is then divided among the total number of regular workers (temporary workers are not covered by the union) either in the form of a fixed cash increase or a percentage increase. It is called *besu-appu*. The union will usually bargain with the firm over its distribution. Generally a portion is divided equally among all employees and another is paid on the basis of age and length of service.

The basic wage, the supervisory position allowance, the family allowance, and the housing allowance reward the older workers with a long record of service. At Takei, for example, a twenty-three-year-old worker averaged 21,000 yen a month, while a forty-year-old worker averaged 40,000 after deductions —nearly twice the salary of the younger man. The Takei wage differences by age are roughly similar to those given in national statistics.[12] The wage increase curve follows the

12. *Ibid.*, pp. 130–149.

actual costs incurred by workers as they move from bachelorhood to family responsibilities. At Takei, the increase curve
levels off after age forty, as it does in other firms of this size.
In larger firms (of more than 1,000 employees) the wage
curve continues to increase until retirement age at fifty-five
but at a slower rate. In smaller firms (30 to 99 employees)
the wage increase curve increases only slightly after thirty and
declines after forty-five.[13] The smaller firms try to maintain
the *nenkō joretsu chingin* system of payment by age and
length of service, but find it difficult because as workers get
older and wage costs increase, their ability to pay becomes
limited.

Another characteristic of the *nenkō* practice should be
mentioned. In most large firms, educational qualifications
serve as cut-off point for differentiating the wages of middle
school, high school, and university graduates. There are three
different wage curves with higher educational achievement
resulting in higher wages at any given age in the work career.
In the auto parts firm, blue-collar wages averaged about 75
percent of white-collar wages. This is close to the differences
reported in national statistics for male blue- and white-collar
employees.[14] Should a blue-collar middle school graduate rise
to a white-collar position or a high school graduate become
a blue-collar worker, such wage distinctions would be reduced. The former instance, in particular, is a rare
phenomenon, especially in large firms like the auto parts
company.

RELATION OF FACTORY PERFORMANCE TO WAGES

That wages and wage increases are determined by length
of service, age, and education and not factory performance
or job competence has been of particular interest to Western
observers. To some, this implied a wage system that falls
outside economic rationality as it is understood in the West.[15]

13. *Ibid.*, pp. 144–145.
14. *Ibid.*, p. 121. Differences are less marked for females.
15. James Abegglen, *The Japanese Factory* (Glencoe: Free Press,
1958).

But this view cannot be sustained if we recognize that one of the main reasons for payment by age and length of service is that with growing age and lengthening service the worker acquires skill and experience and, therefore, increases his value to the firm. A rough check of wages by occupation reveals that, generally, skilled jobs are associated with higher length of service and higher wages and semiskilled jobs with lower length of service and lower wages.[16] There is a Western myth of the unskilled Japanese sweeper and the skilled die-maker making the same wages, having entered the firm at the same time and being the same age.[17] Although conceivable, it is the exception to the rule. In large firms, it is more likely that the sweeper, if he is older, will be a temporary worker with low wages, or the job will be contracted out to a firm paying lower wages.

In short, wage differentials among blue-collar workers in Japan resulting from length of service differences tend to correspond to wage differentials in the West arising from skill differences. This is not accidental. The importance of age and length of service in Japanese society and especially in Japanese factories should not be seen as a unique structural arrangement. Rather, it is a specific elaboration of more generally universalistic features applicable to all human societies. In all societies, age as a qualifying criterion for the performance of various roles is greatly influenced by the cumulative aspect of different types of knowledge. Different kinds of knowledge are required for different roles; the acquisition of this knowledge consumes time, hence implies age progression.[18] In any advanced industrial society, most adult roles are located in hierarchical structures. The distribution of income, prestige, and power in factories, unions, political parties, and churches occur along lines of an approximately age-graded continuum. In the majority of occupations, a steadily upward progression of status appears to be closely correlated

16. Year Book of Labor Statistics, 1964, pp. 163, 171.
17. James Abegglen, op. cit., p. 68.
18. S. N. Eisenstadt, From Generation to Generation (New York: Free Press, 1956), p. 27.

with advances in age.[19] Characteristic to Japan is the explicit recognition of age and length of service in a wide range of decisions affecting workers.

The Japanese company does not leave to chance the young worker's acquisition of skill and productive capacity. The young worker entering the company directly after school graduation is untrained. If he shows promise, he is gradually led through "stages of difficulty." In the beginning he will be assigned relatively simple jobs and then gradually be introduced to increasingly difficult ones over the years. This often involves a complicated system of job rotation. In this way, it is expected that the employee's value to the company increases. It is true, the wage fit with factory performance is not as tight as that found in an American factory. Nevertheless, a clear correlation between wage and factory performance exists, and if it is not as tight, it is because the practice of permanent employment makes it less necessary. That an employee's rewards must be calculated to match exactly his present productive contribution is not relevant in a system of permanent employment. In the major firms a large retirement allowance is designed to help the employee after he retires and to reward him for long years of productive service. In an American firm, where the young worker may quit the next day, it is unavoidable that he be paid for the preceding day's production. But the large Japanese firm, operating with the assumption (not always true as we shall see) that the worker will continue with the firm until retirement, need not reward the worker at the exact moment he makes his contribution and with the exact amount corresponding to his contribution. This suggests that low inter-firm mobility is responsible for introducing economic rationality into the *nenkō* wage system. If we may assume that the employee's productivity rises rapidly until somewhere between thirty and forty, after which it gradually declines, it seems that the *nenkō* wage system underpays young and overpays older workers. The element of rationality is introduced because, presumably, management

19. Norman Ryder, "The Cohort as a Concept in the Study of Social Change," *American Sociological Review*, Vol. 30, No. 6 (December 1965), p. 857.

seeks to cancel out the overpayment of older workers by underpaying young ones. This is achieved by having workers spend their entire career in one company. Building this attachment permits the company to collect on its training investment. A worker separating at an early age costs the company its training investment. Similarly, it is expensive for an older worker to separate from the firm, because his productivity does not justify his high wages and he will have difficulty finding another job at equivalent wages. Only if the worker stays with the company throughout his career will his high wages in later years provide economic justification for the underpayment in his youth.[20]

TENSIONS FOR CHANGE

In recent years a variety of pressures have been at work to undermine the *nenkō* wage system. The force of these pressures has caused the government to support actively a reconsideration of the *nenkō* system. The 1966 Employment Measures Law specifically calls for the elimination of employment practices that prevent workers from making effective use of their abilities.[21]

The extent to which increasing length of service and age correspond to increased skill has always depended on the nature of the industry, the particular company, its growth rate, and its employees' age distribution. In firms where highly skilled jobs are numerous, and long apprenticeships are necessary to learn these skills, the fit is likely to be tight.

Rapid technological change and the rise of mass production industries, however, are changing this pattern. Old crafts give way to new skilled and semiskilled jobs. Young workers are often quicker or at least as quick as the more

20. Conversations with Vladimir Stoikov formerly of the Institute of Labor and Industrial Relations, University of Illinois, in May 1967, were especially helpful in formulating this relation between the *nenkō* wage and permanent employment.

21. An English translation of this legislation appears in Ministry of Labor, *Japan Labour Laws*, 1968 (Tokyo: Institute of Labor Policy, 1968), pp. 161–174. A detailed discussion of the legislation and its implications appears in Japan Institute of Labour, *Japan Labor Bulletin*, Vol. 5, No. 12 (December 1966). See also *ibid.*, Vol. 6, No. 5 (May 1967).

highly paid older workers to acquire and retain the new skills and technology. The story is told how in modern factories imported machines arrive with English instructions which only the young workers can read; an apocryphal story, no doubt, but symbolic of the changes taking place. These changes break down the relation between increasing length of service, acquisition of skills and factory performance. It constitutes a fundamental break with the traditional agricultural society in which the father trains his son over many years in the skills necessary to care for the rice fields until the father retires and the son takes over. These developments upset status relations in the shop; the prestige of older workers declines. In the two factories studied, age and length of service were not sufficient criteria for high prestige among fellow workers. Only when these were combined with skill and experience, did the other workers grant them high prestige and management award such workers extra privileges. It was reported that the practice of gradually introducing workers to harder jobs over the years was rapidly disappearing. Management is increasingly concerned with using the new technology efficiently, particularly because of its high cost. More and more young workers are assigned jobs appropriate to their abilities, and a growing shortage of young workers compels management to use them more efficiently. The practice of not giving young workers difficult jobs survived mainly among white-collar employees in the auto parts plant. This is reminiscent of the American experience when automation was first introduced to the production line (Detroit Automation). Management realized later that the same savings could be made by applying automation to white-collar work.

Other pressures lie behind the recent willingness of Japanese management to reappraise their wage-rate structures and look for alternatives or modifications of the nenkō wage system. The average age of employees in Japanese industry is low (32.6 for males in the manufacturing sector). Although the low age depends on the demographic characteristics of the population, it can also be attributed to the rapid growth of the Japanese economy and the practice of hiring young workers at low pay. As these vast numbers of workers grow older and their wages increase under the *nenkō* system, they become a serious cost problem. Therefore, management is being forced to resolve the inherent contradictions of the *nenkō* system.

Because of the growing manpower shortage, the structuring of the *nenkō* wage according to educational qualification has come under pressure. More middle school graduates are entering high school; their number rose from 50 percent in 1955 to 72.3 percent in 1968.[22] Middle school graduates available to the labor force declined from 960,000 in 1964 to 520,000 in 1966.[23] The number of new middle school graduates who will seek jobs in 1970 is estimated to be only 185,000. Also, the Japanese university, an elite educational institution in the prewar period where only 3 percent of the eligible age group were graduated, is now attended by 20 percent of that age group. The number of university students increased from 700,000 in 1960 to 1,400,000 in 1968. These changes have dried up past sources of blue-collar labor. Like the auto parts firm, many firms are being forced to recruit high school graduates for blue-collar jobs. In 1964 high school graduates made up 16.7 percent of all blue-collar workers as compared to 13.4 percent in 1958. These percentages continue to rise and the increase is noticeable in firms employing over 500 workers.[24] No doubt, this trend works to dilute if not to dissolve wage distinctions between blue- and white-collar workers and points to further weakening of the *nenkō* system.

It is not only the decline in the supply of middle school graduates that has weakened the *nenkō* wage. The productive age population (15 years and over) increased 12 percent during 1960–1965 but the increase fell to 9 percent during 1965–1970, and it is estimated that the increase will be only 6 percent during 1970–1975; a lower birth rate being mainly responsible for these changes. At the same time, the number

22. *Ibid.*, Vol. 7, No. 1 (January 1968), p. 2.
23. *Ibid.*, Vol. 6, No. 9 (September 1967), p. 8.
24. Ministry of Labor, *Chingin Kōzō Kihon Chōsa* (Wage Structure Basic Survey), Tokyo, 1958, 1964. See also Ujihara Shōjirō, "Japan's Laboring Class: Changes in the Postwar Period," *Journal of Social and Political Ideas in Japan*, Vol. 3, No. 3 (December 1965), pp. 63–65.

of jobs is expected to increase at the rate of 1,000,000 a year; this number will be augmented by the need to replace retiring workers. The anticipated lowered rate of supply and the heightened demand will result in an increasingly tight labor market in the future.

These developments are increasing the wages of young workers; this, in turn, has compressed the wage-rate structure. The starting rate for middle school graduates (destined for blue-collar jobs) more than tripled during 1955–1965, while the starting rate for high school graduates has increased more than two and one-half times.[25] As a result, older workers' wage advantages disappear. In manufacturing male blue-collar workers in the forty to forty-nine age group saw their wage advantage over workers under eighteen years diminish from slightly less than four times in 1954 to slightly less than three times in 1965.[26] This is a *de facto* weakening of the *nenkō* wage system. The practice of compensating for the high wages paid to older workers by paying low wages to young ones becomes less possible as young workers' wages rise.

WORKERS AND NENKŌ

To look at the *nenkō* wage system and the kinds of changes discussed above from the viewpoint of the worker gives added perspective. The *nenkō* wage system became firmly established after World War II as much by union demands as by other causes. That the union demands reflected worker views can hardly be doubted. It was a time of severe inflation and worker demands for the "livelihood wage" encouraged the spread of the *nenkō* system.[27] "Livelihood wage" meant workers were paid according to their needs; consequently, older workers with large families and higher living costs were paid more according to age and length of

25. Japan Institute of Labor, *Japan's Labor Statistics* (Tokyo: The Institute, 1967), p. 82.
26. Ministry of Labor, *Rōdō Hakusho 1965* (White Paper on Labor 1965), (Tokyo: Labor Laws Institute, 1965), p. 203.
27. The so-called *Densangata chingin*, named after the electric power union (Densan) set this pattern.

service. With the passing of hard times, length of service replaced age as the more important criterion.

Worker division over support of the *nenkō* wage system was apparent in the Takei diecast union. Each year in formulating the union wage demand, the issue arose over how much should be paid equally to all workers and how much of the union demand should be divided according to the "pay slide scale." An emphasis on the "pay slide scale" has the effect of paying older workers more, hence increasing wage differentials according to age and length of service. The younger workers want the increase to be paid uniformly to all workers while the older workers want it divided according to the pay slide scale. There is considerable dissatisfaction in the age group which has less influence in the union.[28] Moreover, the recent impact of market factors in raising entering wage rates and compressing the wage structure is likely to insure increasing friction in the future. Older workers who seek to recoup their advantages meet with resistance from young workers.

Young workers in unskilled jobs often can look forward to acquiring a skill in the future. They are willing and able to work hard, and with the new technology can often match the productive performance of veteran workers. Hence, they see no reason why older workers should be paid more.

Older workers, as might be expected, usually support the *nenkō* wage. This is particularly true of those who see no chance of moving up in the skill hierarchy of the company. The *nenkō* wage system helps them to maintain a positive occupational image and to provide a source of work motivation. They can still hold their head up doing an unskilled or semiskilled job because they know they are making almost as much as the young skilled worker. As a thirty-four year old semiskilled press operator put it, "Yea, I'd like to work in the die department, but there's no chance, and besides, who needs it as long as I'm making out okay in my pay."

The dissatisfaction of young workers with the *nenkō*

28. Research in American industry has shown that differences between wage rates are almost as important as their absolute levels in causing worker dissatisfaction. Leonard R. Sayles and George Strauss, *The Local Union: Its Place in the Industrial Plant* (New York: Harper, 1953), p. 45.

wage system intensifies as Japan moves from a production-
to a consumption-oriented society. For the young workers
want their money now so they can cash in on the good life
so enticingly described in the mass media. The *nenkō* wage
system combined with the permanent employment system,
acts as a system of deferred wage payment, which does not
sit well with them.

However, the *nenkō* wage system cannot be described
as disintegrating under enormous pressure. At the auto parts
and the diecast company, except for a few articulate workers,
dissatisfaction of young workers took the form of occasional
criticism rather than consistent opposition. In part, this is
because they are not sure how they would like to replace the
nenkō wage system. Opinion polls report young workers to
be sympathetic to a wage structure based on pay by type of
work or ability. But it is one thing to fill out interview forms
and quite another to risk upsetting social relations in the
shop.[29] The dissatisfaction of young workers in shops like
the diecast and auto parts companies, is voiced by demands
for reducing wage differentials based on age and length of
service rather than outright demands for pay by type of work
or ability. Furthermore, young workers also want to be assured a future that includes rising wages, and for many the
nenkō wage system still seems the best way of assuring this.
The unknown is always a dangerous quantity.

One may ask what functions the *nenkō* system fulfills
for workers. First, it brings the industrial world into line
with the rest of Japanese society, where age is highly valued.
In the political world, in the family, and in other institutions,
age insures some degree of respect and prestige. Second,
nenkō serves the interests of workers by bringing order into
management's distribution of rewards. Favoritism is unacceptable to workers as a basis for distributing rewards because
it causes friction and competition. The *nenkō* system insures

29. A 1962 survey reported that 53.2 percent of surveyed workers
under age 30 favored a wage structure based on type of job or ability while
only 26.1 percent of those over age 45 favored such a system. *Rōdō Hakusho*
1962 (White Paper on Labor 1962), p. 213. The results of such surveys,
however, have not always been consistent.

some degree of protection against management discrimination and maintains worker solidarity. Length of service and age are public information and therefore have an objective, indisputable character. This is less true in the assessment of skill and ability.

Nenkō provides employment and wage equities (rights) for employees by defining the scope and boundaries of wage differentiations. This is important in an economy where workers generally must look to the employer rather than to the market for job security and wage improvement.[30] George Taylor, the noted American arbitrator, has made exactly this point in trying to explain why seniority principles develop in some American industries and not others.[31] For these reasons we cannot expect the nenkō system to disappear in Japan simply because modifications are now under way. The nenkō system will persist for precisely the same reasons that the seniority system persists and indeed has grown in American industry during the past 25 years. While American, and increasingly, Japanese workers may accept abstract social values of industrial efficiency, it can be expected that they will maintain an interest in building equity in their job and associated rewards when the market does not provide these to their satisfaction.[32] Societies differ in the ways workers satisfy needs for job security, worker solidarity and order in the distribution of rewards. In Japan, the scope of the seniority principle is far wider than in America, partly because Japanese workers are less able to rely on or control the market. Rather than seeing the universalistic ascriptive characteristics of nenkō as unique, they should be seen as elaborations and variations of age-grading principles present in the institutions of other ad-

30. The low rate of inter-firm mobility in many sectors of the economy will be discussed in the following chapter.

31. George W. Taylor, "Seniority Concepts," Arbitration Today, Proceedings of the Eighth Annual Meeting of the National Academy of Arbitrators (Washington: Bureau of National Affairs, 1955), p. 132.

32. Frederick Meyers, The Analytic Meaning of Seniority. Reprinted from the Proceedings of the 18th Annual Meeting of the Industrial Relations Research Association, 1965 (Los Angeles: University of California, Institute of Industrial Relations, 1966), p. 99. See also AFL-CIO Department of Research, "Seniority-Fair Play on the Job," AFL-CIO American Federationist (September 1961).

vanced industrial countries. It has the strength of all age-grading systems. At a given point in time, there is an unequal distribution of rights and rewards. But age-grading as a mode of institutionalization implies the automatic transfer of positions and rewards to junior sets at fixed intervals. This insures equality of access over time and thereby reduces tension and competition over rewards.[33]

MANAGEMENT AND NENKŌ

Management is in a similar situation. It would like to introduce pay by type of work or ability to make possible a more efficient calculation of wage payment (hard to do under a system of deferred wage payment). It is aware of the increasing wage costs as a result of the present crop of young workers advancing in age. But it hesitates to introduce a system of direct wage payment by type of work or ability that may open the floodgates to changes which in turn will undermine existing social relations and methods of labor control and work motivation. It fears a rapid switchover will result in unusually high costs which could not be deferred. At present economic pressures from falling profits, for example, are not great enough to push management toward drastic innovations. Moreover, although some managers would make personal gains from an increased emphasis on pay by type of work or ability, others have a vested interest in the present system.

The Takei management, like other companies, was experimenting with modifications of the nenkō wage. In 1966 the company suggested to the new union at the suburban plant that the work allowance be replaced by a new achievement allowance. The union leadership was somewhat confused by the company proposal but agreed to accept it. Essentially, the achievement allowance was to be distributed on the basis of a sliding scale according to plant output. It was not to exceed 4,000 yen a month per worker, which was what the work allowance component would total in 1967. A

33. Michael G. Smith, "Pre-Industrial Stratification Systems," *Social Structure and Mobility in Economic Development,* Neil Smelser and Seymour Lipset (eds.) (Chicago: Aldine Publishing Company, 1966), p. 150.

minimum sum was guaranteed on the basis of existing production levels. This was a rather modest start, but Takei's
delicate financial situation and fear that the new plan would
become costly without a stipulated maximum amount made
it reluctant to make bigger changes. The Takei plan was an
attempt to accustom workers to being paid by production as
a forerunner to more far-reaching changes. Workers at the
new diecast plant reacted against the new plan. The opposition came not from tradition-oriented workers dragging their
feet, but from workers who were a step ahead of management. Their main objection was:

> This isn't really an incentive wage. No one thinks produc-
> tion will fall in the future, so the company isn't really pro-
> tecting us against anything with the minimum. What we
> want is to get paid for increased production, which will
> make it worthwhile to go all out.

In recent years, the Gujo Auto Parts Company management also has given increasing consideration to a system of
pay by type of work or ability to complement or in part replace the *nenkō* wage. The conditions at that company are
especially favorable to the introduction of such changes. The
low average age of twenty-four years among its workers means
an absence of the strong resistance by older workers as is the
case in established industries.

In the nineteen-fifties a number of companies experimented with pay by work (*shokumukyū*) formulas, akin to
Western job-classified wage-rate structures. The experience
led to numerous difficulties because the new approach clashed
sharply with existing practices. As an alternative, many firms
established payment by ability (*shokunōkyū*) formulas. These
developments, reflected in government statistics, show that
the percentage of manufacturing firms with a pay by type of
work formula for blue-collar workers in the basic wage declined from 5.8 percent in 1953 to 1.8 percent in 1962.[34]
During the same period there was a marked increase in pay-

34. Ministry of Labor (ed.), *Sengo Rōdō Keizaishi* (Postwar Labor
Economic History), (Tokyo: Labor Laws Association, 1966), pp. 296–297.
It is extremely difficult to measure the increased role of achievement in the
wage system because it is often hidden under vague labels in a highly complex wage-rate structure.

ment by ability formulas. The statistics do not specify exactly the number of firms with pay by ability formulas but it is apparent that these formulas are spreading rapidly.

Like the auto parts company, many firms view payment-by-ability as a compromise between the existing *nenkō* system and the more radical departure represented by the payment by work formulas. Payment-by-ability is different from payment by type of work in that it rewards a worker not only for doing a given job but also for having the ability to perform the job *even if at the time he is not doing it*. This may seem an unnecessary complication but, in fact, serves to maintain the continuity of the reward system in the Japanese factory, while at the same time it opens up greater possibilities for rewarding achievement. Here is an example stated by a Japanese manager: If there are thirteen workers with the same seniority and ability (skill) to operate only ten machines, a Western employer will lay off three of them. But in a Japanese factory, under the *nenkō* wage and permanent employment system, not only should these three extra workers not be fired but, if they have the same seniority as the ten actually doing the job, they should be paid the same wages. For "if they have the same seniority," [35] the payment by ability formula substitutes the qualification, "if they have the ability to perform the job."

Payment-by-ability varies by firm; indeed, this is its virtue from management's point of view. In some firms it is mere window-dressing for existing practices. Such firms make the payment by ability portion of the wage a percentage of the basic wage based on age and length of service. They may also see to it that, though workers are paid by their technical ability, their placement and exposure to training continues to be determined by their age, length of service and educational level. Under such conditions, there is really no substantive change from the *nenkō* practice.

On the other hand, the emphasis on ability and technical qualifications in the payment-by-ability formula of some

35. The American practice of making minute distinctions in seniority as criteria for layoffs or access to jobs does not apply in Japan. For wage distinctions in Japan, the year of entry is relevant and not the day or month.

firms is one step closer to direct reward of achievement. It moves the wage-rate structure toward a closer fit between skill level and reward. As such, the payment-by-ability formula enables employers to modify the *nenkō* practice at their own pace, without the disruptions that result from a wholesale introduction of the pay by type of work formula. There are those who point out how little payment-by-ability actually deviates from the *nenkō* concept, but it is significant that management now finds it necessary to justify existing practices in terms of payment-by-ability. This points to the existence of great tension. It seems possible that once the rhetoric of payment-by-ability is established, it will create pressure for the adoption of the payment-by-ability formula. Managers at the diecast and auto parts company were conscious of recent changes whereby placement, training opportunities and promotion were increasingly awarded on the basis of ability rather than age and length of service. In the diecast company, the slogan was *tekizai tekisho,* which translated means "the right man in the right place." In many firms, formal introduction of the payment-by-ability formula also involved establishing ability grades for calculating that component of the wage. Each grade has a maximum and minimum range, which allows for rewarding age and length of service. For example, gradings for ability may be divided into twenty-five classes, each specifying a monthly cash range. Thus, a semiskilled worker may be assigned to the lower 4,000–6,000 yen class as opposed to a skilled worker who may be assigned to the 10,000–12,000 yen class, but the precise wage of the workers within these ranges will be determined by their length of service.

From these examples, it is clear that the payment-by-ability formula is an important mechanism for firms that seek a means of rewarding achievement and skill directly. The payment-by-ability formula illustrates the talent of Japanese managers to devise mechanisms that maintain continuity in the social structure of the firm, yet permit them to adapt the firm to new social and economic requirements.

Depending on one's viewpoint, the payment-by-ability formula can be interpreted as a support for the convergence hypothesis which holds that industrial societies are inexorably becoming more similar or for the theory which holds that cultural differences will be preserved. However, framing issues in terms of polar opposites obscures the more complex questions. What is the relationship between universal tendencies and national cultural differences? Are there functional equivalents? How does change occur? What is the mediating role played by certain mechanisms like the payment-by-ability formula? What is the emergent mix?

The accommodations and adaptations possible under the *nenkō* system suggest that *nenkō* should be seen as an ideal type that is present in varying degrees rather than as a rigid structure in all firms. For example, the *nenkō* system in large firms is only made possible by its absence in small firms. Its application to regular workers in big firms is only possible because of the large numbers of temporary and subcontract workers to whom the *nenkō* wage does not apply. Its persistence in the future will not be easily measured by formal criteria. As the above examples suggest the principle of *nenkō* system will be interwoven with newly evolving arrangements that emphasize skill and ability.

A GROUP INCENTIVE WAGE SYSTEM

An additional component of the wage-rate structure at the Gujo Auto Parts Company was a group incentive premium system. It accounted for 25 percent of the total wages paid. Monthly production norms were set for each department and a formula was worked out for rewarding workers in those departments that produced over the norm in a given month. How does the system operate in a Japanese context? How do workers respond to it? Group incentive systems are common in Japanese industry. Though the details may vary in firms, the general principle and underlying meaning probably are similar to the system at Gujo.[36]

This group incentive system has not been recently im-

36. On the average, 6 percent of the monthly contract cash earnings of production workers in the manufacturing sector is in some form of incentive wage. The percentage has been higher in the past. *Year Book of Labor Statistics*, 1965, p. 172.

ported from the West but has had a long history at Gujo. Management attributes its presence to the earlier spread of Western ideas to Japan, specifically the theories of scientific management by the American Frederick Taylor. Over the past ten years, the Gujo incentive system has been modernized to make it more effective. Time study methods and their sophisticated use to set production standards were adopted. The use of Western techniques, however, does not mean Gujo management has incorporated the Western system in toto.[37] Important adaptations have been made. For example, the 25 percent of the wage accounted for by the group incentive system is calculated as a percentage of a worker's basic wage. This means that each worker's share is graded according to his length of service and age. In this way, the group incentive system is interwoven with the *nenkō* system. It is a group incentive system rather than one that focuses on the individual; hence, it can draw upon traditional group sanctions in making the individual conform to required standards.

In the case of the clutch assembly, five sections are grouped as one unit, and a total monthly production norm is set for it. The production norm is based on the time allotted for each job, which includes actual work time and 20 percent additional down time (e.g., use of toilet, waiting time for materials, machine breakdown, and preparation time). The actual work time is based on observing a worker turn out 100 pieces. If the production norm is exceeded and instead of the norm of 90 pieces in 60 minutes, 90 pieces are produced in 50 minutes, there is then an efficiency of $\frac{60}{50} = 1.20$. This efficiency rate is multiplied by the agreed upon rate of payment, which is set at .3 for the entire company.[38] If the

37. The first attempt at a time and motion study at the Tokyo die-cast plant was in progress when the research was conducted. Worker reaction to the study was generally not hostile; the workers said they did not yet know what its consequences would be. Left-wing political activists, however, were strongly opposed; they equated time and motion studies with rationalization, by which they meant speed-ups and heavier work loads.

38. This figure, set by a company-and-union agreement, states that profits achieved by producing over the norm shall be divided as follows: one-third to the workers, one-third to the company, and one-third to pay increased costs.

monthly rate is being calculated, the total of .360 (1.20 × .3) is then multiplied by the individual worker's basic wage; if it is 20,000 yen, the worker will receive an incentive premium wage of 7,200 yen. In a typical month, of the fifteen units in the whole plant, three units produced over their production norm, one unit equaled its production norm, and the remaining eleven units produced between 90–99 percent of the production norm.

One way workers may express their views of a group incentive system is by production restriction, namely, by consciously restricting production when it is well within their ability to exceed the production norms. How this is done can be seen in the following research notes, written while working the night shift on a clutch assembly line:

> Crew of six start work at 10 P.M. One of the workers sets belt speed at no. 6, well above no. 4 speed used on the day shift. Work pace is fast until one-hour break for food from 2–4 A.M. Resume work at 3 A.M. sharp. Pace is still the same. Worker at end of line keeps track of production and starts signalling to one of workers up front how rate of production is going. Soon they start yelling back and forth to each other discussing the amount of clutches being turned out. From 3:30 the worker up front starts making occasional trips to the back of the line picking up a finished clutch and putting it up on the top of the line. This slows the work pace for everyone. Despite this, by 4:45, 310 clutches have been completed. At this rate, about 400 clutches will be completed by finishing time at 7. (The production norm for a crew of six for eight hours is 360.) The 5 A.M. break starts at 4:45. Instead of the prescribed break of 15 minutes the break lasts one hour until 5:45. During this time the six workers smoke, drink milk, do some cleaning around their machines and then talk some more as they stand by their machines alongside the 8 meter long belt. The switch is turned on at 4:45 but the belt speed is turned down to about 70 percent of what it was. Finally, the line is shut off ten minutes early at 6:50 instead of running it right up to the last minute as they do on the day shift. Total production at end of shift is 360 clutches, hitting production norm exactly.

From this example and many others in the clutch assembly sections and other departments, it is apparent that a pattern of production restriction is not uncommon in the factory. Depending on the circumstances, it can be organized by one worker, a group leader, or be a spontaneous group action. During the day shift, production proceeded at a steady pace, and there was no indication that workers were holding back. But on the night shift they enjoyed breaking loose for the early part of the evening and then sharply cutting back for the last few hours. The absence of a foreman and high ranking management (one group leader was in charge of five sections) accounted for the workers' ability to change the pattern of production on the night shift. The phenomenon of production restriction is not to be understood in terms of the foreman's absence on the night shift, though it made it visible to me as a conscious act of the workers. It was practiced on the day shift, too.

In some respects, the term production restriction is inappropriate.[39] Many workers simply thought of the production norm as a quota to be met. As an incentive system it was not meaningful to them. To view the production norm as quota was hard to avoid, because the parent firm set daily and monthly quotas for the auto parts firm, and they had to be met or production at the parent firm would be disrupted. To meet these quotas, raw materials were allocated to the different sections in the auto parts firms, often precisely according to the quotas, making it impossible to exceed the production norm. Hence the very setting of production standards operated to inhibit increased production.

Because wages are paid monthly, the incentive system seems somehow "far away" to the individual worker. Moreover, the production unit is often quite large incorporating a number of sections as was the case in clutch assembly, where the larger unit included about seventy workers. As a result,

39. Strictly speaking, production restriction is most likely when workers are paid according to individual piece rates. Yet, even under a group incentive system, when workers reach a consensus to limit production despite management efforts to raise it, the concept seems applicable.

monthly production differences between sections tended to cancel each other out, so the portion of the incentive wage paid was relatively constant. Workers simply thought of the premium as a fixed amount within the wage. They often did not know how it was calculated. There was not the constant pre-occupation whether or by how much they should exceed the production norm ("are you making out") as is often the case among American workers on individual piece-rate systems.[40] In the clutch assembly sections, there was never any talk about how much money they would get from a given production level. Instead, the workers tried to hit the quota set for their operation and let it go at that. If they exceeded it slightly, that was fine, for they figured the other shift or another section would probably fall below. Yet they knew it was well within their ability to exceed the norm as was apparent on the night shift, when they actually exceeded it for several hours.

This behavior is not inherent but gradually learned by the worker as a response to specific situations. Some jobs make it hard to restrict production. Sometimes management can convince the worker that it is unnecessary to do so. But where it exists it is essentially learned by group process. One worker described his early experiences in the factory as the first-machine worker on a four-machine sequence. He often worked so fast that production piled up at the next station; whenever this happened the others told him to slow down as he was making it hard for them. Gradually, he learned the "right pace." The fruits of learning are not shared equally by management and labor. When workers acquire skills and techniques that enable them to increase production without using prescribed methods, they may refuse to inform management. A machine worker explained:

> We change the order of a job or the way of operating the machines to make things go faster so that we can turn out more pieces. I learned these kinds of things from some of

40. See Donald Roy, "Quota Restriction and Goldbricking in a Machine Shop," The American Journal of Sociology, Vol. LVII (March 1952). See also William Foote Whyte, Money and Motivation (New York: Harper and Brothers, 1955), pp. 11–49.

the older guys. The company has a suggestion system and pays 50,000 yen, 25,000 yen, and 10,000 yen according to the value of the idea. But if I suggest a good time-saving idea, the work load would become heavier. And in that case, maybe only I could work well, while the guys on the other jobs (to which mine is connected) could not. This would upset things. So I don't suggest improvements to the company, but we do actually make use of them during the night shift for at least part of the time. We do make suggestions to management, but only when we believe it won't mean a heavier work load.

The reasons workers give for production restriction are important in understanding company attachment and provide an area for cross-cultural comparisons. Past experiences of the clutch assembly line workers strongly colored their views of production. Those who lead in restricting production pointed out that when production increased, management raised the production norm, so there was no money in it for workers. An instance particularly upsetting occurred when the lead man on the line was given a new air-pressure pin-insertion machine, replacing the old hand-lever operated one. His production increased greatly without extra effort, but everyone else down the line was hard put to keep up with him. The production norm was raised on the basis of this innovation, which meant that the other workers were producing more under a heavier work load but earning no more.[41]

Most workers in the clutch assembly sections had no strong feelings on restricting production. Younger workers, in particular, often simply followed the lead of the veterans; they would meet the production pace set by older workers no matter what it was. As one young worker put it, "I have no strong feelings one way or another on holding back production. It is a matter of social relations." Before the conveyer belt was installed two years earlier, workers had individual machines and social relations were not so important. But with the introduction of the conveyer belt, production had

41. Management maintained that the workers had misunderstood their action, but, be that as it may, the worker perception is the most important element here if one is to understand their behavior.

to be better coordinated if it was to run smoothly. Thus social relations became more problematic and older workers
came to set the tone of production.

The above explanations are quite similar to those reported by American workers.[42] The formal logic of the incentive system that higher production means more money is
not always accepted by the workers. Fear that management
will cut rates, fear of working oneself out of a job, fear of a
heavier work load, not believing that the extra effort required
to exceed the norm is worth the money, and the importance
of group solidarity in setting the production pace are the
similarities with American workers. Absent in the auto parts
firm, however, is worker fear of unemployment as a result of
exceeding production norms or making improvement suggestions. This is mainly because Gujo Auto Parts is a growing company and employment security is guaranteed. Different also from research reports of American workers is the lack
of understanding of the purpose and operation of the group
incentive system by many auto parts workers. It is probably
because of the system's focus on the group rather than on the
individual, the newness of the conveyer system and the inexperience of the young rural workers.

The conspicuous absence of the union in the operation
of the premium system recalls an observation by Max Weber
that production restriction serves as a substitute for a strike.[43]
This seems to apply to the auto parts plant, where the union
was so closely integrated into company administration that,
judging by worker statements, there was no vehicle for adequate representation of worker grievances on the premium
system.[44] There was recourse to the foreman but actual worker
behavior in restricting output suggests they found this inadequate. It is significant that union leaders denied the existence of production restriction by workers; they realized that
it constituted a partial rejection of the union. In this respect,

42. Donald Roy, op. cit.
43. For a discussion of this comment in the context of production
control see Georges Friedmann, Industrial Society (Glencoe: Free Press,
1955), pp. 280–284.
44. Production control in this firm must also be understood in the
light of worker dissatisfaction with over-all union wage policy. See Chapter VII.

management was more candid and took the view that without any change in production methods, production could immediately be raised by 20 percent if workers were willing to work harder. It also took the position that the unwillingness of workers to accept the notion that higher production means more pay reflected the short history of a rational labor movement in Japan (i.e., non-political labor movement). Management was optimistic that with education workers would learn to strive for higher productivity.

The production norms may not have been particularly successful as elements in a group incentive system, but they were quite successful in setting production standards for each section. Few workers talked or acted in terms of resisting these production quotas. Management personnel, including the foreman, continually sought new ways to raise production quotas, usually by reorganizing machines, shifting workers, and through technical improvements. This, together with the increasing skill of the young workers, led to rising production over the past several years. It was even true of the Tokyo die-cast plant. Workers at Gujo and Takei knew they were not strong enough to maintain a production level at the status quo ante. Indeed, even if it were in their power, they probably would not do it because of their wish to see the firm survive and grow. Production was not restricted to maintain the status quo, but rather to control the pace at which production quotas were raised, so that workers would not be forced to accept heavier work loads without proper compensation.

Japanese workers, though diligent, by no means identify uncritically with management's production goals. No doubt, interpersonal shop relations contributed to the remarkable industrial success of the Japanese in the postwar period. But to assume that the Japanese have found the key to ultimately successful human relations in industry is the myth of the uninitiated. The Japanese would make no such claims.

In conclusion, the *nenkō* wage structure, with its basis in deferred rewards, has proved remarkably successful in its contribution to economic growth. It cannot be denied that the importance assigned to age and length of service in the wage system is resonant with Japanese cultural traditions and existing social structure. It is not necessary, however, to see *nenkō* as outside economic rationality as it is understood in the West. It is important to recognize *nenkō's* underlying assumption that with increasing age and length of service the worker's value to the firm increases, and that overpayment of older workers is compensated by the low wages paid to young workers.

The combination of a rapidly changing technology and labor market create pressures on the *nenkō* system and tensions that portend change. The ability of young workers to master and adapt to the new technology and management's need to place the most able man on the job to effectively utilize its growing capital investments weakens deferred payment and leads to the direct reward of young workers. The shortage of middle school graduates and the growing shortage of young workers in general has tightened the labor market, increased the wages of young workers and compressed the wage structure. Management is less able to compensate for overpayment of older workers by underpayment of younger ones.

These developments have led management to consider rewarding achievement and performance more directly while retaining some continuity of the wage structure. Increasingly, the pay-by-ability formula is coming to be looked upon as a means of moving toward the direct reward of achievement within the framework of *nenkō*.

Although changes in the wage-rate structure will undoubtedly continue in the direction of convergence with other industrially developed nations, characteristically Japanese arrangements are likely to persist. A variety of alternative institutional arrangements can have similar functional outcomes. The degree to which these alternatives are sustained will depend on human inventiveness and the functional importance of the given area to both the organization and the human actors. Those who emphasize only convergence are too willing to give priority to organizational requirements and ignore the requirements of the human actors imbued with unique cultural and historical orientations. The requirements of human actors are built into the organization and give it a distinctive identity.

CHAPTER IV

WORKER SEARCH FOR
ADVANCEMENT AND SECURITY

I'm going to stay right here till I die unless I'm forced out.
A man eats and defecates. It's a handicap to move away
from the place where you get your food. And it is always a
lot better to defecate in the same place too.

Abé Kobo—*The Ruined Map*

An integral part of the *nenkō* wage-rate structure and
one of the basic rewards open to blue-collar workers is the
system of promotion. Promotion to foreman means not only
additional wages but also a release from the work routine, a
chance to exercise authority over subordinates, and high
status in the shop.

NENKŌ PROMOTION

Incorporated in the *nenkō* concept are payment by age
and length of service and promotion on the basis of age and
length of service. Even regular blue-collar workers—but not
workers classified as temporary—with normal skill qualifications, leadership abilities, and demonstrated loyalty can expect some form of promotion under *nenkō*. Like the wage
system, the promotion procedure is not inherently irrational.
Based on the assumption that with increasing age and length
of service, not only job skills but skill in human relations,
ability to lead people, and status in the shop will have increased, the *nenkō* approach does not necessarily turn out

incompetent supervisory personnel. The *nenkō* promotion procedure controls and channels tensions over promotion aspirations in an equitable way among workers who have relatively little access to the market.

The importance regular workers attach to promotion aspirations offers Japanese managers great possibilities for worker manipulation. A common occurrence in the two companies was to suggest to workers that their chances for promotion will increase if they agree to various changes such as job transfers. Because promotion by age and length of service is, in practice, selective (that is, not everyone gets promoted) and because the timing is flexible, management can pick and choose and so make workers compete for its favor.

This practice has important consequences for social change. Given the highly crystallized age-grading characteristics of Japanese firms, young subordinates must wait a long time for positions of power and responsibility. If they display attitudes or behavior that deviates from the expectations of their superiors, they will not reach even the bottom rungs on the promotional ladder. Conformity to such vertical structures and acceptance of the rewards and duties defined by superiors restricts social change initiated from below. Advance in a particular business firm entails acceptance of the existing order. Innovation occurs within this framework. "Success reinforces the way in which success has been achieved."[1] Similar situations are by no means unknown in the West.[2] But the highly crystallized age-grading characteristics of Japanese firms, low inter-firm mobility, and the transmission of traditional authority relationships give the *nenkō* pattern its particular configuration and strength.

As an age-grading system, the *nenkō* approach to wages and promotion has important consequences for individual worker motivation. This is critical to the understanding of the economic rationality within *nenkō*. Ely Chinoy in his study of American automobile workers found that after age

1. Norman Ryder, "The Cohort as a Concept in the Study of Social Change," *American Sociological Review*, Vol. 30, No. 6 (December 1965), pp. 857–858.
2. *Ibid.*

thirty-five most workers lose their foreman aspirations. After this time aspirations for upward mobility were essentially killed except in their fantasy world and in passing their aspirations on to their children. He explains this loss in terms of limited objective possibilities and unclear criteria for promotion. He attributes the extensive sense of alienation among auto workers to the gap between culturally prescribed success goals of society and the limited structural means in the factory to achieve them. Bureaucratization of the enterprise and technical specialization make it impossible to achieve the success goals. The work cycle is a process of the worker adjusting his aspirations downward as he comes to grips with and accepts such realities of factory life as the fact that he will always remain a worker, and that a young man entering the plant almost immediately will be making as much as he although he has twenty years seniority.[3]

This process of killing American workers' hopes contrasts sharply with the *nenkō* practice through which workers have not only been able to look forward to higher wages as they get older but also toward promotion. At the diecast firm, I was told, worker interest in foreman promotion became especially pronounced at age thirty-five. Generally, this gradual increase in promotion expectation with advancing age must have profound consequences for increasing work satisfaction, reducing alienation and providing effective work incentives.

The gradual increase in promotion expectation combined with the practice of permanent employment leads many blue-collar workers in large firms to view their job as a stage in a career. In other industrial societies, like the U.S., it is reported that careers apply only to a small elite of the labor force.[4] If it is correct that Japanese blue-collar workers, particularly those in large firms, look upon their jobs as stages in a career, this is of major importance. Careers are said to be a major source of stability in modern societies. Every or-

3. Ely Chinoy, *Automobile Workers and the American Dream* (Garden City: Doubleday, 1955), pp. 47–61.
4. Harold Wilensky, "Careers, Life Style, and Social Integration," *International Social Science Journal*, Vol. 3 (Fall 1960), pp. 554–558.

ganization must recruit and maintain its personnel as well as motivate job performance. The prospect of continuous predictable rewards, a feature of careers, creates willingness in workers to train, to achieve, and to adopt a long view and defer immediate gratification for the later pay-off.[5] Provided that expectations are met, career patterns may serve as a major stabilizing influence on a society. Apparently this has been the result of *nenkō* wage and promotion, and the practice of permanent employment in the postwar period. It suggests that the so-called docility and high work motivation of Japanese blue-collar workers must be understood in the context of their career commitments.

Evidence for this position can be seen by further contrasts with practices in the U.S. Tentative results from an investigation of the American auto industry show that American management minimizes the skill differentials that exist among blue-collar workers.[6] This is achieved through narrow wage spreads, job dilution, and the lack of a standardized promotion system for blue-collar workers. In Japanese auto firms with similar technology, these same differences in skill levels are magnified. They have built an elaborately stratified structure based on age and seniority wage payment, promotion, and job rotation. The outcome of the Japanese approach in large firms is a highly motivated labor force with career commitment, no small asset in the struggle for competitive advantage in growth and profits.[7] The American approach

5. *Ibid.*

6. The American evidence for the following statements comes from early research results of a comparative study on industrial firms currently being conducted by Bernard Karsh in Japan and the United States.

7. Contrary to the position of some, the Japanese firm is not run to insure harmony or the maintenance of social relations. Certainly such considerations emerge, but the Japanese firm is perhaps no less concerned than its American counterpart with economic growth and profit, though it may be argued that Japanese management tends to emphasize growth and expansion rather than profit. To finance expansion, there has been large-scale reliance on debt financing which, in turn, means high fixed financial charges. This, no doubt, is a factor in lowered rates of profit. See M. Y. Yoshino, *Japan's Managerial System* (Cambridge: MIT Press, 1968), pp. 139, 143–145, 180.

with its interchangeability of human actors presumably also pays off with high efficiency and productivity. But we may be speaking of different kinds of efficiencies. What are the costs in U.S. firms of extensive training programs resulting from high turnover? What is the toll of alienated workers? The answers to these questions have yet to be assessed. Certainly, it cannot be assumed *a priori* that the Japanese approach of career commitment is less efficient or rational.

The preceding considerations have some implications for the convergence hypothesis which assumes that there is only one way to operate given kinds of advanced technologies and that common attitudes and behavior flow from common technologies regardless of cultural context. The above evidence, however, suggests that cultural contexts influence in important ways the use and impact of given technologies.

Apart from its strength, *nenkō* promotion has a number of devices or safety valves to compensate for its weaknesses. For example, Japanese managers take great care to recruit a labor force with a balanced age distribution so that there will be no concentration at certain ages. As the diecast manager explained,

> It's not good to have all employees recruited in the same year because there would be tremendous competition for foreman promotion, and this would create ill feeling among the workers who do not make it. But if you scatter recruitment in different years, then workers accept as legitimate the promotion of a worker who entered the company before them.

He went on to explain that time would weed out certain workers among a given age group eligible for promotion. For example, of four workers who enter the company at the same time, one will drink, another will show that he is incapable of controlling his men, a third will be recruited as foreman at another company, and finally just one will be left who will be promoted. No doubt, in practice, it doesn't work out as smoothly as this but it is a goal that management tries to achieve.

PRESSURES FOR CHANGE

Management is so accustomed to reap the benefits of the *nenkō* practice in the form of labor control and worker motivation, it finds it hard to abandon *nenkō*. Yet there are increasing pressures for a reappraisal, and indeed many changes have been reported. *Nenkō* promotion commonly results in overstaffing of supervisory personnel. A 1965 survey by *Factory Magazine* found the number of subordinates per foreman or supervisor to be twenty-one in the United States. A comparable survey by the Japan Federation of Employers' Associations in 1968 found the corresponding number in Japan to be seventeen. Such overstaffing and the resultant costs are hard to tolerate in an age of increasing international competition and trade liberalization.

Rapid technological change has subjected *nenkō* promotion to growing pressures. Older foremen find it increasingly difficult to cope with the new technology which makes it hard for them to be effective leaders. With machinery becoming more complicated and expensive, management cannot afford ineffective foremen supervising the job. In the diecast company, several foremen had been demoted for this reason.

In recent years both companies have adopted policies of promoting young qualified workers, and in both, there were many cases of older workers under younger foremen. When the gap was more than a couple of years, it often became a sensitive situation. Most frequently workers would report, "Well, it doesn't bother me, but my foreman is cautious when he talks to me and doesn't order me around." Both in the clutch assembly line at the auto parts firm and in the press section of the diecast firm, the age differences among workers and low-ranking supervisory personnel were the reverse of what one would expect from *nenkō* age-grading practices. In the diecast firm, the new management's first act was to revamp the criteria for promotion and restrict their number. A promotion test was established emphasizing ability; it partially replaced the past procedure of promotion through a recommendation procedure. The thrust of these developments is to give increasing weight in the reward structure to achievement and ability while reducing the role of age and length of service.

WORKER PERSPECTIVES ON PROMOTION

Workers in the two factories were hesitant to admit any aspirations for promotion though they often attributed such aspirations to their fellows. Even workers who were reported by others to be on their way to promotion denied such aspirations or said that they did not think they had a good chance. This reflects the extreme sensitivity of this issue in a Japanese factory and the great importance attached to promotion by workers. To admit such aspirations is considered overly aggressive, which is unacceptable behavior. In describing workers who were being too obvious and trying too hard to be promoted, the workers used a variety of invidious expressions (e.g., brown-nosing).[8]

Generally, blue-collar workers at the two companies believed that section chief was the highest level to which they could be promoted. Most of them, however, thought only of becoming foreman or supervisor. Almost all workers regarded the foreman as a worker. Few believed that being promoted to foreman constituted "getting ahead."[9] They believed it was only a step on the ladder of success that could be followed by promotions to supervisor and then to section chief. To become a section chief meant getting ahead in the world. They were aware of the higher rungs on the ladder, but none thought these were open to blue-collar workers. They discounted chances of being promoted to white-collar positions. When asked what occupation or work they thought meant getting ahead in society, they responded usually with jobs outside the company such as banker. Most workers thought

8. This list includes: *gomasuri, obekka, happōbijin, yōryō ga ii, saba o yomu, betabeta, iinari, neko o kaburu, obenchara, chiyahoya,* and *shippo o furu.*

9. In the formal questionnaire, this was translated as *risshin shusse,* a term with a long history which in many ways is analogous to the ideas contained in the "American Dream," and the "Horatio Alger rags to riches" ideology. In the Japanese context, however, *risshin shusse* originally meant to get ahead and be successful for the good of Japan and one's family.

a blue-collar worker's chances to be promoted to foreman were good. They were not aware that management was trying to reduce *nenkō* promotion, although they were aware that "nowadays a young guy can get promoted easier." The Tokyo diecast workers had firmer opinions on promotion than the auto parts workers, probably because they were older and had more factory experience. Being older, they naturally were more interested in promotion than the younger auto parts workers.

The limited number of rungs on the success ladder open to blue-collar workers does not necessarily mean that the incentive to get ahead is thereby limited. A forty-year-old pressman at the Tokyo diecast plant explained:

> It's still possible for a working man to get ahead. If, when you are young, you make strenuous efforts and give it all you got, you can make it. One way is through getting a higher education. Another way is to make it in the factory. For example, you can take ten young workers who start even but by retirement age one has his own house and has taken care of his family well and is financially prepared for retirement while others haven't progressed at all. Although they are all still receiving the same wages, a gap opened in their standard of living. It's constant striving that makes the difference; it's the difference between the guy who on a hot day squanders his money on beer, while another drinks a glass of milk and saves.

Even when promotion by the company does not take place, workers may still find ways of redefining "success." Ely Chinoy reported a similar phenomenon among American automobile workers.[10]

When asked what it takes to get ahead in the factory the workers generally emphasized technical ability, hard work, ability to lead, skill and a certain craftiness in social relations, and a cooperative attitude toward the company. Interestingly, none mentioned age and length of service; these were felt more to be preconditions than actual determinants. Active union leadership was believed by workers to attract the attention of management in a way which enhanced pro-

10. Chinoy, *op. cit.*, pp. 125–126.

motion chances. A minority in both plants added that being a "yes man" and kowtowing to superiors by doing such things as giving them New Year's gifts was necessary to get ahead. There was also a small minority of young political activists at the Tokyo diecast plant who denied the desirability of promotion, saying it meant more responsibilities and troubles than it was worth. They pointed out that the foreman allowance was only 1,000 yen a month and that foremen were used by management like any other worker.

Worker responses in the two firms generally conformed to the results of other surveys. For example, Odaka Kunio reported that 67 percent of the industrial workers at OKM Manufacturing named either effort or talent as the two most important requisites for success.[11] The emphasis on effort and talent suggests that workers have confidence in their future.

THE STATUS RANKING SYSTEM

We saw how management seeks to decrease foreman promotions—especially those based on *nenkō*—to streamline operations and to reduce overstaffing at the supervisory level. We saw how modern technology levels many hierarchic positions and how it creates a potential conflict situation, because workers continue to aspire to *nenkō* promotion. One way management is trying to resolve the conflict is by developing a status ranking system. This system goes under different names in various companies; the most common names are *shikaku seido* or *mibun seido*. The Takei status ranking system provides a case study of what happens when the requirements of modernization (the need to cut overstaffing and to base promotions on achievement) confront existing practices (worker expectation of promotion based on age and length of service).[12]

11. Odaka Kunio, *Work and Leisure: As Viewed by Japanese Industrial Workers*, paper presented at the Sixth World Congress of Sociology, Evian, 1966, p. 5.

12. The auto parts company had no status ranking system. Management explained it was not yet necessary in view of the relative youthfulness of their labor force. They did anticipate the establishment of such a system

The status ranking system is divided into two categories. One is open to line workers and the other to staff employees (shown in parentheses). Each rank is paid a monthly allowance. Their titles and allowances are as follows:

		Yen	Percent of average monthly wage
Councilor	—	6,000	18.0
Engineer	(Engineer)	4,000	12.0
Asst. Engineer	(Asst. Director)	2,000	5.0
Technician	(Secretary)	1,000	3.0
Asst. Technician	(Asst. Secretary)	500	1.5

Blue-collar workers were found only at the bottom rank of assistant technician. Takei management, however, has future plans to promote blue-collar workers to the technician rank. These ranks and their allowances in no way entitle the recipients to line authority; they were completely separate from line operations and, ostensibly, a device to give recognition to skilled workers. In some companies this aspect of the status ranking system has been combined with increasing use of the payment-by-ability formula. The wage system at Takei Diecast incorporated the status rank allowances into the basic wages of workers.

Takei has two methods of blue-collar worker status ranking: the first is recommendation of the section chief, the second is a test open to all workers. To be eligible for recommendation, a blue-collar worker must have worked seven years if he is a middle school graduate and four years if he is a high school graduate. To take the open test, he must have worked eight years if he is a middle school graduate and seven if he is a high school graduate. The test for the rank of assistant technician includes an interview, a job knowledge and a technical knowledge test.

Before the new management, the status ranking system was quite different in operation and purpose. Appointment

in the future when the advancing age of workers would lead to increased concern with promotion.

was only through recommendation, usually a formality which preceded foreman promotion.

The new management initiated the test procedure and tightened the award of status rank so that it was no longer automatic. It retained the promotion-via-recommendation procedure in order to maintain continuity with past practices. The ratio of blue-collar workers holding status rank to the total number of workers in the press section was 1:6.6; this ratio applied to most sections, but was higher in sections with highly skilled and older workers. In addition, the new management put those with status rank on a monthly wage. Those without a status rank were paid monthly wages on the basis of a daily wage.

The manifest function of the status ranking system is to reward skilled workers. Faced with overstaffing, management is trying to redesign the system so that its latent function will be what one sociologist has called "cooling out the mark." [13] That is, it is being used to "cool out" workers who will not be promoted. They are awarded a status rank and given an allowance so that their monthly pay corresponds roughly to a foreman's. The company rules on the status ranking system read, "The assistant technician rank shall be awarded to employees with the ability to fulfill the official duties of foreman." By granting the worker an allowance, putting him on a monthly salary, and giving him status, management raises him a step above his fellow workers. The ranking is also designed so that the worker may show outsiders how highly the firm regards him. The system's purpose is to minimize disappointment, provide a nominal promotion, and maintain the worker's loyalty to the company. Management said it is also a device to "cool out" demoted foremen by raising their status ranking so that demotion will mean no loss of pay.

Worker reaction to the status ranking system at the Tokyo diecast plant varied. The key variable that seemed to differentiate worker attitudes was age. Among workers under

13. The "mark" is the victim. Erving Goffman, "Cooling the Mark Out: Some Aspects of Adaptation to Failure," *Psychiatry*, XV (November 1952), pp. 451–463.

twenty-five years of age, two different views were apparent. The left-wing politicals or those influenced by them labeled the system as just one more attempt by management to deceive and manipulate the workers. The largest group of young workers, however, were apathetic to the system and had little knowledge of its purposes or operation. The views of older workers were more varied. Those who had foreman aspirations saw it as the first step up the promotion ladder. Others took the view that because the money payoff was insignificant the system was not worth much. Still another group identified with company purposes. One, a forty-two-year-old piston maintenance worker who had a status ranking and little chance of promotion, explained, "The status ranking system is good. It rewards people who can do their job. It gives me a good feeling." Whether the status ranking system will achieve the desired effect is difficult to judge. For most young workers it was not yet a meaningful issue; though they are less likely to confuse status with authority and cash.

The status ranking system is not unique. Firms in America also devise titles for employees they do not wish or are unable to promote to line authority. However, in Japan status ranking is not an *ad hoc* action but is an institutionalized response to the conflict between the perceived requirements of economic modernization and worker aspirations based on past practices. Like the payment-by-ability formula, the status ranking system reflects the ability of Japanese managers, in their quest for modernization, to make concessions to existing cultural expectations and behavioral patterns. The status ranking system works with minimum interference of production; and contributes to production insofar as it mobilizes worker loyalties.

We must examine not only if national identities reflected in aspirations and social structure survive in advanced industrial societies, but also their meanings and roles. The Japanese experience may be relevant to technologically underdeveloped countries to the extent that it provides a model for solving acute problems of reconciling national identity with industrial imperatives. Ann Wilner, for example, could well have written about a Japanese factory when she described the constraints imposed by nationalism in an Indonesian factory: "The Javanese managers seek to adopt policies which outwardly satisfy cultural expectations while achieving the goal of maintaining efficient operations in the factory." This involves employing "the circuitous Javanese modes of behavior" for their objectives.[14]

THE INS AND OUTS OF PERMANENT EMPLOYMENT

The remaining pillar in the *nenkō* system is the practice of permanent employment (*shūshin koyō*).[15] Permanent employment generally means that the worker enters a large firm after school graduation, receives in-company education and training, and remains in the same company until the retirement age of fifty-five.

The meaning and historical development of the permanent employment practice is much discussed by Western and Japanese scholars. Some, like James Abegglen, see the practice growing out of traditional social relations.[16] In recent years, however, a growing number of scholars, especially Japanese scholars, have concluded that it was institutionalized only during and after World War I.[17] These explanations, particularly in the work of Taira Koji, seem to imply

14. Ann Wilner, "Problems of Management and Authority in a Transitional Society: A Case Study of a Javanese Factory," *Readings in Industrial Sociology*, William Faunce (ed.), (New York: Appleton-Century-Crofts, 1967), p. 118.

15. The term *shūshin koyō* is actually a new word popularized by the translation of James Abegglen's book into Japanese. Historically, the practice of lifetime employment has been rendered by the term *shōgai koyō*. Present-day workers do not use either term but simply emphasize the obligation of the firm not to fire them.

16. James Abegglen, *The Japanese Factory* (Glencoe: Free Press, 1968).

17. Samples of such analyses may be seen in the following: Taira Koji, "Characteristics of Japanese Labor Markets," *Economic Development and Cultural Change*, Vol. 10 (January 1962), pp. 150–168; Sumiya Mikio, "The Development of Japanese Labour Relations," *The Developing Economies*, Vol. 4, No. 4 (December 1966), pp. 499–515; Ōkochi Kazuo, "The Characteristics of Labor-Management Relations in Japan," *Journal of Social and Political Ideas in Japan*, Vol. 3, No. 3 (December 1965), pp. 44–49; Odaka Kunio, "Sangyō no Kindaika to Keiei no Minshuka," (Modernization of Industry and Democratization of Management), *Chūō Kōron* (Central Review), (July 1961), pp. 26–44.

that a sociological explanation emphasizing the traditional elements of permanent employment is incorrect and that only through an economic explanation can we understand the emergence of this practice. It is not our intention to take up this historical debate here. Nevertheless, our interpretation of recent Japanese scholarship on this subject leads us to conclude that a number of traditional elements clearly went into the formation of the permanent employment practice.[18] These elements served both as structural precedents and sources of ideological legitimation.

At present, it is difficult to delimit exactly the number of workers covered by the practice of permanent employment. Government statistics are ill-suited for this purpose because of their more nebulous category of regular workers. Apart from such special categories as temporary workers, Japanese labor contracts generally bind the contracting parties together for an indefinite period of time. Permanent employment has been established as company practice and employee behavioral pattern, reinforced by the distribution of rewards according to age and length of service and strengthened by social and judicial pressures. The rapid economic growth of postwar Japan further clouds the issue of whether employees have permanent employment or whether employers are simply in a better position to guarantee continuous employment.

No doubt, rapid economic growth in the postwar period spread the practice of permanent employment by making it possible for employers to grant it. In the context of present-day Japanese values, a *de facto* situation of continuous employment among regular employees is interpreted by management and workers alike as evidence of permanent employment. This spread of permanent employment in a period of rapid economic growth somewhat confounds the expecta-

---

18. The work of Hazama Hiroshi is particularly relevant. Hazama Hiroshi, *Nihon Rōmu Kanrishi Kenkyū* (Studies in the History of Japanese Labor and Management Relations), (Tokyo: Diamond Press, 1964); *Nihon-teki Keiei no Keifu* (The Genealogy of Japanese-Style Management), (Tokyo: Nōritsu Kyokai, 1963). The work of Prof. Hazama has recently been made available to the English-reading audience in a brief and lucid presentation by M. Y. Yoshino, *op. cit.*, pp. 65–84. See also Robert E. Cole, "The Theory of Institutionalization: Permanent Employment and Tradition in Japan," *Economic Development and Cultural Change*, forthcoming.

tions of economists that high turnover will be associated with peak levels of demand. It should be kept in mind, however, that Japanese postwar economic growth has occurred, at least until recently, in a labor-surplus economy.

Notwithstanding the difficulties inherent in any attempt to measure the present scope of the permanent employment practice, it is generally agreed it applies to regular employees in large-scale enterprises in both the private sector and the public bureaucracy. Taira Koji estimated that in the early nineteen sixties permanent employment covered about one-fifth of all wage earners in Japanese manufacturing.[19] Tominaga Ken'ichi, in a 1960 study of occupational mobility in Tokyo, reported that 12 percent of all employees sampled still were employed by the firm that gave them their initial employment.[20] This percentage is no doubt lowered by the wartime disruptions suffered by older workers. The practice of permanent employment is least applicable in the small-scale private sector, where working conditions are poor, bankruptcy rates high, product demand unstable and capital funds often in short supply.

There was an annual separation rate of 17 percent (monthly rate 1.4 percent) at the 2,500-employee auto parts company and 23 percent (monthly rate 1.9 percent) at the 500-employee diecast company; these rates were for all employees and would be higher if only blue-collar workers were considered. The rates are prior to the 1965–1966 slowdown, when the (voluntary) quit rates dropped sharply. Looking at statistics for the manufacturing sector in Table 4, the rates at the two firms seem quite representative.

As shown in Table 5, the U.S. rate is almost twice as high as Japan's. The gap narrowed in the early 1960's and then widened again. However, the Japanese separation rate from 1965 onwards is underestimated because it refers only to wage and salary earners in firms with thirty or more employees. The ratio of employed persons changing jobs gives a more direct

19. Taira Koji, "Characteristics of Japanese Labor Markets," p. 167.
20. Tominaga Ken'ichi, "Nihon Shakai to Rōdō Idō," (Japanese Society and Labor Mobility), Gijitsu Kakushin to Ningen no Mondai (Technological Innovation and Human Problems) Odaka Kunio (ed.), (Tokyo: Diamond Press, 1964), p. 302.

TABLE 4
Annual Average Monthly Separation Rate for
Production Workers By Size of Firm, Manufacturing Sector

Scale of firm	Separation rates for 1960
All firms	2.3
500 employees and more	1.7
100–499	2.5
30–99	3.0
5–29	2.7 [a]

SOURCE: Ministry of Labor, Sengo Rōdō Keizaishi (Postwar Labor Economic History), (Tokyo: Labor Laws Association, 1966), p. 62.

[a] This monthly rate is for all employees and would be slightly higher for just production workers.

TABLE 5
Annual Average Monthly Separation Rates for Wage and
Salary Employees, Manufacturing Sector

Year	1959	1960	1961	1962	1963	1964	1965	1966	1967
Japan	2.0	2.1	2.5	2.4	2.3	2.6	2.3	2.2	2.4
U.S.	4.1	4.3	4.0	4.1	3.9	3.9	4.1	4.6 [a]	4.6

SOURCES: Sengo Rōdō Keizaishi (Postwar Labor Economic History), p. 62. Japan Institute of Labour, Japan Labor Bulletin, Vol. 7, No. 5 (May 1968). Employment and Earnings and Monthly Report on the Labor Force, U.S. Department of Labor, Bureau of Labor Statistics, Vol. 15, No. 1 (July 1968), p. 92. The definitions used in calculating the separation rate are rather similar in both countries. They both refer to temporary as well as regular workers and include employees transferred to another establishment in the company, employees on leave without pay, retirements, voluntary quits and discharges. One difference is that in Japan employees not receiving pay during the survey period because of labor disputes are included in the separation rate; this is not the case in the U.S.

[a] The rise in 1966–1967 U.S. separation rates derived from the unusually high economic growth and inflation created, in part, by American involvement in Vietnam. This 4.6 percent represents the highest separation rate since 1953.

measure of labor mobility. This ratio has been reported in Japan and the United States in the one-year-period from 1965 to 1966. The ratio of U.S. males changing jobs (9.9 percent) was more than twice as high as that for Japanese males (4.7 percent); U.S. females, however, enjoyed only a small advantage

(6.9 percent) over their Japanese counterparts (6.5 percent).[21] We should be cautious about seeing the United States as representative of advanced industrial societies. If we compare the labor turnover rates in manufacturing of Japan, England, and Germany, it appears that the Japanese rate is only slightly below that of the latter two.[22]

TAKEI DIECAST AND PERMANENT EMPLOYMENT

At the diecast company the conditions for dismissal listed in the work rules were:

1. When an employee's attendance at work is not regular owing to physical or mental disorders or owing to physical weakness or chronic disease.
2. When an employee's work ability or efficiency is conspicuously inferior to the general level and is not expected to improve, even if he receives education, training, and guidance.
3. When it becomes clear during the period of employee suspension that he cannot return to his original work.
4. When an employee is absent from work for more than one month in succession, owing to reasons other than sickness and injuries, and is not subject to suspension.
5. When an employee is not ordered to return to work even when his term of suspension expires.
6. *When there are superfluous personnel because of readjustment and curtailment of business, rationalization of operations and other unavoidable reasons, and these personnel are not absorbed through personnel realignment, changes in type of work and other means.*[23]
7. When an employee is subject to a disciplinary dismissal.
8. When there are other reasons corresponding to one of the above items.

21. Economic Planning Agency, *Economic Survey of Japan* (1967–1968) (Tokyo: The Japan Times, 1968), p. 152. The Japanese ratios are not entirely representative of the current situation for, as we have seen, 1965–1966 was a period of lowered rates of economic growth and reduced voluntary quit rates.
22. The data is for the early nineteen sixties. Organisation for Economic Co-operation and Development, *Wages and Labour Mobility* (Paris: OECD, 1965), p. 50.
23. Italics added.

What is striking about these criteria for dismissal, especially number six, is the similarity to what one might expect in an industrially advanced Western country. But as is often the case in Japan, Western-sounding rules conceal a way of doing things that is characteristically Japanese. In practice, management's dismissal right at the Takei firm was far more limited and not necessarily because of worker pressures, though indeed workers exhibited strong feelings on this matter. Despite the formal existence of a wide latitude in firing, a management official explained: "My idea of a good manager is one who does not fire workers." Notwithstanding its attempt to gain more leeway in discharging workers, management was limited in what it could do, being caught up in its rhetoric of traditional values.

When asked to list acceptable grounds for firing, workers in the diecast and auto parts plant generally agreed that the breaking of company rules, such as stealing or willful destruction of company property were legitimate grounds for discharge. They believed that firing a poor producer was unacceptable, because "the company could always find some useful slot for such workers." Particularly offensive to most workers was a rule which would permit the company to fire workers because of an economic slump. These feelings were summed up best by a former miner who had been "voluntarily retired" before coming to the diecast company. He explained, "My idea of a good company is one that when it gets into economic difficulty doesn't fire but asks the workers to go all out, and everyone works together to solve the problem."

For the workers, the bond between company and worker was not to be taken lightly and broken for purely economic reasons by the company. Permanent employment, then, does not have a fixed meaning; rather it has different meanings for different categories of people. It is mainly these different perceptions by workers and management that have led to some of the most bitter and violent postwar strikes in Japan, particularly in the coal industry.

THE BACK DOOR TO PERMANENT EMPLOYMENT

Managers generally said that they would not fire workers except under the most exceptional circumstances. Westerners have been particularly impressed with Japanese management statements such as, "We have the right to fire but it would not be right to do so." [24] These views, however, are subject to considerable modification depending on the company, industry, and economic climate.

Management tries to screen out incompetents during their trial period before they become regular employees. Once the probation period is past, a number of other devices are available for dealing with regular workers should they become undesirable. An employer may simply transfer undesirables and incompetents to harmless positions where they do not interfere with production. This was not uncommon in the diecast plant, particularly at the supervisory level. Devices designed to make workers quit are numerous. This is not to say that Japanese executives are lying when they explain to their foreign visitors that they do not fire as a general rule. In part, this is a problem of translation. Managers will reserve the term *kubikiri* or *kaiko* for firing or discharge. They would prefer, however, in many cases to use the term *yamete morau* which literally translated means, "the company has received the quitting (of someone upon its request)." This is a euphemism for firing when the company leaves the worker no alternative but to quit.

The desire to choose the softer way of expressing a discharge probably comes from the generalized acceptance of the norm of permanent employment in Japanese society, the solidarity of social groups, and a desire of employers not to violate this solidarity. At the same time, employers like to end their relationship with the employee on a friendly note and if possible not to endanger the employee's chance for another job. To write "fired" on an employee's recommenda-

24. See, for example Everett Hagen's comments on his meeting with Japanese executives. Everett Hagen, "Some Implications of Personality Theory for the Theory of Industrial Relations," *Industrial and Labor Relations Review*, Vol. 18, No. 3 (April 1965), p. 344.

tion form would make it hard for him to get a new job, so they prefer to say he quit.[25]

There are many techniques for getting an employee to quit. For example, a professor had been looking for a way to fire his secretary. One day he came into the office and found she was absent without telling anyone in advance. He saw his chance and feigned great anger in front of the office girls. The next day when the secretary came to work she heard from the other girls that the professor was upset. Embarrassed that the professor did not think more highly of her, she said, "Well, if that's the way he feels about it, I quit." The following day the girls announced that the secretary had quit. Undoubtedly, the professor would have said the same. By choosing such an indirect way of firing, he avoided a lowering of morale in his office staff. Though this may strike the Westerner as a terribly inefficient and circuitous way of getting things done, it probably comes as second nature to the professor.

The above device is less likely to work in a factory, where, with their livelihood at stake, workers cannot afford to be as sensitive. To give an extreme example, an oil refinery worker employed at a major corporation is not likely to quit because his feelings are hurt when he knows that he cannot obtain another job at the same high wages. One of the characteristics of the Japanese dual economy is that employees who quit large firms are less likely to be employed at other large firms. Instead they will often end up working at a smaller firm for lower wages. For example, of the 118,400 employees who left their jobs in firms with over 500 employees between January and June 1965, only 19 percent were rehired in firms employing over 500.[26] At the big firms, this is a powerful incentive for not quitting over relatively minor matters. In short, the availability of alternative employment at similar wages and working conditions is a key factor in determining worker response to such management

25. Essentially, this blurs the line between voluntary quits and involuntary quits which, for one thing, makes economists terribly unhappy.

26. Ministry of Labor, Year Book of Labor Statistics, 1965, (Tokyo, The Ministry, 1966) p. 34.

tactics.[27] The worker's need to maintain his livelihood normally outweighs the consideration of losing face, notwithstanding Western stereotypes to the contrary.

There are still other devices used by management to get workers to quit. Constant job transfers or the threat of them, assignment to dirty, low-status jobs, making it known to the worker that he has no chance for promotion, or that his yearly pay increment will be lower than his fellow workers', are some of the more common techniques. Working in a low prestige job under the eyes of one's former colleagues can be so humiliating that the worker will soon decide to quit. This is particularly true if the worker is young and skilled (i.e., the labor market situation is favorable for him). The mere threat of such tactics by management may be sufficient to significantly increase work performance. Ann Wilner has described a similar process in Indonesia in her study of a Javanese factory. She sees such a pattern emerging out of a combination of nationalism and traditional elements. Since workers can no longer be fired outright in post-colonial Indonesia except for grave offenses such as theft, techniques embodying "the utmost Javanese finesse" have evolved.[28]

One way to reduce employment sharply is that of "voluntary retirements." James Abegglen was impressed with its voluntary nature, but from the worker's point of view it often borders on firing.[29] The employer may hold out inducements such as double the normal severance pay, making it clear that if the worker does not accept he has no future in the company, and that he will be paid a much lower severance allowance if he waits past the deadline for "voluntary retirements." This pressure is augmented by the practice of "patting the shoulder" where the supervisor will strongly urge the worker to retire.

It is clear, then, that a variety of devices fall short of direct firing but nevertheless may force the worker to quit. In such a way, management may rid itself of incompetents,

27. On this point, conversations with executives from the Toa Nenryo oil refinery company were particularly helpful.
28. Wilner, *op. cit.*, p. 119.
29. Abegglen, *op. cit.*, p. 20.

agitators, and, to some extent, surplus personnel. In extreme cases, however, such as existed in the postwar coal industry or the reorganization of the auto industry in 1955, large-scale direct firing may take place. During the 1965 slowdown, employers experimented with what was dubbed the Japanese-type layoff system. In the electric appliance industry, for example, employees were sent home for periods of up to six months but continued to draw 60 to 70 percent of their basic wage.

A pattern of permanent employment exists in Japan which gives management considerable flexibility in shedding undesirable personnel without forcing it to engage in direct firing. There are, in short, some functional equivalents for firing. In addition, the rapid growth of the economy in the late nineteen fifties and the nineteen sixties mitigated many problems for which employers had to use indirect means to reduce the labor force. The slack was taken up in many industries. Moreover, the large number of temporary workers, casual workers, subcontract companies, and within-company subcontract workers, all give the company considerable leeway in dealing with the ups and downs of the economic cycle. As Taira Koji so aptly expressed it, the number of permanent (regular) employees is limited to a cyclically justifiable minimum.

PRESSURES FOR CHANGE

There is growing evidence of increased inter-firm mobility among Japanese blue-collar workers. The ratio of employed males in nonagricultural industries changing jobs shows a fairly steady increase from 2.7 percent in 1959 to 4.4 percent in 1968 (See Table 6). Because this increase occurred during rapid economic growth, it reflects an increase in voluntary quits rather than involuntary discharges. Moreover, blue-collar workers accounted for 62.7 percent of all male job-changers in 1968—a considerable increase over the 51.1 percent in 1962.[30] In short, the inter-firm mobility of

30. Office of the Prime Minister, Shūgyō Kōzō Kihon Chōsa Hōkoku: 37 (1962 Employment Status Survey), (Tokyo: The Office, 1963), p. 225. Ibid., 1969, p. 258.

blue-collar workers is increasing faster than that of other occupational groups. Furthermore, the rate of inter-firm mobility declined in small firms and increased in large ones between 1959 and 1965; during this same period the number of employees who moved from small firms to large firms increased.[31] A recent survey conducted by the Ministry of Labor examined the work histories of 950,000 recent graduates of middle schools over a three-year period from 1965. It disclosed that 20 percent of the newly employed left their first job within one year after employment and 52.5 percent after three years of employment.[32]

TABLE 6

Ratio of Employed Males 15 Years and Older Changing Jobs in One Year, Nonagricultural Industries
(In thousands)

Year	Continuing same job	Changed jobs	Employment-change ratio [a] (in percent)
1959	17,072	470	2.7
1962	19,112	770	3.9
1965	21,101	865	3.9
1968	23,401	1,087	4.4

SOURCES: Based on Office of Prime Minister, Shūgyō Kōzō Kihon Chōsa Hōkoku, 34 (1959 Employment Status Survey), (Tokyo: The Office, 1960). Ibid., 1962. Ibid., 1965. Ibid., 1968. This survey is conducted every three years beginning in 1955. The categories used in 1955 were different from subsequent years so that the 1955 totals were not available for comparison.
[a] The ratio of employed males changing jobs is calculated as follows: the number of persons who changed jobs (persons whose job as of the listed year was different from that of the preceeding year) divided by the total number of those who have not changed jobs plus those who have changed jobs.

We can identify a number of sources of tension in the present labor market arrangements which point toward change: Rapid economic growth, rising technological levels,

31. Ministry of Labor, Rōdō Hakusho 1966 (White Paper on Labor: 1966) (Tokyo: Labor Laws Institute, 1966), pp. 124–125.
32. Ministry of Labor, Shinki Chūgakukō Sotsugyō Shūshokusha no Shūshoku Rishoku Jōkyō Chōsa (Research on the Circumstances of Employment Separation of Recently Employed Middle School Graduates), (Tokyo: The Ministry, 1969).

demographic changes, and trade liberalization create numerous imbalances, lags, and shifts in the employment structure. Both management and labor are reassessing permanent employment to see whether it serves their interests.

Managers are now more open to the lesson of foreign models and more willing to question the advisability of tradition-oriented solutions to present problems. In 1965, with great fanfare, the Japan Federation of Employers' Associations announced its support for the establishment of an American-style layoff system—though it was to be adapted to Japanese conditions. Unions and workers, however, showed strong resistance and were able to hold the line. While workers are enjoying the benefits of increased inter-firm mobility because of a growing labor shortage, they obviously want their mobility to be on a voluntary basis. Although management would like to move toward new solutions for present problems that serve its own interests, it is forced to move slowly and to develop a *modus vivendi* with workers and their unions.

Another source of tension is the shift away from cultural values that emphasize loyalty to the corporate group and that stress its role in mediating and defining the nature of rewards. Behavior based on these values initially supported the institutionalization of permanent employment. Contemporary democratic and mass consumption based values now emphasize the direct gratification of individual needs. Loyalty to the corporate group becomes a more instrumental value to be turned off and on in accordance with perceived self-interest. Under these circumstances, the legitimating ideologies that once supported the institutionalization of permanent employment no longer operate to produce this outcome. Instead, democratic and mass consumption based values conflict and compete with those values upholding the permanent employment practice. It is not a matter of tradition simply fading away; rather a process of competition goes on inside each individual.

The Japanese practice of permanent employment was institutionalized partly as management response to high labor turnover during World War I and as a union and worker response to job scarcity in the post-World War II period.

Now workers once again find it in their interest to move to different firms to improve their economic position. Permanent employment succeeded for a time in offering sufficient psychic and material inducements as well as negative sanctions to keep certain categories of employees tied to one firm throughout their work career. But the changing socio-economic environment has eroded such inducements and sanctions in recent years. The growing labor shortage, caused by the expanding economy and demographic changes resulting from a declining birth rate, pressures the permanent employment practice and encourages workers to look for alternative job offers. The structure of the labor market increasingly comes to resemble that of other advanced industrial societies.

With increasing mobility workers gain a better bargaining position *vis-à-vis* their employer. When workers know they can move to new jobs, they are in a better position to resist managerial authority and demand higher wages and improved working conditions. This contributes toward a more democratic society in a country where historically employers have had the upper hand in a labor surplus economy. The conditions of a growing labor shortage indicate that job mobility will grow in the future, enhancing industrial democracy. This is not to suggest that high job mobility automatically induces industrial democracy. Because the job mobility rate is far higher in the U.S. than in Japan, it does not mean there is a correspondingly higher level of industrial democracy in the U.S. Such a conclusion would be ludicrous given the differing cultural traditions and the many factors that build industrial democracy. It suggests, however, that increased job mobility in Japan creates an important precondition for insuring workers equal bargaining strength with management.

The extent of recent changes should not be overestimated. The job-changer as a percentage of new hirings each year did not increase between 1956 and 1966.[33] Indeed, there was a decline from the peak of 58.8 percent in the boom

33. Ministry of Labor, *Rōdō Idō, Sengo no Suii to Genjō* (Labor Mobility: Present Conditions and Changes in the Postwar Period), (Tokyo: The Ministry, 1968), pp. 256, 265. Totals are for all industries but limited to firms with over thirty employees.

year 1961 to 44.7 percent in the recession year 1965. Obviously, these changes were a response to timing in the business cycle rather than part of a clearly discernible trend in labor mobility. Large employers still view hiring of those with previous job experience as a last resort to be undertaken only during labor shortage conditions. The recent increase in female participation in the labor force also accounts for some increases in labor mobility. Finally, there is no appreciable increase in the percentage of employees moving from large firm to large firm.

That the permanent employment practice has not withered away under "modern" pressures is not so surprising. We know the factors that bring about a structural pattern are not always those that maintain it. Although the initial resources that crystallized the permanent employment practice are being diverted, it is not conclusive evidence that the practice will disappear. The Japanese may yet develop new equivalent resources to support permanent employment. The move of Japanese business into the labor surplus area of Southeast Asia represents just this search for alternative resources.

The resilience of Japanese tradition insures that traditional elements will be represented in the emergent new pattern. One can already discern, in medium-scale industry, a piecemeal solution that is likely to spread to larger firms. It means a reinterpretation for regular employees so they can maintain their right not to be fired during a downturn in the business cycle but assert the right to quit should alternative job offers prove attractive. If this favors worker interests, it should be remembered that growing labor shortage increasingly favors worker interests. Managers still retain the flexibility in reducing their work force in slack periods. For management to assert its right to layoff workers in times of business decline attacks the foundation of Japanese-style enterprise unionism and arouses workers as no other issue can; this, the Japan Federation of Employers' Associations discovered in 1965. Even if such a move were successful, the costs in lowered worker morale and loyalty make such an attempt by management hazardous, except in those firms threatened with bankruptcy. Of course, much depends on whether Japan will maintain high rates of economic growth in the future.

It would be a mistake to examine the prospects of the permanent employment system simply in terms of strength or weakness of tradition. It is fashionable to see the permanent employment system as unique to Japan; it constitutes, after all, the basic element that goes into forming the firm as a semi-closed corporate group. The core of the permanent employment practice, however, is present in any ongoing industrial society because the industrial organization must be based on the commitment of key personnel such as skilled workers and able management executives on whom it depends for continued success. It must have devices to penalize movement out of the system; otherwise training and other related costs become unmanageable. Likewise, workers develop psychological and economic stakes in their employment; therefore, labor market arrangements must guarantee some degree of employment tenure if they are to motivate workers.[34] The elaborations surrounding this core structure depend on the political, social, and cultural heritage of a country and its specific labor market situation. The current Japanese situation suggests that we may anticipate increased inter-firm mobility in the future, while permanent employment will continue to exist in some form. Present trends do not portend eventual disappearance.

WORKER RIGHTS AND REALITIES OF THE LABOR MARKET

Dissatisfaction with wages and working conditions, poor promotion possibilities, poor prospects for company growth or survival and the belief that they can make a better economic bargain elsewhere are some commonly given reasons for voluntary quits. Other firms raided the diecast company

---

34. While the Japanese talk about modernizing their labor market arrangements and the need to accept increased inter-firm mobility, American Teamster Union officials have begun to talk about a guaranteed lifetime job to be established through collective bargaining. They see this as a step beyond the guaranteed annual wage to secure workers' livelihoods in an age of rapid technological change.

for experienced workers. The average quitting age at the diecast company was twenty-five. About half the workers quitting go to other, often smaller, diecast companies. They are
lured by more overtime, promises of promotion, the per-
suasion of friends who formerly worked at Takei, and a
general promise of greener pastures. Rarely do these promises
materialize. Lured during peak periods the workers short-
sightedly forget the future troughs. Besides, at the smaller
diecast companies the hours are long and vacations few.

Few of those quitting return to Takei. The company
indicates they would be welcome, but the workers say that:
"A guy couldn't hold his head up among his fellows if he
came back after having failed elsewhere—you make your decision, cut your ties and if you fail it's not easy to swallow
your pride and return." Ely Chinoy reports that often American auto workers come back to their old company if their new
jobs do not pan out. One possible explanation for this difference in behavior is that in a Japanese firm length of
service is more important for establishing social capital over
time. Once a man quits, this social capital is destroyed and
it is difficult for him to come back. It is an established
practice when a worker quits that fellow employees chip in
for a farewell party and gift. These parties are often rather
moving affairs which include spontaneous testimonials from
fellow workers thanking the employee for his friendship and
help. The farewell party as a formal practice shows the importance attached to severing the bonds of the firm as a social
unit and symbolically accomplishes the act of separation.

We should also examine the practice of permanent employment by studying the factors that limit inter-firm mobility and affect worker consciousness of mobility chances.
As in the U.S., increasing length of service means increasing
commitment to the company as fringe benefits build up. In
Japan, this commitment seems especially strong given the
scope of these benefits and the fact that wages explicitly increase with length of service.

We saw that if an employee leaves a large firm, it is
likely that he will be forced to take employment in a smaller
firm which pays lower wages. Until recently, a worker chang-

ing jobs could also expect to be assigned to temporary employee status in his new firm for at least one year, which means lower pay and other disadvantages in working conditions. Even if the new employee gets regular employee status, because of his shorter length of service his wages often will be only about 80 percent that of other regular workers. In addition, he faces a difficult task of gaining acceptance by other employees, especially in larger firms where the *nenkō* system is well institutionalized. In this context, Nakane Chie has written:

> The individual's status in a social group depends on the duration he keeps the contact with the group. This actual contact is itself the person's social capital. And the capital, by its very nature, cannot be transferred to other groups. So it is a great loss for individuals to change (their) group from A to B. Even if the seniority rule is abolished and one can get the same or higher salary when one changes job from A to B, there still remains a social loss in the loss of his contact.[35]

In conversations with employees who had changed jobs I was impressed by the ambivalent feelings which their status gave them. Their lowered status led to feelings of inferiority and of being an outsider; but it also led to a stronger attachment to the company and a strong competitive drive to prove themselves in order to rise in the company. It is not surprising, therefore, that job changing, especially among older workers, is regarded as a very uncertain venture filled with many pitfalls.

At the diecast plant, worker consciousness of mobility chances focused around age thirty as the turning point. They believed it was hard to get a job at another company once you were much past thirty, because companies want young workers who have high productivity and can be paid low wages. As evidence, workers pointed to newspaper advertisements which called only for workers under thirty. National statistics tend to support these beliefs. Eighty percent of

35. Nakane Chie, "Towards a Theory of Japanese Social Structure: An Unilateral Society," *The Economic Weekly* (Bombay) Vol. 17 (February 1965), p. 203.

the 1,362,000 job-changers in 1965, whose previous occupational status was employee, were under thirty-four years old.[36] Thirty-four percent of all job changes occurred in the twenty to twenty-four-year-old category.[37] Moreover, these statistics conceal the "quality" of the new jobs in the over-thirty category. Many of these new jobs are filled by workers who suffer a worsening of wage level and working conditions; this includes workers who retire when they are fifty-five years old from one company but take lower paying jobs at another company. These prospects and the unwillingness of employers to hire workers much over thirty at age-determined current wage-rates lead to a similar result. Most diecast workers, except for the skilled workers, viewed the period around age thirty as a crucial turning point.

The structure of the labor market which makes it hard for workers to change jobs after their early thirties is probably one of the more restrictive features of the contemporary industrial relations system in Japan. It is, of course, not unique to Japan that as workers grow older they are less able to move and become more dependent on company benefits. These conditions, however, are greatly strengthened in Japan. It is commonly said in the U.S. that "when a guy passes forty nobody wants him." Japanese workers substituted age thirty as the critical time. This, then, is not a researcher's abstraction but was consciously felt by the diecast workers. Once workers accept that they no longer can move, it means that they must tie themselves tightly to company policies and look for promotion within the company. Resistance in any form

36. *Year Book of Labor Statistics*, 1965, p. 38.
37. From a comparative perspective, it is reported in a nationwide survey of the U.S. labor force in 1961 that only 20.5 percent of the job changes were in the twenty to twenty-four age category. In Japan, only 19 percent of the newly hired employees in 1965 who previously had been employees were thirty-five years old and above. This contrasts with the U.S. where 15 percent of the job changes in 1961 were accounted for by males forty-five years and older and females fifty-five years and older. One should be cautious in drawing conclusions from these statistics, however, since the totals are affected by differing age compositions in the two labor forces. *Year Book of Labor Statistics*, 1965, p. 38. The American source is: Gertrude Bancroft and Stuart Garfinkle, "Job Mobility in 1961," *Monthly Labor Review* (August 1963).

to management policies is extremely difficult where no alternative employment opportunities exist.

An extreme example was the case of the ex-miners who were recruited to the suburban diecast plant. Their average age was thirty-three, most had family responsibilities and few had any marketable factory skills. Leaving the mines had filled them with the deepest apprehension about the future. Their unbounded appreciation at receiving jobs at the diecast plant and subsequent almost slavish devotion to the company can only be understood in the light of their perceived lack of alternative employment opportunities. The strength of this commitment was notorious among other employees who passed around such stories as, "Those guys would rather leave here dirty than waste the company's money by using its soap."

WORKER ASPIRATIONS OUTSIDE THE COMPANY

Worker aspirations are central to understanding worker motivation and the operation of permanent employment, for their hopes and dreams also explain the nature of their commitment to factory employment.

Workers were asked whether at the time of their entry into the firm they viewed the job as permanent and intended to stay until retirement. Among the diecast and auto parts workers a majority said that at their time of entry they had doubts about remaining until retirement. This was especially pronounced at the diecast company. Those who were past the low thirties at their time of entry usually defined the job as permanent from the beginning; those under thirty were less likely to do so. Workers who did not believe at their time of entry that they would stay until retirement, commonly gave these reasons: "Wanted to learn a skill not possible in this company," "Wanted my own business," "Wasn't thinking about the future in those days," "It was hard times and tough to find any job in those days so I just took this one thinking it would be temporary," "Expected to go back to the country and take over father's work," and "My work was boring." As to why they stayed so long despite these initial doubts, the usual answers were: "Things just dragged out," "For economic reasons," and "The situation at the company improved."

At the time of this research, except for some older workers who had nowhere to go, few of the Tokyo diecast workers believed they would remain until retirement. The situation was particularly hard for the large number of workers in their middle thirties who had as much as ten years seniority. They were quite sure they could not find equivalent wages elsewhere, yet lacked confidence in the company's survival. Some elected to stay on, but each year, as they drew higher wages, they further depressed their potential market value because of their advancing age. At any rate, many of the Tokyo diecast workers who had initially defined the job as permanent were actively searching for new jobs by the end of 1965. The poor economic position of the company, the unpleasantness of company-union relations, and the uncertainty of the future were given as reasons. At the auto parts plant, on the contrary, workers who originally thought they would soon leave because of the poor economic position of the company changed their minds. Because of the improving economic position and growth of the company in recent years they now expected to stay with it. In both cases, although the change was in opposite directions, worker commitment to their company depended on their assessment of its future growth. They had in mind not only employment security but also promotion prospects and company ability to pay high wages.

Throughout Japanese industrialization, there has been much movement between the laboring class and the large number of small manufacturers and other categories of self-employed. Ujihara Shōjirō reports that in the past blue-collar workers showed a high degree of identification with the petite bourgeoisie and vice versa.[38] Together they constituted the lower part of the dual structure. The employment structure, however, has changed in recent years. From 1960 to 1966 among nonagricultural and nonforestry employed persons,

38. Ujihara Shōjirō, "Japan's Laboring Class: Changes in the Postwar Period," *Journal of Social and Political Ideas in Japan*, p. 66.

the self-employed increased by 200,000; family workers declined by 80,000; and employees increased by 6,540,000. Overall, this means a decline of self-employed persons from 17.4 percent of all nonagriculture and nonforestry employed persons in 1960 to 14.5 percent in 1966.[39]

Despite these changes, a majority of the diecast workers still had aspirations about owning their own business. These businesses, ranged from machine consultant, diecast shop, grocery store, flower shop, book store, auto repair shop, doll maker, to guitar teacher, etc. Some of these businesses drew upon skills acquired at Takei Diecast, though a number of them were quite unrelated. For some workers, these were concrete objectives they took steps to realize, for others only fanciful dreams.[40] For workers over thirty such aspirations were commonly just an expression of their fantasy world. Those under thirty with such aspirations had, for the most part, still hopes of realizing them. Often, workers could point to former workshop friends who had left the shop and been successful in starting their own business. Just as often, however, they had heard about the failures. Most of the young workers with such hopes showed a keen awareness of the difficulties in establishing their own firm, including the high rate of bankruptcy among such companies. They talked about the great amount of capital needed to start a business nowadays and how it was increasingly hard to make a go of it, or that the high cost put it out of their reach. This intuitive awareness of the changing structure of Japanese employment dimmed the hopes of many young workers.

Workers gave the following reasons for wanting to own businesses: "Because the harder I worked, the more money

39. *Year Book of Labor Statistics*, 1964, pp. 10–11. *Ibid.*, 1966, pp. 14–15.

40. The desire of workers to own their own small business was also apparent in the larger auto parts plant. It would be interesting to see the responses in the truly giant corporations where the practice of permanent employment is well established and the company future secure. It may well be that the workers' desire to own a business will still be extremely important because the blue-collar workers in such firms are subject to more rigid bureaucratic discipline. However, their security may put off such desires until retirement. Workers in the major firms usually receive large retirement allowances, which are sometimes used to set up a small business.

I would make," "I would have time for myself," "A grocery store isn't affected by good times or bad, people always have to eat—I never heard of a grocer going bankrupt," "A book store would be good because I like books," "I'd be my own boss and whether I succeeded or not would be my own responsibility." The independent life described reflected what workers believed they lacked in the factory. Insofar as it provides a rough measurement of alienation in the factory, it shows that workers are not entirely committed to factory life. Their widespread desire to own small businesses, despite their awareness of the difficulties, indicates considerable disdain for their employment as blue-collar workers.

In summary, not only does the concept of permanent employment have different meanings for workers and management but a worker's objective performance (service at same firm until retirement) can be quite different from his private hopes and dreams.

I have shown how *nenkō* promotion commits the worker to the firm with the expectation that increased length of service will result not only in higher wages but also promotion. Together with the practice of permanent employment, *nenkō* promotion leads to the worker viewing his job as a stage in a career. This appears to be a major factor in strengthening work motivation and attachment to the firm.

Recent developments, however, have shaken the foundation of the three-way tieup between *nenkō* wages, *nenkō* promotion, and permanent employment. The increasing installation of modern technology undermines *nenkō* promotion and favors immediate reward of young workers who are quick to master the technology. Recent labor market developments lead to increased inter-firm mobility. Growing job opportunities make the protection offered by permanent employment less important. These developments point toward an increased democratization of Japanese society. Deferred rewards, despite their effectiveness in work motivation, lend themselves to manipulation by the employer, and lack of alternative job possibilities makes a mockery of the formal rights of workers to quit.

Still, there is a flexibility in the present arrangements, as reflected in the conversion of the status ranking system to "cool out" workers and the various ways in which permanent employment is not really so permanent. This flexibility suggests that though no radical changes are in the offing, a steady stream of concessions, compromises, and adaptations are the order of the day.

CHAPTER V

UNITY AND CLEAVAGE
AMONG WORKERS

> You get ahead of your fellow workers and dance attendance
> on your superiors. Even fellows who don't have any hope
> for advancement try to pull the others down. They're all
> mixed up together like so much fluff.
>
> Abé Kobo—*The Ruined Map*

Coalitions and breaks among workers derive from a
number of sources. We expect that the nature of the firm's
reward system, method of worker classification, work assignments, age of workers, and the cultural values of a society
will constrain and shape social relations among workers.

IN-GROUP UNITY

The appearance of unity among blue-collar workers in
both firms was quite striking. On closer examination, however, this tightness of social relations should be understood in
the wider context of in-group orientation. The firm as a corporate group stressing integrative principles binds its members closely together. There is, of course, another type of
worker solidarity that binds workers together out of common
interest *vis à vis* the firm and is commonly expressed in the
labor union, but this subject shall be left for a later chapter.

This overlaying of worker unity with attachment to the
semi-closed world of the company is reflected in a fluidity in
worker social relations. Workers known to be strong antago-

nists were often seen passing the time of day together. It was not uncommon, in the Tokyo diecast plant, to see a Communist leader idly chatting with a foreman who tried to split the union or to see a worker who had angrily given the foreman hell at a section meeting offer him a cigarette on a break the next day. By the same token, one saw rival union faction leaders, who disliked each other intensely, casually stroll away from the factory after work. These were everyday occurrences, notwithstanding strong conflicts between the principals. Workers explained that their differences on such matters as union policy were one matter and personal friendships another. Under such circumstances one would expect to find an American worker saying, "The hell with the bastard, I won't have anything to do with him." But in Japan there appears to be an ideological pragmatism, as one Japanese scholar labeled it, which stems from a number of sources. On the most fundamental level, the view of the firm as a corporate group dictates that its members are under great pressure to make accommodations in order to live with one another. Ideological pragmatism prevents the tensions within the organization from solidifying into a "we" against "they" attitude and thus serves to maintain the organization and prevent it from being torn apart. This is of special importance when workers expect to make their life career in one company.

Under these circumstances, there is a continuous co-optation of the opposition. The militant Communist says he keeps on talking terms with even the most company-oriented worker or foreman to keep in touch with the worker viewpoint. From management's point of view, there is every reason to maintain a dialogue with left-wing workers, as it knows from experience that age can cure the most militant worker. There is the willingness of management to forget "past sins." Having once been left-wing activists, many of the low ranking management personnel know the process by which young radicals change and are skillful at playing upon this knowledge. Without extensive access to the labor market, cooptation makes the most of limited human resources while neutralizing an enemy.

The above behavior may also be viewed from the situational ethic that workers apply to their evaluations. The workers did not think in terms of absolute good and evil; they saw no contradiction in passing the time of day chatting with another worker whom in private they would call a "two-timing so and so." This posture makes possible an eventual shift, should circumstances demand one, without great psychic damage. Westerners who believe in integrated behavior, however, are more likely to make full-time enemies, with any conversion to the other side resulting in great psychic stress for the converted and the strong possibility that the converted will be branded a traitor by his former fellows.[1] In the Tokyo diecast plant, for example, the reaction of the press workers to the only press operator who quit the union during the crisis was not the ostracism one would expect. Rather it was sympathetic understanding that this worker was older than the rest and it was therefore harder for him to resist management pressures and he also had to consider his family's future. At another time, however, they were not above ostracizing a ratebuster. But these same workers later accepted him as their informal group leader after the production level evened out and the reason for ostracism disappeared. In a society known for its strong consensus norms, it is important to analyze how the Japanese handle dissent without ripping apart the social fabric. The fluidity in social relations described above gives us one important clue toward understanding this.

This "covering of all bets" is often looked upon by Westerners as insincerity; but the Japanese look upon it, if done circumspectly, as the behavior of a man of wisdom.[2] The element of self-interest, of course, should not be ignored, for by spreading wide the web of contacts (e.g., keeping on talking terms with everyone) one increases the likelihood of

1. This explanation is based on Ruth Benedict's delineation of Japanese national character. Ruth Benedict, *The Chrysanthemum and the Sword* (Boston: Houghton Mifflin, 1946).

2. This has implications for the researcher doing participation observation, for he has considerably more leeway in which to operate than his Western counterpart. He can move among different worker groups and factions with less fear of being identified with one or the other. However, he will also have a more difficult time understanding what he sees.

being able to receive help in time of need, whether it be for a new job, help at work, or borrowing money.

Worker unity was also reflected in the mutual consultation among workers. In the Tokyo diecast plant, this was often based on knowledge and skill, but was overlaid with status considerations of age or seniority. One electrician explained, "In the Tokyo plant, when you have a job to do, you sit down with two or three guys, each expresses his ideas about the best way to do the job; then gradually you sort out the best proposals and a decision is made." The diecast workers participated in a variety of organizations, many worker-formed. These included the union, labor bank, travel club, camera club, youth section, mutual financing association, and the friendship associations organized by each section. Such organizations reflect a self-reliance among blue-collar workers that modifies the image of the paternalistic company doling out benefits.

However, the many worker organizations in the Tokyo diecast plant should be interpreted with caution. One worker made the astute observation that the press section's friendship association was a sign of weakness in human relations, because among true friends "organized friendship" would not be necessary. The friendship society, besides being a way of collecting contributions for sickness, marriage, birth, etc., was a way of controlling the size of donations. The 50 yen a month contribution spread the cost over time so that a worker would not have to make a large lump sum donation. The friendship association represented more systematic mutual aid but did not necessarily reflect greater worker solidarity.

One way of examining worker unity is to consider the amount of leisure time workers spend together. There were significant differences in the two companies studied. The Tokyo diecast workers, particularly the unmarried workers under thirty, often went out together after work, spent holidays together, and went on outings sponsored by the union's youth section. But they also had friends outside the company and spent their leisure time with them as well. These friends outside the company usually were work mates from an earlier employment or former school mates. Married workers over thirty spent less of their leisure time with their fellows and more with their families. In general, the absence of company recreational facilities at the Tokyo diecast plant reduced the amount of leisure time workers spent together. In the auto parts company, the tendency of young workers, especially those living in company dormitories, to spend leisure time together was pronounced.[3] Extensive company recreational facilities meant that workers spent a great portion of their leisure time together on company premises. Sports, dances, celebrations, outings, sightseeing trips, movies, and game facilities—all were part of this. The youth section in close cooperation with the company and union sponsored many of these activities. A relative lack of friends outside the company further intensified worker dependence on such programs. Worker unity occurs within the all-embracing arms of the company.

In both firms, the carry-over of worker friendships to off-the-job association suggests that the firm as a corporate group still tends to make work and work-established relationships central to the workers' lives.[4] For male workers, co-worker ties take precedence over neighborhood ties. This contrasts with the U.S., where, we are told, the centrality of work in the culture is being eroded. Work, especially for American industrial workers, is increasingly seen as a means to an end, and the end being leisure time consumption designed to produce a certain style of life.[5] This is consistent with the results of other research in which Americans were asked the comparative importance of neighbors to co-workers. Unlike the Japanese workers, almost all segments of the American population list neighbors before they list co-workers.[6]

There is a Western stereotype of the Japanese as being

3. It would be difficult to generalize about the married auto parts workers over thirty since there were so few of them.

4. Ezra Vogel came to rather similar conclusions in his study of Japanese white-collar employees. Ezra Vogel, *Japan's New Middle Class* (Berkeley and Los Angeles: University of California Press, 1963).

5. David Riesman and Warner Bloomberg, Jr., "Work and Leisure: Fusion or Polarity," *Research in Industrial and Human Relations*, C. M. Arensberg *et al.* (eds.), (New York: Harper and Brothers, 1957).

6. Morris Axelrod, "Urban Structure and Social Participation," *American Sociological Review*, Vol. 21 (February 1956).

always polite and never revealing emotion. It bears little relation to the reality of the Tokyo diecast plant. The workers were gregarious, spontaneous, quick to anger, and quick to express joy. Only once during the three-month work period was a worker seen bowing, and this occurred when his mother-in-law died and he was thanking the foreman after taking three days off work. The colorfulness of factory language is quite different from the Japanese one hears in more polite middle-class circles. For example, the workers had a variety of onomatopoetic words to describe working at a rapid pace.[7]

One is struck by the informality of the language at the factory in a society noted for the minute status distinctions imbedded in its language. The more polite verb forms were seldom used in worker-to-worker relations notwithstanding age and skill differences. The informal personal pronouns *ore* and *omae* predominated. Address to foremen and supervisors by workers, though more polite, was not excessively so. If one judged by language alone, the factory is one of Japan's more democratic institutions.

The absence of language formality among blue-collar workers reflects a streamlining of social relations so as not to interfere with productive efficiency. This phenomenon also fits the universalistic trend reported by linguists for inferior-superior distinctions of a status society to be replaced in open-class societies by a solidarity norm that distinguishes between intimates and non-intimates. The language previously designed for inferiors becomes the language used for intimates. The industrial revolution levels many of the old status distinctions such as that between craftsman and apprentice and the solidarity norm steps into the breach. Workers in a firm like Takei view themselves as intimates and address each other with informal language, but address the employees of the firm across the street, non-intimates, in more formal fashion. The choice of plain, polite, or deferential styles of address depends on the speaker's attitude toward the person being addressed. The linguist Samuel Martin, suggests that

7. Among the words they used were: *jan jan, don don, gichi gichi, bakasuka bakasuka, tattakata tattakata* (sound of army bugle), *gatsu gatsu, gatta gatta,* and *bari bari.*

the criteria for choice in present-day Japanese in order of importance are: *outgroupness,* social position, age differences, and sex differences.[8] Within the firm, there are a minimum of status distinctions expressed in the language by blue-collar workers, not only because old status distinctions have broken down but because egalitarian ideals have penetrated postwar Japan. In the Japanese case, the old hierarchical distinctions of the status society are replaced by the solidarity norm of the corporate group. The hierarchical in-group orientation is replaced by a more egalitarian one. The change is from one type of in-group orientation to another but not necessarily from a collectivity orientation to individualistic orientation.[9]

WORKER CATEGORIES

As in other industrial countries, one of the key cleavage points in the Japanese factory is that between blue-collar and white-collar employees. In pre-World War II days the gap between the two categories was much wider than it is today. White-collar employees enjoyed a great advantage in wages and benefits. For instance, they were paid semi-annual bonuses and retirement allowances; blue-collar workers usually had none or if they had, the benefits were only a small proportion of those received by white-collar employees. The latter were paid on the basis of a salary, which, in 1935, was almost double the average monthly wage of blue-collar workers. They had access to company welfare facilities not open to blue-collar workers; if such facilities existed for blue-collar workers they were "separate but not equal." Promotion was easier for white-collar employees. Furthermore, blue-collar workers with little education could not hope to be promoted

    8. Samuel Martin, "Speech Levels in Japan and Korea," *Language in Culture and Society,* Dell Hymes (ed.), (New York: Harper and Row, 1964).
    9. Yoshiharu Scott Miyamoto comes to a similar conclusion on the basis of nationwide public opinion research on Japanese attitudes toward family, work, village life, and political leadership. He sees the Japanese moving toward a new set of egalitarian collectivity values. Yoshiharu Scott Miyamoto, "Contemporary Japan: The Individual and the Group," *Transactions of the American Philisophical Society,* New Series, Vol. 50 (Part I, 1960).

to white-collar jobs.[10] These distinctions were formalized in a status system (*mibun seido*) with the white-collar workers known as *shokuin* and blue-collar as *kōin*. The system mirrored general community attitudes toward the two groups. The *kōin* was looked down upon as inferior, and the term itself took on negative connotations.[11] The *shokuin*, with greater employment security, higher wages, and better working conditions, held a prestigious position in society. This status distinction was established early in life as a result of differentiated educational channels for the two categories.

In the postwar period, the gap between the two categories narrowed. This pattern can be seen in most advanced industrial countries of the world. With advancing industrialization, white-collar employees, once a small minority in the labor force, gradually increase their numbers and their high wages and benefits become a liability for the company. The company tries to hold down their wages and its task is often made easier by the absence of white-collar unions.[12]

In Japan, the gap between blue-collar and white-collar workers is closing in a somewhat different way. Soon after the war, the white-collar employees joined with blue-collar workers in the same enterprise unions. These unions, with a majority of blue-collar workers, were often led by ideologically committed white-collar employees who were usually from the bottom prestige and wage level of the white-collar group, having only a high school education or a degree from a second-class university. They had been deprived of company benefits relative to the more privileged white-collar group. Under such slogans as "democratize management," the unions called for an end to the old discriminations based on *shokuin* and *kōin*. The wage gap was greatly reduced, bonuses were established

10. Though certainly inter-generational mobility was possible.

11. To this day, the term *kōin* continues to have deprecating connotations and is seldom used by workers to describe their own position in society. Instead, they prefer more neutral terms such as *wareware* (we), *wareware rōdōsha* (we workers), and *hataraku mono* (working people).

12. For a treatment of white-collar unionization in Japan, see Solomon B. Levine, "Unionization of White-Collar Employees in Japan," in *White-Collar Trade Unions*, Adolf Sturmthal (ed.), (Urbana: University of Illinois Press, 1966). For an account of the private life of white-collar workers see Ezra Vogel, *op. cit.*

and increased for blue-collar workers, welfare facilities were thrown open to all employees, and the permanent employment guarantee was made available to regular blue-collar workers. It was a move toward egalitarian in-group solidarity.

These changes are symbolized by the dress of blue-collar workers. In both firms studied, the blue-collar workers commonly arrived and left the factory in a suit, white shirt, and tie, in contrast to the not-so-distant feudal times when each class had its own prescribed clothing. Now, in the subways, restaurants, and other public places, the blue-collar worker is almost indistinguishable from the white-collar employee. It is symbolic of the democratization process in an emerging mass society which permits the blue-collar worker to move more freely through society without discrimination.

Although much progress has been made in upgrading the status of the blue-collar worker, there is still considerable social stigma attached to being one. One indication is that, with the emerging manpower shortage, management has difficulty filling blue-collar jobs with high school graduates. These high school graduates are reluctant to go into the shop because they had gone to high school to escape blue-collar work and obtain higher paying, more prestigious jobs. The auto parts company reported exceptionally high quit rates among high school graduates assigned to blue-collar jobs. It is apparent, too, that conflict still exists between the two categories. Most Japanese unions are faced with the problem of how to divide the wage increase among white-collar and blue-collar employees. At the Gujo Auto Parts Company, the union denied that such controversy existed. But it is significant to note that in each election the union carefully selected a balanced slate, providing the appropriate number of representatives for blue-collar workers, technicians, and white-collar employees. If no basis for conflict existed, such care in selecting a balanced slate should not have been necessary.

While the social stigma may still be there and wage differentials still exist, a continued movement toward equalization seems guaranteed in the future. The rising levels of education and the increasing use of high school graduates in blue-collar jobs undoubtedly will reduce still further the gap between the two groups. In the same way, the increasing use of sophisticated machinery to be operated by blue-collar workers will also raise their status.

In general, blue-collar workers at Takei Diecast associated with other blue-collar workers, although it was not unusual to see them go out with white-collar employees after work. At the auto parts company, and to a lesser extent the suburban diecast plant, however, worker interaction occurred more exclusively within the blue-collar and white-collar classifications. The reasons for this difference lie above all in size and complexity of organization. In the smaller diecast company the distinctions based on job duties, wages, and educational level between white-collar and blue-collar workers were not as sharp as in the more bureaucratized auto parts plant. What blue-collar and white-collar workers shared in both companies was a deep concern and identification with the financial position and future of their company. Despite all other differences, this was a source of strong unity among them.

Temporary employees (*rinjikō*) constitute an exception to this commitment. In 1966, there were some 1,530,000 temporary employees and 1,120,000 additional day workers. These two categories alone made up over 8 percent of the total employees in nonagricultural industries.[13]

As a rule, temporary employees are recruited for blue-collar jobs, but they obtain few of the benefits that accrue to those with regular employee status. Low wages, unskilled work, low employment security, and lack of union protection are the distinguishing characteristics of the temporary employee status. It is estimated that the average wages of the temporary employees are about 60 percent those of regular blue-collar employees. Although the postwar labor movement has greatly reduced the differences among blue-collar and white-collar categories, there has not been a comparable development with regard to the rigid distinctions between reg-

13. Ministry of Labor, *Year Book of Labor Statistics*, 1966 (Tokyo: The Ministry, 1967), p. 16.

ular and temporary blue-collar workers.[14] In smaller firms like Takei Diecast there is less discrimination against temporary workers by management. This also is apparent in worker interaction; regular blue-collar workers regularly associated both on and off the job with temporary employees at the Tokyo plant. In larger firms, like the auto parts company, management treatment of regular and temporary workers is more differentiated and worker interaction also occurs more exclusively within these formal classifications.

In recent years, there has been a marked decline in the role of the temporary and day worker employees in the Japanese economy. The ratio of temporary and daily workers to regular employees in all industries declined from a peak of 6.4 percent in 1962 to 4.1 percent in 1965.[15] The percentage of new hires in all industries made up of temporary and daily contract workers declined from a high 31.0 percent in 1956 to 14.0 percent in 1965.[16] Moreover, there has been a marked increase in the willingness of employers to promote temporary workers to regular status. This reached a peak in 1964 when the ratio of temporary employees promoted to regular status to all temporary employees reached almost 20 percent.[17] A falloff to 10 percent in 1966 indicates that by this time employers had been successful in converting most temporary and daily contract workers who had the proper qualifications and who desired regular employee status. At both Takei Diecast and Gujo Auto Parts, a regularized procedure had recently been established for the promotion of temporary workers to

14. For a brief historical sketch of the relations between regular blue-collar workers and temporary workers see Sumiya Mikio, "The Function and Social Structure of Education: Schools and Japanese Society," *Journal of Social and Political Ideas in Japan*, Vol. 5, Nos. 2–3 (December 1967), pp. 134–135.

15. The ratios are based on surveys of firms with thirty or more employees. Temporary and daily contract workers are defined as those employed for a fixed period who worked more than eighteen days for each month during the two months prior to the date of the survey or who worked sixty days during the six months prior to the survey. Ministry of Labor, *Sengo Rōdō Keizaishi: Kaisetsuhen* (Postwar Labor Economic History: Explanatory Volume), (Tokyo: Labor Laws Association, 1968), p. 140.

16. *Ibid.*, p. 141.

17. *Ibid.*, pp. 44–45.

regular workers. The auto parts company instituted a two-stage transition period during which these employees are on probation for one year; then, after passing a routine test, they are promoted to semi-regular employee status. After one additional year, if judged desirable by service record, loyalty, and personality, they are granted regular status. Not only are the relative number of temporary employees decreasing, but the once rigid lines between classifications show signs of becoming more fluid.

A major cleavage exists between male and female workers. The treatment of female workers and their work cycle is different enough from that of male workers to demand special attention, especially since discussions of blue-collar workers generally deal with male blue-collar workers and ignore the increasingly large category of female blue-collar workers.

Women play a large role in the economic life of the nation. They accounted for 18,830,000 or close to 40 percent of the total employed labor force in 1965.[18] In the manufacturing sector, it is estimated that they account for approximately one-third of all production and related employees. Today it is considered normal for girls to take a job after graduation. Most, however, stay in the labor force only until they marry or give birth. Consequently, the average length of service for women is 4.1 as compared to 7.7 years for men, and their average age is 26.3 years as compared to 32.8 years for men. The younger age combined with shorter service means less access to skill and leads to more limited chances for promotion as well as to lower wage levels for women. It is estimated that their average wage level is still less than half that of male workers.[19]

The shorter service of female workers is partially based on company retirement policies. A Ministry of Labor survey in 1965 reported that 9.4 percent of the firms investigated

18. The term total employed labor force includes self-employed and family workers as well as employees. *Year Book of Labor Statistics, 1965,* p. 6.

19. Akamatsu Hanami Tadashi, "Women Workers and Retirement after Marriage," *Japan Labor Bulletin,* Vol. 8, No. 5 (May 1969).

had formal rules requiring the retirement of women once they were married. Another 7.5 percent of the firms, though lacking a formal rule, indicated that they followed it in practice. Some 27.9 percent of the firms reported the existence of a separate retirement age system for women; this means generally earlier retirement ages for women. Given the age-seniority system of wage increase and promotion dominant in many Japanese firms, separate retirement ages for women prevents their use in responsible positions and contributes to their low wage level.

In 1966, the District Court of Tokyo ruled against the retirement age system of Sumitomo Cement Company on the grounds that it violated the provision of the Constitution guaranteeing equality between men and women and the freedom of marriage.[20] This may well mean the gradual disappearance of separate retirement age rules for women. Recent manpower shortages also work in that direction. In 1968, for the first time in the course of Japanese industrialization, the number of ever-married women in the labor force exceeded the total number of single women. This does not mean that the employment status of women is automatically raised. Few married women employees achieve regular employee status. Particularly noticeable in recent years is the increase of part-time workers, most of them married women.

The lowly status of women employees was seen at Takei Diecast. Those working on the shop floor were generally married women in their late thirties, who took the jobs to supplement family income. Despite their age and length of service which was often three or four years, they were paid under 20,000 yen a month—little more than an eighteen-year-old boy earned on entering the company after graduating from high school. Women's jobs on the shop floor were concentrated in low skills such as the inspection line, packing section, and hand-breaking of excess metal from castings. At Takei, the work rules specified the retirement age for women as 50; this contrasts to 55 for men. The auto parts firm fixed the retirement age for women at 30 as opposed to 55 for men.

20. Ibid.

SOME BASES OF WORKER COALITIONS

As might be expected, in the two firms studied, worker coalitions were formed on the basis of similar workshop, similar interests in sports and hobbies, common age and marital status, roughly equivalent wage levels, and similar skill levels. There is much overlapping of memberships, and conflicts often arise out of competing commitments.[21]

There were other bases of worker friendships. Of particular interest was the workers' tendency to form coalitions by regional ties and common year of entry. These coalitions often carried over to after-work activities. Larger companies such as the auto parts company usually establish regional patterns of recruitment. Every March, for example, Gujo recruits graduating middle school students from the same areas. Sometimes these workers knew each other as schoolmates; indeed, they may have decided together to join a certain company. In other cases, workers arrive at the company and gradually draw close to others recruited from their prefecture. Similar regional dialects and social customs, which set them apart from their fellows, are a powerful factor in worker coalitions that persist throughout their work careers. These coalitions serve as a bridge between management and workers as some are promoted to foremen and supervisors while others remain ordinary workers. In this way, workers' friendships are transformed into ties binding them into the firm. They are a basis for the vertical cliques that in some companies extend from top-level management down to blue-collar workers. A variation of this phenomenon occurs where older workers from the same school or region will take younger workers under their wing and guide them in the correct behavior.

Another basis of worker coalitions, often overlapping with and strengthening friendships based on regional ties, is common year of entry. Strikingly symbolic was the case of the

---

21. Such factors and the resultant conflicts have been reported in the American context. See Robert Dubin, *The World of Work* (Englewood Cliffs: Prentice-Hall, 1958), pp. 94–107; and Leonard Sayles, *Behavior of Industrial Work Groups* (New York: John Wiley, 1958), pp. 144–145.

three Takei Diecast workers at the Tokyo plant who celebrated their ten-year anniversary at the company by going out drinking together after work. They had entered the company as temporary workers ten years earlier and advanced to the status of ordinary workers. They remained close friends even though they worked in different sections, one had been promoted to supervisor, and another had supported the Communist faction. This tendency of workers to form coalitions on the basis of year of entry is yet another way to unite and bind them to the company. Maintaining friendships with supervisors who entered the company at the same time keeps workers informed of pending management policy, keeps management informed of worker views, and results in an obligation for higher-ups to be lenient in their treatment of workers. It is also a subtle form of labor control.

Coalitions on the basis of year of entry also generate worker dissatisfaction with company policies and affect union activity and quit rates. Workers in larger companies take as their reference group those who entered the company at the same time. Throughout their work career they compare their own treatment by the company to the treatment accorded others who entered the same year. This may prove particularly decisive on the matter of promotions. Seeing a fellow worker who entered the company at the same time being promoted, while they are left behind, may cause strong resentment, culminating perhaps in increased union activity or with the offended worker quitting. In the Tokyo diecast plant, there was a chain reaction of quits, each successive quit leaving the remaining workers recruited in the same year feeling more and more isolated until they also quit. This pattern of quits is most likely to occur among young workers whose friendships with fellow workers constitute a key element in their attachment to the company.

Apart from the *nenkō* wage system, one reason for the formation of coalitions on the basis of year of entry is the solidarity of the social group in the factory. Because it often takes years to gain acceptance, workers turn for friendship and sustenance to those who enter at the same time. Each year adds an additional ring on the "tree" and workers are conscious to which ring they or others belong. It is particularly true in large firms like the auto parts company where yearly recruitment is more systematic and the pattern more fixed.

An additional factor cementing relations on the basis of common year of entry and regional ties is dormitory life. This is especially true in large firms, such as the auto parts company, with extensive company housing. Each year newly hired workers recruited from distant prefectures are housed together, giving them a chance to build friendships on the basis of year of entry and regional ties. They may live in the company dormitory for as long as ten years before marrying. It is an ideal base for forming worker friendships. In some big firms, marriage may simply mean moving from bachelor dormitories to married company housing.

While dormitory housing may cement relations among residents, particularly on the basis of regional loyalties and year of entry, it may also serve to divide them from fellow workers living outside the dorms. In the auto parts firm the break was along the lines of the local residents versus the distant recruits housed in company dormitories. This break was reinforced because the local residents were closer to urban types on the urban-rural continuum, whereas the distant recruits were generally from strongly rural backgrounds. In the suburban diecast plant, the basic division of workers was also geographic. Worker association was sharply divided into three groups: workers from the neighborhood of the plant, the Kyushu Island recruits (subdivided into former miners and new school graduates), and the former Tokyo plant workers.[22]

PRESTIGE RANKING OF JOBS

One aspect of worker cleavage and coalition is determined by job assignment and work group. On the basis of their own experiences and those of others, workers tend to

22. During one section meeting at the Tokyo plant, a worker rejected his supervisor's request for transfer to the suburban plant saying that no one wanted to go there because of the disunity among these three groups. The supervisor retorted, "But we are all Japanese." Suddenly one of the workers pointed to me and everyone laughed. Apart from the importance workers attached to such divisions, this also shows how they forgot about my presence except in unusual situations.

develop rankings of jobs and work sections. These rankings provide an important basis for evaluating the nature of worker cleavages and coalitions.

In the Tokyo diecast plant, the main section rankings in order of worker preference were: diemaking, maintenance, diecasting, and press. These rankings roughly followed the skill order of the majority of jobs in these sections. In the auto parts plant, the status rankings of sections were less clear. The auto parts workers showed high agreement on the best sections such as the experimental section and the worst sections such as the press section. In general, machine jobs were preferred to assembly line sections. A common comment was that a worker was too closely tied to his work on the assembly line, but in the machine section he could move around.[23] However, the auto parts workers did not have as strong views about the middle-ranking sections as the Tokyo diecast workers. Again the explanation for this difference lies in the inexperience and youth of the auto parts workers combined with the large size of the plant, which made it hard to know the content of some jobs. It is also possible that greater identification with the company and the inclination to view their skills as property of the company led the auto parts workers to make less sharp distinctions among jobs.

In the Tokyo plant, the diemaking section, containing the most skillful jobs in the firm, received the highest ranking from almost all workers. They valued it highly because of the skilled work and because the learned skills were saleable in other firms. To work in the diemaking section, therefore, gave the workers a certain independence. In fact, there was a growing trend for groups of diemakers to quit and set up their own independent companies selling dies both to Takei and other companies. The diemaking section was also

23. The prestige of machine and maintenance jobs over line jobs fits with American research results in the auto industry. Ely Chinoy, *Automobile Workers and the American Dream* (Garden City: Doubleday, 1955), pp. 65–74. One factor in worker prestige rankings in America that was not present at Gujo Auto Parts was the strong preference for jobs or sections which guaranteed steady employment. At Gujo, the practice of permanent employment and the growing firm made this concern less necessary for regular employees.

ranked highest because the work pace was relaxed and it was hard for management to control the rate of production. It had no daily production totals like the press and diecasting sections. The diemakers were not tied to one particular machine but moved around to different ones as the die moved through different stages. As each die was different in some way from the preceding one, the element of routine was not as pressing. The tighter social relations among diemakers also appealed to other workers. They were the only section that had an organized baseball game during the lunch recess. The absence of similar characteristics corresponds with the lower prestige assigned to the other sections. The solidarity and high prestige of the diemakers was also reflected in the union, where the diemakers were the most active along with the smaller design section.[24]

The diecasting section was unusual in a number of respects. It was ranked low by most workers, but the casters tended to rank themselves just behind the diemaking section in the prestige hierarchy. This was in contrast to the press workers who were ranked low by others and ranked themselves low. The diecasting section was also ranked higher by former casters and by a number of young workers.

The way the diecasting section is described by other workers and by the casters themselves suggests a situation analogous to one reported by Alvin Gouldner in his study of the American gypsum factory.[25] Gouldner notes that the surface workers in the gypsum factory looked down upon the miners but also held them in awe. The reasons for this similarity are not hard to find. The casters, like the miners, worked at a dangerous job where the accident rate was higher than in any other section. The casting job required strong young men who could bear the intense heat. Like the miners, they had the highest absence rate in the firm. The three foremen

24. Sayles and Strauss in their study of American local unions found that a large proportion of leaders and those who participated in the union were skilled workers with high seniority who had high prestige in the plant. Leonard Sayles and George Strauss, *The Local Union: Its Place in the Industrial Plant* (New York: Harper and Brothers, 1953), pp. 143, 203.

25. Alvin Gouldner, *Patterns of Industrial Bureaucracy* (Glencoe: Free Press, 1954).

were closer to the workers than those in other sections; sharing a common danger and hard physical conditions created a strong *esprit de corps* among the casters. They liked to brag about the furious work pace and how much tougher and more demanding their job was. Like mining, casting held a central position in the operation of the firm. They created the product, with other sections either feeding them or depending on their output. When the diecast company hired the ex-miners in their suburban plant, the younger ones were concentrated in the casting section. Evidently, management believed they would not balk at the tough working conditions and would be more accustomed to the type of social relations in the casting section. One management official explained, "Those Kyushu workers willingly work a three-shift system because they think everyone is doing it."

The difference in prestige accorded to different jobs and work groups is a natural basis for forming worker coalitions and cleavages. As one welder explained, "I don't like to bother with those unskilled guys. Except when it is required by my job, I associate only with skilled workers like myself." Technology, by determining the type of skills required, the size of the work group, the work pace, and the nature of worker interaction on the job, affects the prestige accorded to jobs, sections and people. It is thus a major factor conditioning the shape of worker coalitions and cleavages.[26]

AGE: A FOCAL POINT OF COALITION AND CLEAVAGE

Age was a major source of worker cleavage and coalition in the two firms studied. In all rapidly changing industrial societies, we expect generational differences to develop and mutual understanding to be difficult to achieve between young and older workers. Where pay is according to the nature of work or work achievement, coalitions are more likely to be formed along skill levels. Where strong industrial unions have reduced wage differentials, we expect generation differences to

26. Robert Blauner has made a convincing argument on this point based on American data. Robert Blauner, *Alienation and Freedom: The Factory Worker and His Industry* (Chicago: University of Chicago Press, 1964).

be held somewhat in check. But in Japan, where payment is explicitly according to age and length of service with marked wage differentials developing between young workers and older workers, the break between generations is heightened. It is not only the different wages but the uneven spread of expenses throughout a worker's career that makes a meeting of minds difficult. The economic obligations felt by workers in bachelorhood are quite different from those of the married worker, who is generally over thirty, has children to support, and is thinking of saving for retirement. The differential incomes by age and length of service and the differential obligations create different life styles. In Japan, in the middle sixties, the gap was further accentuated because of different educational experiences. Young workers are participating in the expanding educational system of an advanced industrial society. This isolates them from the adult population and contributes to a significant cultural cleavage. Blue-collar workers over thirty-five received their formal education in prewar schools and were shaped by community and family attitudes which are in many ways strikingly different from the postwar experiences of young workers. Young workers did not know the hardships of war and the immediate postwar period. They were raised in a more democratic environment with a freedom to experiment seldom seen in the prewar period. They are not caught as tightly in the web of social obligations as older workers. They are more oriented toward the expanding consumer economy. These differential experiences intensify young workers' identification with others of the same age with similar wages, values, and life styles.

The two companies provided striking confirmation of these differences. The generation gap was a persistent topic of conversation among workers and management. Management continually complained of trouble in understanding what young workers think nowadays.[27] In their answers to

27. Japanese consciousness of the generation gap can be seen in government statistics and public opinion surveys, which invariably collect and report data according to the age of respondents. There is also a wide literature on problems of young workers. The Japan Federation of Employers' Associations, *Seishōnen no Rōmukanri* (Personnel Management of Youth), (Tokyo: The Federation, 1963).

research questions about factory behavior, workers often mentioned age differences.

The common practice of establishing a youth section in Japanese companies institutionalizes and accentuates generational differences. Youth sections usually loosely affiliated with the enterprise union, are designed to serve unmarried workers. They organize sports activities, hiking trips, and dances for members. In the Tokyo diecast plant, the youth section was also a mechanism for political education, with the Communist youth group, Minseidō, exercising major control; this is not an uncommon practice. In the auto parts company, the youth section was firmly controlled by the union leadership. They saw to it that loyal workers were elected to its offices so that the youth section would not become a center where dissenting workers crystallized their opposition.

WORKERS AND THE WORK CYCLE

One way of approaching age cleavage is to follow the worker through the work cycle. The blue-collar worker entering the Takei Tokyo factory, particularly the eighteen-year-old high school graduate, comes in with high ideals. These are not ideals of political and industrial democracy or socialism but of higher wages, shorter hours, and a chance to be promoted; their sources are varied. The extremely low wage paid the entering worker is one necessary though not sufficient explanation. Workers say their high ideals are formed by newspapers, television, and other mass media, and by past experiences and talks with friends at other companies as well as school and neighborhood friends.[28] They make detailed comparisons of work conditions and benefits that the companies offer. Undoubtedly, the postwar educational system with its emphasis on democratization, modernization, and civil rights helps to form these high ideals directly and indirectly. However, these ideals are not only creations of post-

28. While this research was conducted, a television program appeared on the life of the Australian worker. It attracted the attention of the Tokyo diecast workers who were amazed at the affluence of these workers. It is not hard to see how programs of this nature heighten the aspirations of young workers.

war reconstruction. The cultural values inherited from the Meiji period which emphasized the importance of making Japan a modern industrial country are easily adapted to contemporary demands for higher wages and better working conditions in the factory or to political action for social reform. There are also the persisting historic values expressed in the concept of *risshin shusse* which results in children being taught in the family that "you have to be better than we are."

These ideals affect young workers' behavior. They are willing to unite, sacrifice, and take risks to achieve these ideals. Worker solidarity is strong in their early years. It is particularly true of the present crop of young urban workers because the labor market is good and job changes are possible.

Given the workers' high ideals during their early years of employment and their inclination toward worker solidarity, it is not surprising that they often turn to leftist political leaders.[29] The leftists promise to fight for higher wages and better conditions in the shop and are less inclined to concern themselves with company ability to pay. A common view among the young workers in the Tokyo diecast plant was that older workers were not able to stand up to the company or march in political demonstrations because they could not afford to lose overtime work and were concerned about their future. Consequently, they believed that it was their mission to take the place of the older workers in the struggle for higher wages, better working conditions, and a better society.

The young workers' appraisal of their own situation is not favorable. They are conscious of what their low wages can buy and the good life offered in the mass media and the gap between the reality of factory life and their high ideals. They are aware of the discrepancy between their low wages and their high productivity. Yet in terms of the whole work cycle, the age before marriage is the most favorable with respect to available cash wages relative to economic obligations.

29. This was not the case in the auto parts firm because of the rural labor force; they did not have the same high ideals, organizational ability, or sophistication as the urban diecast workers. In the auto parts plant, the young workers' leaders, being well over thirty, were clearly in the company orbit and set the tone for young workers.

Although the young unmarried worker cannot afford to use his leisure time the way he wants or buy the material goods he wants, he is not saddled with the financial obligations that come later in life. Indeed, this is responsible for the freedom of action the young worker has. The higher absence rate and lower overtime worked by young workers in the Tokyo diecast plant was clear testimony to their more favorable economic position. For married workers the freedom to accept or reject overtime in the Tokyo diecast plant was more academic than real, as overtime provided them with the margin necessary to make ends meet.

Most Japanese workers marry late. In the firms studied, the proper age for getting married was estimated by blue-collar workers to be twenty-eight or twenty-nine, with the wife being twenty-five. This is in line with our general knowledge of Japanese society, which shows blue-collar workers on the average marry at twenty-eight with the first child coming at thirty-one and the second at thirty-three.[30] Two children are the expectation and, with the diffusion of birth control methods, become the rule. A national sample of married women under age 50 in 1965 reported 52 percent currently using contraception and 33 percent having experienced induced abortion. Class differences are not large. For example, 57 percent of wives with white-collar husbands were reported using contraception while 50 percent of laborers' wives reported current use.[31]

Workers explain late marriage in terms of the low pay to young workers. They believe they cannot afford to get married until their late twenties, when their wages rise and they

30. An extensive study by Chubachi Masumi and associates of blue-collar workers at a major steel corporation bears this out. For some of the published results see Morioka Kiyomi, "Rōdōsha Kazoku ni okeru Jidō Yōikuhi no Kenkyū, (I): Kazoku Shūki kara mita Sekatsu Kōzō o Chūshin ni" (Study on the Childrearing Expenses of the Worker Family, Part I: Analysis of Life Organization in Terms of Family Cycle), Kikan Shakai Hoshō Kenkyū (Quarterly of Social Security Research), Vol. 2, No. 3 (December 1966).

31. Mainichi Shinbun, August 21, 1969, pp. 10–11. Institute of Population Problems, Selected Statistics Concerning Fertility Regulation in Japan, Ministry of Health and Welfare, Research Series No. 181 (December 15, 1967), pp. 50–51.

have had time to accumulate savings.[32] Generally, age thirty as the time of marriage and child-bearing sees the sharpest rise in financial obligations in the work career. It is a time at which the fit between rewards received and actual needs is worst. In the U.S., Harold Wilensky suggests that this same "trough" exists between 22 and 35 years of age.[33] For the Japanese worker, however, the trough is probably shorter, partly because of the late marrying age.

The time for marriage and child-bearing coincides with another very important change in the worker's life. As discussed in Chapter IV, it is extremely difficult to change jobs after thirty. Even if a job change is possible, it often means lower wages, which workers are not willing to accept once they have family responsibilities. This is a time for settling down and thinking of the future. The worker becomes more concerned about the financial position of the company and is more susceptible to management appeals. Company benefits are lopsided in favor of those over thirty and if the worker does not step out of line he can cash in on them.

The forces impinging on the worker around thirty require the most crucial adjustment since he first entered the factory. It is a time for scaling down of the high ideals of youth and adjusting to supporting a family on factory wages. Company loyalty and family ties are strengthened at the expense of worker solidarity. The amount of leisure time spent with fellow workers declines as more time is spent with the family or working overtime to support the family. The shift in worker loyalty to the company with increasing age is not unique to Japan but has also been reported in the U.S.[34]

32. The median age at which American males marry has slowly declined from 26.1 in 1890 to 23.1 in 1964; recently there has been a leveling off. In 1947, by occupational status of the husband, the median age at first marriage for those married less than five years was 22.9 for laborers (except farm and mines), 23.4 for operatives and kindred workers, and 24.0 for craftsmen, foremen and kindred workers. These median ages can be presumed to have dropped still further in recent years. Paul Glick, *American Families* (New York: John Wiley, 1957), p. 118. Hyman Rodman, *Marriage, Family, and Society* (New York: Random House, 1965), p. 291.

33. Harold Wilensky, "Work, Careers, and Social Integration," *International Social Science Journal*, Vol. 12 (Fall 1960), p. 549.

34. Robert Dubin, *World of Work*, p. 254.

What is unusual is the convergence of the various forces noted to make the shift around the age of thirty sharp and decisive for Japanese blue-collar workers.

The shift from worker solidarity to company loyalty moves the worker into competition with his fellow workers as he seeks to demonstrate his loyalty. This competition becomes stronger as workers approach their late thirties and early forties and aspirations for promotion intensify. Friendships, which were a key factor in the young worker's attachment to the company, decline in importance relative to a more direct attachment to the company. As might be expected, worker attitudes and behavior toward their union often change radically. Workers are less willing to support the union in making strong demands on the company. Given the difficult economic circumstances which confront the worker after thirty, one would expect them to press their union to demand higher wages. On the contrary, the difficulty of finding another job and the promise of security and economic benefits in the long run turn them in the opposite direction. If there is a militant left-wing union, the workers are particularly susceptible to behind-the-scenes company maneuvering to organize a second union more sympathetic to management. Whether it actually happens, however, depends on a variety of factors such as type of management, age composition of the entire work force, economic position of the firm, and relations between blue- and white-collar workers. In particular, the demographic structure of the firm—the result, at a given point in time, of recruitment, turnover, and biological aging—strongly conditions the degree of worker militancy. The unusually low age of the Japanese labor force must always be kept in mind when seeking explanations of contemporary worker behavior.

The shift from worker solidarity in the under-thirty category to a preoccupation with family and orientation toward the company is most noticeable among the left-wing union leaders. The thirty-one-year-old leader of the right-wing socialist faction advocating a more cooperative attitude toward Takei, only four years earlier had been a leading member in the shop of Minseidō, the Communist youth group. A large number of foremen and supervisors in the Tokyo plant had also been former left-wing union leaders, but had undergone similar conversions around age thirty. The simplistic notion that age turns young radicals to mature conservatives is far from adequate in explaining this behavior. I have tried to identify the structured pressures in Japan which produce a sharp break around age thirty.

The shift in the early thirties is not necessarily a transformation from carefree to scared and economically oppressed workers. There may be no noticeable shift in companies with a labor force composed mainly of recent rural recruits. But in a company such as Takei Diecast, where a left-wing union exists, the shift is more noticeable. Even there the shift from worker solidarity to company loyalty can be a relatively smooth role transformation. The ideological pragmatism of workers discussed earlier undoubtedly eases the change. Most workers are aware of the process and the pressures that account for it, so they develop a certain passive acceptance of the phenomenon. It mitigates much of the bitterness that one might expect.

Between age thirty and forty-five, Takei workers receive gradually rising wages in line with their increasing length of service. But rapidly increasing expenses leave little margin for saving or indulging in new products on the consumer market. Increased housing costs absorb part of the higher wages as the worker seeks larger quarters to accommodate his growing family. Television, refrigerator, washing machine, electric fan, and sewing machine are items increasingly viewed as necessities. When the worker is thirty-seven his first child will enter school. Then educational expenses will be added to the family budget.

For male blue-collar workers in 1965, Table 7 reports the average monthly income and expenditures in cities with a population of 50,000 or more:[35]

35. Office of the Prime Minister, *Family Income and Expenditure Survey* (Tokyo: The Office, 1966). A more complete analysis is presented in: Office of the Prime Minister, *Annual Report of the Family Income and Expenditures Survey*, 1965 (Tokyo: The Office, 1966), pp. 168–171.

TABLE 7
Average Monthly Income and Expenditures for Blue-Collar
Workers in Cities of 50,000 or More, 1965
(In yen)

Income			52,803
Expenditure			45,107
Living Expenditures			
Food:			
Cereals	4,333		
Other foods	12,300		
TOTAL FOOD		16,633	
Housing: a		4,692	
Fuel and light:		1,856	
Clothing:		4,542	
Miscellaneous:			
Medical care	1,038		
Education	1,292		
Reading and recreation	2,289		
Social expenditures	2,193		
Other miscellaneous	7,232		
TOTAL MISCELLANEOUS		14,044	
Total Living Expenditures:			41,767 b

a Housing includes rent, repairs, improvements, furniture, and utensils.
b The difference between total expenditures (45,107) and living expenditures (41,767) included earned income taxes, other taxes, and social security.

The 52,803 yen income derives from 1.64 earners per family and the average age of the household head is forty-one. For a large number of blue-collar families the additional wage earner is usually the wife. The average family size is 4.11. Some of the above totals gloss over important differences. Housing costs, for example, vary widely depending on whether the employee has access to company housing. These totals also conceal the differences between blue-collar employees in large firms who receive higher wages and those in small- and medium-scale firms like Takei Diecast. There are additional disbursements, other than expenditures, which include net savings, insurance premium payments, debt payments, and installment credit purchase payments. In 1965, the monthly average disbursements were, respectively, 7,575, 2,028, 1,009, and 3,916 yen.

The majority of firms (about 80 percent) set their retirement age at fifty-five; the number of firms raising the age to fifty-six, fifty-seven, and sixty has increased in recent years, however. Company retirement allowances may be paid to those who leave the company before retirement age, but the total allowance is usually constructed on the basis of final base pay so that it strongly favors those with long service. The retirement allowance encourages commitment to the firm. Generally, the allowances are lower for blue-collar workers, because their base pay is lower.[36]

In the present-day average blue-collar family, the children will be twenty-five and twenty-three years old when their worker father reaches the retirement age of fifty-five. At best, the worker will be fifty when his second child graduates from high school, which leaves him five years to concentrate on saving for retirement, assuming none of his children go on to higher education. The difficulties of saving before retirement, the leveling off of the wage increase curve in the later years, the inability to rely on children for aid or support, low old age pensions, increased life span, and the low retirement pay in small and medium firms, mean that most blue-collar workers continue to work after the official retirement age. At Takei Diecast, blue-collar workers said they could not rely on the pension, did not expect to retire at age fifty-five, and would probably "work until I drop." They expected to work as special employees at Takei or some other company. In either case, they were likely to have much reduced income and irregular employment. Gujo Auto Parts made it a practice to rehire favored retired employees at lower wages to man their welfare facilities such as their canteen and employee discount store. The practice of selecting favored employees undoubtedly contributes to employee competition to demonstrate their loyalty to the company, and works against resistance to the company by older employees. The circumstances at the two firms were quite typical. For example, a recent Ministry of Labor survey of workers who had reached

36. For example, in a 1962–1963 survey conducted by the Kansai Federation of Employers' Associations at firms with more than 500 employees, the retirement allowance after thirty years of service was: 3,960,000 yen for university graduates, white-collar; 2,802,200 yen for high school graduates, white-collar; and 1,968,400 yen for middle school graduates, blue-collar.

retirement age reported: 74 percent were still working as employees, 8 percent were self-employed, and 18 percent were without regular employment. Of those still working as employees, 76 percent received an income lower than that before retirement. Blue-collar workers, it is estimated, are receiving only 75 percent of their pre-retirement income. Almost half of those employed after retirement age were forced to move to smaller firms to earn their livelihood.[37] An examination of the employment structure of nonagricultural industries by age and size of enterprise reveals that the overwhelming number of employees over fifty-five are working in firms with fewer than 300 employees.[38] Essentially, the larger firms "rationalize" their enterprise by dumping their older labor force onto small and medium companies.

Worker loyalty to the company is likely to remain strong after thirty until retirement. Three factors can upset this pattern, however. The first is the failure to achieve promotion, and the second a threat to living standards when income does not keep up with rising prices. Older workers have not shared equally in the rising real wages during the past fifteen years. Whether the absolute increase in living standards continues in the future obviously depends on the maintenance of a high economic growth rate.

Failure to achieve promotion may remain a matter of personal dissatisfaction or affect labor-management relations. Whether it becomes a social issue depends on many factors, the most important of which are employee age composition, rate of firm expansion, and effectiveness of the status ranking system in "cooling out" workers. The third factor affecting older workers' loyalty to the company is the threat of dismissal in companies that are forced to "rationalize" their operations. In such cases, older workers often look to a militant union to defend them against the company, because the firm tries to force out the highly paid older workers.

37. Japan Institute of Labor, *Japan Labor Bulletin*, Vol. 7, No. 8 (August 1968), p. 2.

38. Office of the Prime Minister, *Shūgyō Kōzō Kihon Chōsa Hōkoku*, 40 (1965 Employment Status Survey), (Tokyo: The Office. 1966), pp. 60–61.

WORKER COMPETITION

There is an image of Japan as a society in which joint decision making, consensus, and tightly integrated social groups predominate. Although it would be wrong to deny the existence of these phenomena, their emphasis distorts the role that competition plays in Japanese society. There is indeed an enormous amount of competition in Japanese society, but it is often carefully controlled, channeled, and manipulated by higher authorities. Perhaps the most striking example of competition on a national level are the annual university examinations or, as it is called, "examination hell," which attracts the attention of the whole country during the months of February and March. At the prestigious major universities perhaps only one out of ten applicants will be accepted. The competition is high and the stakes are enormous: one's very career hangs on the outcome.

In the factory, too, competition is high, and although the objective consequences may not seem as momentous to the outside observer, they often are so to the participant. The competition occurs throughout the work career, but is especially pronounced in the over thirty age group. The competition among blue-collar workers is intensified by the priority given vertical relations at the expense of horizontal attachments. It is hierarchical relationship which is decisive, not worker solidarity. Seen from a comparative perspective, in the U.S. factory, competition among workers over promotion, overtime, job assignments, etc., is decided to a high degree by relatively objective criteria such as skill or seniority. Favoritism, though not unimportant, plays a limited role; one of the major achievements of American unions is the strong plant organizations which diminish such treatment. In Japan, once minimum standards of seniority and skill are met, worker competition often is decided by a worker's vertical relationship to his superiors.[39] Great emphasis is placed on

39. The Japanese have two widely used terms to describe this vertical relation, *jōge kankei* and *ue-shita no kankei*. We do not seem to have a counterpart in the English language; we could say superior and subordinate

impressing superiors, on flattery, and behind-the-door deals. It increases friction among workers and makes it difficult to develop deep horizontal friendships and worker solidarity.

The above interpretation is supported by the views and behavior of the Tokyo diecast workers. The workers often stated that they could not make close friends in the factory as they could in school. School, they said, is where you make your life-long friends. Competition at Japanese schools is focused on the period of entrance; it diminishes during attendance; a pupil rarely is expelled or held back, which means absence of competition and minimization of conflicting interests among peers. In school one does not advance at the expense of others. The teacher is not seeking to play one student against another. But this situation does exist in the factory and weakens worker solidarity. In both factories, when workers were asked to name their best friend, it often was an old school friend rather than a fellow worker. Moreover, a worker usually met his school friend only once a month, if then.

Workers spoke quite freely about competing in contrast to the caution with which they spoke of production restriction. Most Tokyo diecast workers, however, believed that competition among the workers was good from management's point of view but bad from the worker's. What management regarded as cooperation was, in effect, often viewed by workers as the result of internal competition and, therefore, destructive of worker solidarity.

Management was adept at tactics designed to increase the competitive spirit. Encouragement of promotion expectations was one device. In the suburban diecast plant, management started the practice of posting the daily production of each worker on a bulletin board. There was no doubt among workers that it was designed to set up competition in order to increase production. Management was also adept at converting competition with other firms into loyalty to their own to strengthen work motivation. Competition is not eliminated by shifting the arena from intragroup to inter-

relationships but these are not expressions in the popular idiom like the Japanese terms.

group rivalry, but merely redirected. Difficulty in establishing industry-wide unions is one indication of the success of this strategy.

Worker competition may be for scarce material or nonmaterial resources; it often operates as a zero-sum game. This is the case with promotion and its associated rewards, where the winner takes all. Competition for prestige in the shop takes a similar form. In this case, the "loser" is expected to display proper deferential behavior to his "superiors." These kinds of competitions were quite apparent in the two factories in terms of short-term and long-term calculations. For example, the Tokyo diecast workers pointed to the competition among them for securing a good merit rating. What seemed to be competition over an immediate scarce reward, was also part of a long-run competition to demonstrate loyalty to the company and to secure a promotion.

Competition among workers was particularly stimulated when age, length of service, and nature of work were relatively similar. It is more than competition over scarce rewards, it is a dispute over the criteria for awarding them. For instance, there was strong rivalry between two workers in the maintenance section of the Tokyo plant; one worker was one year older, the other had one year's longer length of service.

Workers competed not only for scarce rewards but for competition's sake. The Tokyo diecast workers displayed strong competitive feelings, although they claimed they disliked competition. They said competition often came from the individual's personal feelings. But their pervasive competitiveness reflects internalized cultural values. One worker explained his feelings as follows:

> There are all sorts of areas where you don't want to be defeated. You don't want to be defeated when it comes to work or by people you work with. You don't want to be defeated with respect to your own personality, so you read books and study society. . . . What I mean is not that you want to be more of a big shot than the other guy but that you want to have a feeling of superiority over the next guy even if it's only a little. For example, someone tells me that so and so has made so many pieces today. Well, then, for

that guy to have done so much may be very important for
him and give him a feeling of superiority. But if he says
something about it, I get a stirred-up feeling inside me and
want to show that I can do better.

Significantly, he was a left-wing union militant who, despite
his belief in worker solidarity, could not restrain his competitive drive.

Worker competition was not unlimited. Management
controlled worker competition so it could direct it. It was also
in the workers' interest to limit it. The role of *nenkō* in reducing competition has already been discussed. In the Tokyo
diecast plant, which was declining, the workers feared an in-
ternecine struggle as they scrambled to insure their jobs in
the future. The Tokyo union sought to minimize such situa-
ations for they destroyed worker solidarity.

Without relying on the union, the auto parts workers'
restriction of production was an attempt to control potentially destructive competition. In the press section of the
Tokyo diecast plant, the press operators reported each averaged between 2,000 and 2,500 pieces a day. Without formal
decision workers agreed on a general restriction of production; it was an informal understanding of the right pace for
a day's work. The piece total had been gradually raised over
the preceding three years as workers became accustomed to
the new presses and improvements in die design. A gradual
reduction of employees in the section pressured the remaining operators to compensate for lost production. In this way,
production was raised without serious competition.

Three years earlier, however, a problem arose when one
press operator constantly outstripped the others in daily production. At that time there were thirty workers in the press
and press maintenance section, and ten young workers ostra-
cized (*murahachibu*) the offending man. They stopped talking to him, offered him no help in his work, and avoided him
during the lunch period and after work. The matter was
resolved when the man became disillusioned with company
policy and relaxed his work pace, and technical improvements
raised the production of the other operators. Unlike the

Tokyo press operators, the auto parts workers did not resort to ostracism of their "quota buster." The clutch assembly line was group work so the auto parts worker who constantly tried to raise production could not do it on his own or in a way that would embarrass his co-workers with management. It would have been hard for them to ostracize him anyway, because he was older (twenty-eight), more aggressive and more experienced than the others on the line, who averaged twenty-three years of age. The union commitment to raise production made it harder for them to take public action.

We can say competition among workers to demonstrate loyalty to management and satisfy inculcated competitive cultural values is a recurring theme among blue-collar workers. As a major factor contributing to worker motivation, it is one of management's strongest weapons. Viewed from the workers' side, it is a source of weakness that dilutes their solidarity. The balance between competitive behavior and worker solidarity is conditioned by age, marital status, place on the urban-rural continuum, and the nature of work as well as the growth rate of the firm, industry, and national economy.

The question of unity and cleavage among Japanese workers must be understood within the context of the in-group orientation of members of the firm. It is this orientation which sets the tone for coalitions or cleavages. This is true in any industrial society, but it is especially so in Japanese firms where there are strong centripetal forces. We observed this in-group orientation in the fluidity of worker relationships, the informality of language used in the factory, the nature of participation in shop organizations, the type of leisure time consumption, the type of social relations between blue- and white-collar workers, and the importance of intergroup as against intragroup competition.

Primary group attachments among industrial work groups are critical to work performance. The axes along which primary groups form in Japanese factories show the expected bases. When we examine friendship groups, work groups, and interest groups, we see worker coalitions and cleavages develop along the lines of job assignment, skill levels, job prestige, wage levels, age, and similar interests. Beyond these, however, we find key bases for worker coalitions and cleavages in Japan are year of entry, regional ties, and dormitory life. These distinctive bases give industrial work performance in Japan a particular configuration. They are three avenues through which traditional social relations enter to commit the worker to the factory. The kinds of social groups formed on this basis are not voluntary or accidental but the result of management decisions on recruitment, housing, and nature of the reward system. Of particular importance is the fact that the workers' reference groups tend to be composed of those who enter the factory in the same year, creating unity with those of the same year and cleavage from those of different years. Later in the work career, however, the unity with those recruited in the same year may diminish as competition over factory rewards grows.

Age coalitions and cleavages have special importance in Japan by virtue of a combination of factors: the *nenkō* wage and promotion system, a prewar and postwar generation with significantly different values and perspectives, the permanent employment practice, and the late marrying age of Japanese workers.

Competition among workers in the factory is strong and of necessity destructive to worker solidarity. It is particularly intensified after age thirty by virtue of reduced alternative job possibilities, marriage, and an increase in promotional aspirations. It is an important source of work motivation. Because it is difficult to speak of one society being more competitive than another given the ambiguity of the concept, it is not suggested here that Japanese workers are more or less competitive than American workers. There is certainly a great deal of the competitive spirit in Japan despite contrary popular conceptions abroad; although it lies along different axes than in the U.S.

CHAPTER VI

THE WORKER AND THE COMPANY:
THE SHAPE OF PATERNALISM

"The Round-Trip Ticket Blues" is what they want to sing.
Abé Kobo—*The Woman in the Dunes*

If we described the American and Japanese worker's fundamentally different view of his company in one sentence, we would say: The U.S. ideology is that your work should get hold of you; the Japanese, that the company should get hold of you. Although ideology is not necessarily reflected in practice and attachment to work and company overlaps in both countries, the statement indicates a significant difference in ideal orientations. Another possible meaning of company to the Japanese worker is to compare it to caste in India. Consider the following description of caste by J. H. Hutton:

> From the point of view of the individual members of a caste the system provides him from birth with a fixed social milieu from which neither wealth nor poverty, success nor disaster can remove him, unless of course he so violates the standards of behavior laid down by his caste that it spews him forth—temporarily or permanently. He is provided in this way with a permanent body of associations which control almost all his behavior and contacts. His caste canalizes his choice in marriage, acts as his trade union, his friendly or benefit society, his slate club and his orphanage; it takes

the place for him of health insurance, and if need be provides for his funeral.[1]

With some modification we may say that the functional consequences of the Indian's relation to his caste are the same as those of the Japanese worker's relation to his firm. Such characterization is most accurate for permanent workers in the major corporations and in stable small family enterprises.

In earlier chapters we documented the commitment, or over-commitment as some prefer to see it, of the Japanese worker to his firm. The extent of worker acceptance of company goals in Japan is seldom seen in an American factory, except, perhaps, in declining industries and by workers over forty.

There are a number of other indicators which reflect Japanese blue-collar workers' consciousness of strong subordination to the company. The workers at Takei and Gujo commonly referred to their company as *uchi* (literally translated means "we within"), which has the connotation of "our family circle." Using household-kinship as a model for other social relationships in Japan, we have the following analogy: The head of the household is the father who corresponds to the head of the company, the company is the house and the worker is one of the children under the authority of the parents. In the nationalist parallel the Emperor was the father, the state the house, and the people were members of the family. In the factory, the household-kinship terminology, as legitimating ideology, reinforces the hierarchical relationship of management in a superior and the workers in an inferior status.

A striking example of adherence to the authority of the employer was the behavior of two self-styled left-wing militants that I met in a working class-student bar. The two workers often spent their weekends drinking beer in a sing-along bar. The standard fare included Viet Cong liberation songs led by singing waiters dressed in Russian peasant costumes. One of them explained:

1. J. H. Hutton, *Caste in India: Its Nature, Function and Origin* (London: Oxford University Press, 1951), p. 111.

We like to sing here on weekends and march in demonstrations because it gives us a release from the tensions built up while working a sixty-hour week. And by doing this we go back and put in a hard day's work on Monday again. . . . We don't need a union at our shoe factory because our boss is a guy we can talk to, and, besides, we will never make it into a big successful company if we have a union.

As a sociological phenomenon, this compartmentalization is not unique. Many cultures have periodic "moral holidays" for temporary waivering of conventional restraints and norms. Controlled deviance probably reduces nonconformity and prevents the emergence of more disorderly types of social change. Marching in weekend demonstrations, as it turns out, is relatively harmless behavior which does not require a confrontation with one's employer. The exception confirms the rule, and the rule is strict adherence to the authority of a paternalistic employer.

These indicators, however, cannot be taken at face value. Changes in language often lag behind changes in behavior; attitudes, and kinship analogies can be misleading, and indirect indicators and examples should not be confused with systematic behavioral evidence. The remainder of this chapter, therefore, will be devoted to a systematic attempt to lay bare the meaning of paternalism in the two firms. In particular, we will focus on the question of worker motivation and its relation to paternalism. Is paternalism to be understood in terms of the traditional benefits proffered by employers and the traditional duty of workers to respond with hard work? Are management and worker decisions and actions taken as pragmatic responses to changing environmental conditions? The evidence to be presented suggests there is a subtle interaction between these two seemingly polar alternatives.

SOME ASPECTS OF THE HISTORICAL
DEVELOPMENT OF PATERNALISM

Historically, the Japanese employer was dominant in the factory and the scope of management prerogatives was wide. Workers' struggles won few benefits. Existing worker benefits were bestowed first by benevolent employers and, secondly, by the postwar U.S. occupation forces. Both facts strongly color Japanese industrial relations and undoubtedly contribute to a certain submissiveness among workers. A number of factors contributed to the Japanese firm assuming wide authority and responsibility over its employees' lives in addition to its function as a producer of goods. Some major factors are: chronic overpopulation and scarce resources and jobs, the need to commit an industrial labor force in a short period of time, uneven economic growth, high priority government investment in selected industries and defense, low priority investment in social services, and, last, World War II and its aftermath.

The firms' assumption of wide responsibilities fits well with the values of the *shūjū* (lord and vassal) relationship of the feudal period; and it is likely these values worked toward acceptance of the role. The historical link during the early stages of industrialization was the labor contractor (*oyakata*). The continuous movement to the city and industrial employment, despite its many dislocating effects, was seen by many Japanese as an opportunity for achieving individual and family success and a contribution to national strength. Two popular slogans of those days illustrate these motivations: *fukoku kyōhei* (prosperous country, strong military) and *risshin shusse* (make something of yourself). The company was a firm element in this configuration; its role was conceived by employers and accepted by workers as contributing to these goals. This differs sharply with the experience of the first industrializing country, England. There the enclosure movement (especially pronounced between 1760 and 1820), the wars, the Poor Laws, the decline of rural industries, and the counter-revolutionary stance of British rulers propelled rural dwellers off the land and into the growing industrial areas. Industrial work and factory life were identified with deprival of independence and coercion. This was especially true for the estimated 400,000 (by 1841) inhabitants of Great Britain who had been born in Ireland and the many more born in Britain of Irish parentage. E. P. Thompson, in pointing to the exceptional violence during the course of British industrialization, suggests that it was a process that "was unrelieved by any sense of national participation in communal effort, such as is found in countries undergoing a national revolution. Its ideology was that of the masters alone." [2] In such a situation, employers are less willing to offer employees extensive protection and workers less willing to accept wide management authority over their lives.

Many benefits offered particularly by larger Japanese firms have already been mentioned. Some of the more basic benefits are: recreational facilities, health facilities, company housing, cafeteria and lunch subsidies, company discount stores, job training and retraining of employees, saving institutions, and permanent employment.[3] These practices have been partly responsible for attaching the "paternalistic" label to Japanese management. Management engaged in these practices mainly because it viewed them as pragmatic solutions to its problems, but expressed them publicly as requirements of familism and *noblesse oblige*. Yet, it was not simply a matter of pragmatic decisions being made and then legitimated by an ideology emphasizing traditional elements. The continued existence of pre-industrial values and practices made management choice of these policies and worker acceptance of them more likely. However, the very existence of this role over the years deprived workers of their initiative and made them more subordinate to company policy.

Worker and union reaction to extensive company benefits, however, has not always been a passive acceptance of benevolent paternalism, especially since the end of World War II. Company benefits are now a subject of collective bargaining. For example, at Takei and Gujo the union de-

2. E. P. Thompson, *The Making of the English Working Class* (New York: Random House, 1963), pp. 198–199, 444–445.

3. Company saving institutions pay higher interest rates than commercial banks. Worker participation in company saving plans is common in Japan and a source of company investment funds. Firms find it cheaper to borrow from employees and pay high interest rates than to borrow from banks at still higher interest rates. Scandals in the middle nineteen sixties, when some large firms went bankrupt causing workers to lose their savings, led the government to seek a stronger control over these savings.

manded increased company housing. The workers and their leaders explained the demand as an economic need: They could not get adequate housing on the open market because of high costs and their low wages. Nor did political activity seem capable of delivering cheap housing. In the past, the semi-annual bonuses were viewed as a sign of management generosity and paternalism. They are now an integral part of union wage bargaining. The more militant Takei workers consciously avoided the term *bōnasu* in favor of (end of season) lump sum payment (*kimatsu*) *ichijikin* to indicate that it was not a gift but a right to which they were entitled. Benefit programs, then, do not always reflect a passive subordination of workers to authority or to the management view that rank imposes obligations. They are a response to needs of workers and management defined in economic terms. In the postwar period, it has become increasingly hard to cloak benefits in paternalistic ideologies, which are becoming less acceptable to Japanese workers.

It is difficult to speculate on future developments, but it seems likely that paternalistic company benefits to employees will decline in a relative if not absolute sense. The government's increasing role in guaranteeing social services and expanding the national educational system as well as increasing inter-firm mobility point in this direction. Rising expenses from company maintenance of extensive facilities such as housing make employers reluctant to take on new responsibilities. The benefit programs are hard to justify at a time when management is concerned with rationalizing operations.

Yet, Japan has reached an impressive level of industrialization, while maintaining these practices. The Japanese social security system has respected paternalistic welfare practices of large-scale firms. As the growing labor shortage makes it harder to recruit workers, companies will be tempted, despite high costs, to expand various benefits in a competitive effort to secure their desired labor force. However, the benefits will have to be legitimated in universalistic and achievement oriented terms; they will become more similar to Western fringe benefits.

The relations between personnel section employees and blue-collar workers are of special interest in a discussion of Japanese paternalism.[4] The history of the personnel section in Japan is such that workers do not identify it as strongly with the "opposition" as American workers do.[5] The personnel section chief of the auto parts firm—a company of 2,500 employees—often paid money out of his pocket to help out in funerals and weddings of workers. This is the image of the paternalistic superior looking after his charges. In some companies the personnel section takes the workers' side in matters of pay raises and other demands. Sometimes personnel sections support union wage demands in negotiations with the accounting section, which generally resists the increase. In that case, top level management (board of directors) makes the final decision. The personnel section sometimes is called the left-wing faction of management.

An indication of the closeness between workers and personnel section is that its staff members, except the head, usually are unionized. This was true of the forty member personnel section (including fifteen women clerks) in the auto parts firm. In fact, the wage and salary supervisor in personnel was the president of the auto parts union.[6] A personnel section employee commented,

> Because it is an enterprise union with white- and blue-collar workers in the same union, the personnel section employees would have no protection if they were not in the union. As for the wage and salary man being president of the union, why not? After all, he knows more about wage policy than anyone else.

4. Interview with Shirai Taishirō of Hōsei University, Tokyo, October 14, 1965.
5. One consequence for participation observation research is that the dictum "don't be caught dead talking with the personnel man" does not have the same important significance as it does in an American factory.
6. Article 2 of the Trade Union Law excludes from union membership, "workers at supervisory posts having access to confidential information relating to the employer's labor relations plans and policies so that their official duties and obligations directly conflict with their loyalties and obligations as members of the trade union concerned and other persons who represent the interest of the employer." Ministry of Labor, *Japan Labour Laws*, 1968 (Tokyo: Institute of Labor Policy, 1968), p. 16.

This relation between personnel section, union, and workers protects worker interests by relying on the traditional paternalistic obligation of superiors to take care of their own. However, the pattern is changing. The personnel section, as the left-wing faction of management, is associated with the militant unionism of the immediate postwar period. With the decline of militant unionism and the efforts by major companies to rationalize operations, personnel departments are becoming agents of top management and find it harder to play the mediator role.

A manifestation of company paternalism is control over the leisure time of blue-collar workers. This was also a practice of Western countries, but declined with advancing industrialization, having been viewed as interference with worker privacy and a violation of their civil rights. In Japan, a good deal of worker leisure time still revolves around the company. In the auto parts plant, after the 4:00 P.M. quitting buzzer, workers often moved to the end of the assembly line to sit down and play Japanese chess. It is hard to imagine an American automobile worker doing that. For the American blue-collar worker the break between work hours and private time is sharp and decisive.[7] The Gujo Auto Parts workers, living in company dormitories just minutes from their work place, have their leisure time suffused with an omnipresent company. Whitehill and Takezawa in their study of the perceptions of American and Japanese workers concluded that one of the most significant differences lay in the involvement of the Japanese company in the total life of the employee. Worker acceptance of this involvement is seen by them as basic to understanding the high motivation found among the Japanese surveyed.[8]

In the past, long hours and great physical efforts required by labor intensive work methods undoubtedly contributed to a fatigue which left the worker less time and

7. This "segmentation of social experience" by American workers is documented by Robert Dubin, "Industrial Workers' Worlds: A Study of the 'Central Life Interests' of Industrial Workers," *Social Problems*, Vol. 3, No. 3 (January 1956).

8. Arthur Whitehill, Jr. and Shin'ichi Takezawa, *The Other Worker* (Honolulu: East-West Center Press, 1968).

strength for leisure activities. Moreover, low wages and the high cost of public entertainment brought about a reliance on company-sponsored leisure activities. The dormitory system, developed in the late nineteenth century as a protection against high labor mobility, further intensified worker dependence on such programs. Leisure time was often filled with educational lectures designed to instill appropriate values of responsibility, hard work, and loyalty to the company.

In recent years, rising real wages, declining work hours, physically less tiring work, and changing values have contributed to increased leisure and reduced dependence on the company. Since the nineteen fifties there has been a marked diffusion in television sets and an increase in the number of amusement places such as *pachinko* (vertical pinball) halls, bicycle racing tracks, baseball stadiums, dance halls, cabarets, bowling alleys, golf courses, ski resorts, etc. In addition, cars and modern highways are becoming more commonplace. The company is less able to compete with these attractions. Recent research notes the rising valuation of leisure as opposed to work-related pursuits. Industrial workers are reported to attach more importance to home life ("a happy home") as the focus of leisure.[9]

These developments increase the distinction between company work time and private leisure time. It will be logical to expect them to weaken the ties of the worker to the company. Gujo management reported that older workers' lives revolved more around the company than younger workers'. It pointed out that young workers think of lunch time and after work hours as their own, not company, time. But older workers often work on company problems during lunch time or take problems home with them and come back next day with an answer.

Worker reliance on company-sponsored leisure time is

9. Odaka Kunio, *Work and Leisure: As Viewed by Japanese Industrial Workers,* paper prepared for the Sixth World Congress of Sociology, Evian, 1966. See also Komai Hiroshi, *Changing Pattern of Japanese Attitudes Toward Work: A Consequence of Recent High Economic Growth* (Tokyo: Institute of Population Problems, 1969).

not only to be explained in terms of the paternalistic obligations of management and the internalized docility of Japanese workers but by economic factors. The growing debate
that surrounds the introduction of the five-day week provides
an example. In 1960 few firms had a five-day week, but since
then many major corporations have adopted this schedule.
The initiative to introduce the five-day week came from management. Employers are eager to adopt it because experience
taught that it leads to increased production and efficiency,
lowered overhead costs, and a decrease in accidents. Surveys
indicated, however, that workers do not believe they will
draw great benefits from the shorter work schedules; although
they were not opposed, most said they spent their extra time
doing nothing. The reason for this lukewarm support is lack
of money. Ten percent of the total household budget of the
average Japanese family is spent on recreation. This is a rather
large proportion but not much as an absolute sum of money,
given the high cost of public entertainment and the low
level of wages. Most workers on a five-day week have to stay
home on their days off. An Asahi Evening News editorial
reporting these developments concludes that from the economic standpoint Japan is not yet ready for the five-day
week.[10] The editorial further noted that some major firms
expanded leisure facilities to cover the increase in workers'
leisure time. Though not objecting to this development, it
called for the government to raise public standards of culture
and health rather than leave the problem to be solved by a
paternalistic employer.[11]

In the Tokyo diecast plant, the workers, particularly the
left-wing militants, were inclined to insist that their after
hours behavior was their own business and of no concern to
the company. A minority, however, expressed a nostalgia for
the good old days "when the company did things for the
workers." In the auto parts firm, the dormitory residents sel-

10. *Asahi Evening News* (AEN), July 26, 1965. This editorial, written in an English edition, is a direct translation of the editorial appearing in
the Japanese language *Asahi Shinbun* (Tokyo), one of the largest and most
influential Japanese national newspapers.
11. *Ibid.*

dom emphasized the importance of separating private leisure time from company time, though the commuters sometimes did. The dormitory system plays a key role in preserving company organized leisure time activities; this suggests that the reduction of ties with the company will be gradual. TV-watching, a major leisure time activity, can just as easily be pursued in company dormitories. Flexibility in the administration of company-sponsored leisure activities makes them amenable to the democratic impulses of the postwar period. Gujo management pointed out that in prewar days company officials made the important decisions on the administration of the recreational facilities, but that since the war the workers took over more of the planning and organizing of events. This permits workers to determine their own leisure time, but keeps them within the company sphere of influence. We can therefore say this is a move from a hierarchical in-group orientation to an egalitarian in-group orientation rather than to egalitarianism of an open-class society.

One oft noted aspect of Japanese paternalism is the "Japanese worker's sense of duty and need to avoid shame, which causes him to work effectively." [12] Historical evidence suggests a basis for this. In the early stages of industrialization, the original commitment of samurai daughters in the silk industry was based on the traditional duty the samurai father felt toward the government. The father, as a samurai, was still receiving stipends from the government at this time. Notwithstanding the stipends, the difficult economic circumstances of many samurai explains the willingness to send their daughters into the factory. The daughter entered the factory as a result of her obligation to obey her father. She worked hard so as not to injure the family honor, and morale was high. Since many of these samurai daughters were relatives of management officials or had friends of the family in management, working conditions were tolerable. But landless farm worker daughters soon replaced the samurai daughters and the quality of work quickly declined. The new replace-

12. Everett Hagen, "Some Implications of Personality Theory for the Theory of Industrial Relations," *Industrial and Labor Relations Review*, Vol. 18, No. 3 (April 1965), pp. 343–344.

ments were less inclined to worry about injuring family honor. Because they were not related to management officials, management did not feel obligated to provide good working conditions. As a result the sense of duty and the desire to avoid shame to the family declined as motivating factors.[13] There are, however, other ways in which a sense of duty may affect present-day worker behavior; these will be considered later in the chapter. The important question is: duty to whom and for what? We may also speak of cultural sources for high work motivation. Secular views on work are said to have been conditioned by Buddhism and Confucianism.[14]

If the worker believes in the existence of permanent employment, what motivates him to work hard when he knows he will not be fired? It is true that management has ways of getting rid of undesirables. It is also plausible, as we will show, that the worker's sense of duty is an important factor. There is, however, another explanation that is compelling in its simplicity. It is precisely because regular workers anticipate permanent employment that they want to make a good future for themselves in the company and consequently are motivated to work hard. Because much of the worker's social life revolves around the company, he naturally wants to make the best of it and be accepted and respected by management and fellow workers alike. The view that it is desirable to make one's entire work career in one company understandably heightens promotional aspirations within the company and increases the incentive to work hard. Shirkers do not win respect in the factory; the prestige hierarchy of workers, as noted in the preceding chapter, ranks high the skilled worker who knows how to do his job and does it.

13. This decline was not necessarily immediate, as firms, particularly smaller companies in rural areas, were able to recruit family friends and relations for many years. Sometimes villages were bound by contract to supply labor so that poor work performance by the daughters could disgrace their families in the village and threaten renewal of the contract. For this historical account, I am indebted to Fujita Yoshitaka of the Japan Federation of Employer's Associations.

14. For an English source see: Robert Bellah, *Tokugawa Religion: The Values of Pre-Industrial Japan* (Glencoe: Free Press, 1958).

In short, elaborate explanations of Japanese worker motivation in terms of traditional duties are not sufficient and indeed not always appropriate. Japanese paternalism must be understood in a context much wider than the benefits bestowed by a tradition-oriented employer and the duty of tradition-oriented workers to reciprocate with hard work. At the same time, pragmatically based actions occur in a cultural and structural context that shapes options and limits actions.

THE WORKER AND THE FOREMAN

To get at the precise meaning and content of worker subordination to the firm, it is necessary to describe and analyze specific points of contact; for a start, the worker-foremen relationship.[15] This relationship, the point at which the worker meets management, is the most crucial for understanding worker attachment to the company.

In any ongoing factory, the foreman or some functional equivalent constitutes the bottom link of a hierarchical structure transmitting management authority. Foremen are often described as marginal men caught between identification with management and identification with their subordinates.[16] If an effective ongoing relationship is to be established between worker and foreman, some degree of reciprocity must be established. For example, in the Tokyo diecast plant, it was common for foremen to trade rule enforcement for worker

15. The Japanese title, *kumi-chō*, was translated here as foreman. Some authors have preferred the translation of sub-foreman or group leader. It is a difficult problem because titles and job duties vary according to the company, and supervisory levels tend to gradually blend into the ordinary work force. The next higher level, called *kakari-chō* in the diecast firm and *shunin* in the auto parts company was translated here as supervisor. It seemed inappropriate to call the *kakari-chō* "foreman" or the *kumi-chō* "sub-foreman," because it was the *kumi-chō* who directed day-to-day operations. The *kumi-chō* was on the shop floor perhaps 95 percent of the time and it was to him that workers turned for help when a problem arose. The *kumi-chō*, while sometimes helping in production, had no assigned job duties. The *kakari-chō*, however, spent most of his time performing paper work in his office with occasional tours of the shop floor to make sure everything was running smoothly.

16. Donald Wray, "Marginal Men of Industry: The Foreman," *American Journal of Sociology*, 54 (January 1949).

cooperation. This should not be seen as an example of the unique Japanese informal approach to solving problems of motivation, for similar practices have been reported in the U.S.[17] To be successful, a foreman must secure the cooperation of his work crew, and this requires some consideration of worker interests. In return, an acceptable productive performance is expected of workers. This is the minimum necessary for the foreman to establish legitimate authority and to maintain the industrial work organization above a coercive level.

From this basic minimum, we can proceed to describe and analyze the elaborations of the Japanese model. What is notable in Japan with respect to the hierarchical structure of statuses in the factory, and the reciprocal relations between foreman and worker, are: the affective intensity of the reciprocal relationships among those who fill these statuses at any given time; the marked asymmetry in personal relations among individual participants, which is relatively undiminished by combination from below such as in union organization; the formalization of expected behavior between superiors and subordinates; and the high priority assigned to the maintenance of such relationships.

In prewar Japan, the hierarchical structure of statuses was not limited to the factory but extended in pyramid fashion to the whole society, culminating in the Emperor. This structure has been greatly weakened in the postwar period with the secularization of the Emperor's role. In the factory the relative affective intensity and formalization of such hierarchical relationships, though no doubt diminished, remains strong. The subordinate to such a reciprocal relationship is obligated to his superior for favors received and is duty bound to repay in hard work and loyalty. The superior, in turn, is expected to look out for the interests of his subordinates, take responsibility for their errors, and protect them from the discipline exercised by higher ranking authorities.

This pattern does not lead to the construction of a

17. See Alvin Gouldner, *Patterns of Industrial Bureaucracy* (Glencoe: Free Press, 1954), pp. 172–174.

democratic infrastructure within the company. It deprives the subordinates at each level of the initiative to protect themselves and exposes them to the arbitrary will of management should the fortunes of the company turn bad. There is a Japanese proverb that expresses well this lack of initiative of subordinates. The proverb advises the subordinate to "Be wrapped up in something long" (*Nagai mono ni wa makarero*), meaning that his safest course of action is to put himself completely under the power of an influential person such as his superior. If the superior says black is white then indeed the wise course for the subordinate is to agree. In return, the subordinate can expect that his interests will be taken care of by his superior.

Under these conditions, workers are reluctant to stand up to management and defend their interests, fearing that this would endanger the security that was built under the superior-subordinate relationship. In ideal form, these social relationships are "harmonious" in the sense that a dispute is not expected to arise that would disturb the relationship. Should a dispute arise, however, it is expected that it will be settled by mutual understanding (reconciliation) between the superior and subordinate without the subordinate turning to a third party such as the union for satisfaction. A section chief in the auto parts company explained, "It is an exceptional case where the supervisor does not discuss workers' complaints with them and successfully resolves the matter."

The foreman does not necessarily resolve problems in an arbitrary or paternalistic way with the worker passively "wrapping himself in something long." Insofar as the foreman's obligation to take care of his workers requires that he effectively represent their interests toward other sections and higher ranking management, an element of fair treatment and democratic consultation is insured. The actual extent of democratic consultation between worker and foreman depends a good deal on the company, industry, nature of the technology, foremen, and workers. Where management puts strong pressures on the foreman for increased production or where management lifts the authority of the foreman to

186

make decisions higher up in the company hierarchy, the scope
of consultation is greatly reduced. In the diecast company,
where there was highly centralized power among management officials, the foreman had little leeway to negotiate with
workers. The foremen in the Tokyo diecast plant complained
that when it came to changes planned by management they
were as much in the dark as the workers.

One indication of the presence of democratic consultation was that the image of the arbitrary foreman, curbed in
America by the rise of strong unions in the shop, was conspicuously absent among the workers in the two firms. An
almost universal feeling among the workers in the shop was
that foremen were workers and not management representatives. Foremen thought of themselves as workers, though
they also thought of themselves as management representatives. Supervisors were split, with many denying they had
worker status. The view of foremen as worker has historical
antecedents deriving from the lack of distinctive origins of
the supervisory group and the centralization of management
authority at the top leaving foremen to make common cause
with workers. This view was strengthened further in the
postwar period with the spread of egalitarian values and the
reduction of wage differentials.[18] This is not to say that at
present Japan does not have its share of arbitrary foremen,
but it was an established practice in both factories for the
foremen to consult with workers on planned changes or
worker complaints. There is a parallel to the Japanese family
where the father, as head of the household, holds the decision-
making power, but in practice consults extensively with the
rest of the family to determine their wishes. Finally, management in deciding on promotion takes into consideration the
amount of support a worker has from his peers. This element
is built into management's search for leadership qualities.
The new foreman is thus in debt to his subordinates for his

18. Okamoto Hideaki, *Nihon no Genba Kantokusha* (Shop Floor
Supervisors in Japan), No. 57, Industrial Training Association, Tokyo, 1964.
Okamoto also contributed an outstanding comparative study of the origin
and roles of foremen: Okamoto Hideaki, *Kōgyōka to Genba Kantokusha* (Industrialization and Supervisors), (Tokyo: Japan Institute of Labor, 1966).

very position; this helps insure that he will take their interests seriously.

The presentation of a specific worker-foreman relationship should help make clear its content. The press foreman in the suburban diecast plant was thirty-two years old and the press workers averaged twenty-two years. The foreman explained there was a family-like relation between him and the workers; the workers consulted with him on work matters as well as various personal issues and he offered help and advice. They would talk over these matters with friends, the foreman said, but they needed the judgment of an older man before they could make a firm decision. For example, at the time of the research, he was counseling two workers who were thinking of quitting. Even though one decided to quit, the foreman prevailed on him to wait several months until he could get a replacement. The foreman regarded this kind of consultation as an indispensable part of his job, and believed his job would not be good without it. At the same time, he pointed out that it was mainly the middle school graduates living in the dormitory, separated from their family, who desired to consult him. Once these press workers matured, married, and had a family, they would be less likely to rely on his advice on personal matters. Therefore, foreman involvement in the personal affairs of workers is especially strengthened by the Japanese practice of recruiting young middle school graduates from distant prefectures. For these workers, the foreman serves *in loco parentis.*

This same foreman in the press section of the suburban plant said that he held worker conversations with him confidential. He resisted higher management demands for production increases when he believed he could not justify them to the workers. The pattern that emerges is one of the foreman representing his workers toward the company. Workers in both the firms studied were aware of this role and valued it highly. At the same time, the foreman was very conscious of his obligation as a management representative to raise production and constantly sought new ways to achieve this.

In both companies there was a trend toward integrating the foreman more firmly in the management hierarchy and weakening the ties between him and the workers. It was more evident in the diecast company but also present in the auto parts firm. The basis of this trend lies in the changing technology and modern ideas of management which are becoming increasingly popular in Japan. In both firms, the practice of having foremen work alongside their men was declining; more of their time was being spent on paperwork. Their talents are needed to supervise the new forms of mass and process production that replace individuals working on separate machines.

With the separation of foremen from direct production, management seeks to draw them more firmly into its orbit. In the diecast company, management established monthly supervisory training sessions that sought to achieve this. Supervisors were excluded from the new union in the suburban diecast plant in accordance with the policy of the parent company. They were put on monthly salaries and given an increase to replace overtime pay. Foremen, however, continued to be union members; but the trend was clearly toward integrating both categories more firmly in the management hierarchy.

This trend has significant implications for the future of Japanese industrial relations, assuming it also applies outside the two firms studied. Foremen are likely to get more detailed instructions on company policy from both management and the growing ranks of industrial engineers. This reduces the scope for democratic consultation (in a paternalistic mold) between foremen and workers. With the new expensive technology, errors have to be located faster and management must have assurance that they will not be repeated, or losses would be substantial. It becomes harder for superiors to cover up and take responsibility for the errors of subordinates. As this occurs, the vertical bonds between worker and foreman are weakened. The foreman has less to offer the worker and is less able to take care of him.

In the postwar period, management exploited the two-edged position of the foremen as leaders of the workers and as management representatives to insure that the unions adopted conciliatory policies toward the company. The foreman's leverage in the union is that as a member of the management hierarchy he can articulate the obligations of his superiors to take care of those below and he can command the loyalties of workers. But since the foremen are to some extent management representatives, they are subject to manipulation by management in their role as leaders in the union. This two-edged position is present in most foremen roles in Japan. Japanese unions undoubtedly would be much weakened if foremen were excluded, but they would probably become stronger in the long run, because management would be unable to put strong pressure on union leaders to compromise union militancy.

Nowhere is the present role of foremen more striking than in the formation of second unions. In the diecast firm, the supervisory group played a key role in building a union dedicated to cooperation with the company.[19] With the increasing integration of foremen into the management hierarchy, however, such tactics may be less viable in the future because workers will view foremen more as management representatives and less as workers. This will encourage workers to develop their own leaders and bring about a greater democratization of labor-management relations. The rewards the foreman continues to hold out to the worker insure that there will be no sudden change. Moreover, management is not likely to integrate foremen in the line organization to the same extent as supervisors. Thus foremen still will be able to command the loyalties of workers though not to the same degree as in the past.

RECRUITMENT AND THE WEB

Historically, the recruitment process has been one of the more important mechanisms for the establishment of strong vertical social ties in the factory. Its importance in the present-day economy and the nature of changes in the

19. See *The Role of the "Second Union" in Labor Management Relations in Japan*, Occasional Papers of Research Translations, Institute of Advanced Projects, East-West Center, Translation Series No. 3, Honolulu, 1964. In Japanese, the standard work is by Fujita Wakao, *Dai Ni Kumiai* (The Second Union), revised edition (Tokyo: Nihon Hyōron Shinsha, 1960).

postwar period will be examined later. The extent to which employees get jobs through friends, acquaintances, and relatives may be seen in the government statistics noted in Table 8.

TABLE 8
Number of Newly Hired Employees by Channel of Accession
January–June, 1964
(in thousands)

	Total	PESO a	Referred by school	Personal relations	Advertise- ment	Others
All industries	2,211	503	491	661	314	243
Percent	99.7	22.8	22.1	29.8	14.1	10.9

SOURCE: Ministry of Labor, Year Book of Labor Statistics, 1964 (Tokyo: The Ministry, 1965), p. 30.
a Public Employment Security Office.

Almost 30 percent of all new employees stated they entered their job through some form of personal contact. This probably understates the total, because some who said they got their job through other sources such as school reference undoubtedly also had a personal contact in the company they chose. There is no way of telling from these totals whether differences existed between blue- and white-collar workers except to note that in the two firms studied there was no appreciable difference.

These statistics also underestimate the role of personal relations in recruitment particularly in larger firms, because they are limited to the job applicant's perception. They report only personal relations as measured directly between applicant and employer. An additional way personal relations operate is that employees of government employment agencies may establish strong connections with officials in particular firms; this has even led to cases where newly established firms will offer bribes to local employment agencies, to insure a regular labor supply. Personal relations also play a strong role at schools where the employment counselor often wields great power and can direct students to apply to certain companies. These counselors establish strong ties with particular companies and are courted by them so that they will be favored. They may spend their summers visiting several companies, ostensibly to check on their former students, but they actually go to make the rounds of company entertainment, picking up gifts along the way.

Among the 300 workers in the suburban diecast plant in 1965, management estimated that 90 were recruited as friends, acquaintances, or relatives of employees. This amounted to 30 percent of its labor force and conformed to national survey results. Management in the larger auto parts company estimated that 10 percent of its labor force each year was recruited through personal relations but that they accounted for 15 percent of all employees. About half of these were relatives of employees, the rest friends and acquaintances. The difference between the percentage recruited each year and the actual percentage employed is not accidental. Management explained those recruited through personal relations worked harder, were not as likely to quit as other workers, and in general made less trouble for the company. In short, the connection-hired employees were more committed to the company and more subordinate to management than others.

The employee who introduces a new worker to the company takes the responsibility for guiding him in the right behavior and advising him when he engages in inappropriate behavior. This includes matters relating to work, union activity, and, conceivably, off-the-job behavior if it is believed that it might embarrass the company.[20] The basis of this relation-

20. With respect to union activities, a bank employee who tried to organize fellow employees in a union reported the following major problem: Workers were reluctant to join mainly because they were afraid it would put the person who recommended them in a bad position vis à vis the company. In this case, the organizer was eventually successful. In one case at the diecast plant, the leader of the socialist faction reported that when he first started engaging in union activity, strong pressure was put on him through his sister to stop. It seems that a Takei employee, a friend of the sister, had gotten him the job. The patron now complained that union activity on the part of the brother was weakening his position in the company for he had been responsible for the brother's entry. In this case also the union leader resisted pressures and continued his activities. He reported, however, that it was one of the hardest decisions he ever had to make.

ship is that the recipient of employment is obligated to his patron for getting him the job and repays him by seeing to it that his behavior in the firm does not embarrass the patron. This means, above all, that he has a duty to work hard. It is a hierarchical power relation with the job recipient obligated to subordinate himself to his patron. The patron, in turn, is obligated to look after his charge (*mendō o miru*). The patron also has an obligation to the company for granting him the favor of accepting the new recruit for employment. Because the patron risks his reputation in the company and is obligated to look after his charge, he does not incur such an obligation lightly, but carefully selects those on whom he will confer his benefits. Perhaps he may expect some service the new recruit or his family can provide him in return or he simply seeks to gain prestige which will accrue to him for having introduced a competent employee into the firm. Often, however, he chooses to recommend a new employee in response to an obligation he has to kin or acquaintances. In such cases, he may be forced to sacrifice his own interests in the company.

An example of this pattern was reported by one of the young auto workers. His father's friend, a white-collar employee at the auto parts firm, had secured him the job. He explained he felt obligated to this individual not to cause any trouble in the company nor to quit. In the past, he had had some quarrels on the shop floor, after which his supervisor went directly to his patron, who stopped off at his house the same night. There, the patron consulted with the father and the young worker to resolve the problems. This course of action was taken rather than the supervisor directly approaching the worker on the shop floor to deal with the matter. The young worker in question saw nothing unusual about this procedure and appreciated having his father's friend look after his interests.

On a somewhat different level, young workers will refer to certain older workers as *senpai*, a term difficult to translate into English. Literally, it means senior or elder; in the factory it refers, first of all, to someone who entered the company earlier; it often has the connotation of a patron who protects, countenances, or supports his junior, the *kōhai*. The terms suggest a hierarchical relation which binds young and older workers together. The older worker may be from the same village or school; may have helped the young one to get his job; or for a number of other reasons taken the young worker under his wing.

In effect, recruitment through personal relations in the context of Japanese social relations insures docile workers subordinate to management and committed to the company. It is a form of labor control that permits management to exercise worker discipline through the workers themselves. From management's point of view, it is an ideal situation when it can get the workers to exercise self-discipline without requiring company expenditure of time, effort, and money. Conflict and dissent are dissipated as dissidents are forced to compromise to maintain their mutual obligations.[21] This relationship multiplied millions of times explains why Japanese industrial workers never participated in either a bourgeois or Marxist revolution. Connection hiring strengthens human ties—the network that binds worker to worker and worker to company. It is a major factor in worker motivation and strengthens the authority structure within the firm. Hiring through personal contacts is certainly not unique to Japan, but given Japan's hierarchical social structure its consequences are profound.[22] To get a job through a friend or relative in Japan obligates one to a tight, prescribed social relationship.

In an earlier stage of industrialization when sources of livelihood were more limited, hiring through personal contacts was even more important than it is today. A key role was assigned to the labor contractor, who supplied the firm with industrial recruits. In return for a job, the recruit was expected to reciprocate by working hard at low wages. The factory gave

21. John Bennett, "Tradition, Modernity and Communalism in Japan's Modernization," *Journal of Social Issues*, Vol. 14, No. 4 (October 1968).

22. One study of American manual workers in a local labor market showed that 42 percent of the young workers sampled learned about their first job through relatives and acquaintances and 11 percent went to work for relatives or acquaintances. Lloyd Reynolds, *The Structure of Labor Markets* (New York: Harper, 1951), p. 129.

the rural worker protection from the overpopulated countryside. To be chosen for factory work from the many able-
bodied job seekers was often a favor of major importance.[23]
Such selection was often based on the particularistic connections of families to labor contractors and their sub-contractors
in the rural villages. Understandably, the worker felt a strong
obligation to work devotedly and to do everything in his
power to support his patron. Advancement in wages or position depended on demonstrating unswerving loyalty to one's
patron. No doubt, connection hiring and the social relations
which flow from it played a significant role in bringing about
rapid industrialization in Japan. They contributed to the recruitment of a labor force that worked hard at low wages
with minimum complaints. The critics of nepotism or similar
practices should carefully consider their role, as transitional
mechanisms for securing labor commitment and control.

CHANGING PATTERNS OF RECRUITMENT

In the postwar period the labor contractor was legally
banned; many of his functions already had been absorbed by
the company in major industries. Since democratization workers believe it is their right to be employed. Article 27 of the
new constitution states, "All people shall have the right and
obligation to work." When workers come to think of factory
employment as a right instead of a favor dispensed by a superior, then vertical social ties are critically weakened. The
notion of employment as a right appeared soon after World
War II, but it was not until the nineteen sixties that an
emerging labor shortage gave actual substance to the view of
one's job as a right. In a similar fashion, with the rural labor
force less able to serve as source of industrial manpower the
role of vertical ties in committing rural workers to the factory
declines. Viewing the job as a right rather than a favor obviously has far-reaching consequences beyond simply weaken-

23. Particularly in the early years of industrialization, however, factory
labor was often looked down upon and workers were sometimes forcibly
conscripted with the worker dormitories resembling detention homes. Sumiya
Mikio, *Social Impact of Industrialization in Japan* (Tokyo: Japanese National Commission for UNESCO, 1963), pp. 39–41.

ing worker obligations to the one who introduced him to the job. It militates toward a subtle reduction in the over-commitment to the firm which has been characteristic of Japanese workers. These changes suggest that what we label as traditional relationships often persist as a function of scarcity conditions rather than being a reflection of the independent strength of traditional values.

Rapid technological change has also contributed to a weakening of the ability of older workers to command the respect of young workers. As antagonisms over wage payment, job assignments, and promotions increase, young workers become unwilling to follow the lead of older workers. This specifically weakens the ability of patrons and *senpai* to serve as key agents in labor control policies of the company.

The extent of connection hiring varies according to the timing of the business cycle. A high-ranking management official in the auto parts company explained he preferred connection hiring because of its role in insuring docile workers. In good times when a rapid expansion of its labor force is needed, however, the company turns to more impersonal forms of hiring. In times of recession when jobs are in short supply, connection hiring increases over impersonal hiring. The rapid growth of the postwar Japanese economy has meant an over-all decline in the role of connection hiring. The Employment Status Survey has regularly questioned employees about their channel of accession since 1955. A comparison of the survey years shows a steady decline in those employees listing personal relations as their channel of accession. From the 43.9 percent listing personal relations in 1955, there was a decline to 27.1 percent in 1965.[24] The decline was most noticeable in the hiring of new school graduates; job changers, to the contrary, showed a greater willingness (and need) to rely on personal connections throughout the survey period. Large-scale business organizations, where more and more employees are concentrated, require a flexible labor supply. This means a reduced role for connection hir-

24. Office of the Prime Minister, *Shūgyō Kōzō Chōsa Hōkoku*, 31 (1956 Employment Status Survey), (Tokyo: The Office, 1957), p. 243. *Ibid.*, 1959, p. 283. *Ibid.*, 1962, p. 241. *Ibid.*, 1965, p. 264.

ing. Yet, connection hiring is not likely to disappear. For the individual job seeker, it is still commonly seen as the preferred way of gathering reliable job information, securing entry, and gaining good treatment. More impersonal methods may be a last resort when personal contacts are not available as is often the case with new school graduates. This may be no less true in America than in Japan.

OYABUN-KOBUN RELATIONS

A consideration of vertical social ties in the Japanese factory requires an examination of the *oyabun-kobun* or patron-client relationship. *Oyabun-kobun*, literally translated as parent-child role, is a dyadic relation based on intensified vertical ties among specific individuals. It is exclusively a hierarchical power relation with one party in superior and the other in subordinate status. Ideally, this relationship would be suffused with spontaneity. In rural Japan it was a means by which poor families sought powerful protectors in the village in return for loyalty and service. Based on local economic and political situations in which households are implicated, it is said to have declined in the twentieth century, losing its economic basis under the impact of industrialization and the postwar land reform.[25] Apart from its weakening in rural areas, however, evidence suggests it played an important role in urban areas during the course of Japanese industrialization. Master-apprentice relations, labor contractor-worker relations, foreman-worker relations and the present day recruitment process—all may be understood in terms of patron-client relations. In all there is a pattern of continual dependency of the *kobun* upon the *oyabun*; the pattern being sustained by normative pressures of the community and fellow employees as well as lack of alternatives for problems of economic security.

Patron-client relations are found most often in certain industrial sectors peripheral to the key industries associated

25. Fukutake Tadashi, *Japanese Rural Society*, Ronald Dore (tr.), (London: Oxford University Press, 1967), pp. 69–70. See also Nakane Chie, *Kinship and Economic Organization in Rural Japan* (New York: Humanities Press, 1967), pp. 123–132.

with modern industrial development. They are found in construction, longshoring, and forestry where the labor contractor continues to play a key role. The pattern is especially
conspicuous in those industries with large numbers of unskilled workers. Such industries usually lack a permanent
labor force, are dependent on irregular business orders, and
are seasonal or luxury industries. Often there is a continual
dependency of the *kobun* upon the labor contractor, who is
able to terminate the employment of his followers at any
time. It is no accident that labor racketeering in America is
also strong in similar industries such as longshoring and the
entertainment industry.[26] But the patron-client relation also
is found where traditional craft skills survive and long periods
of apprenticeship are required.

In modern industries, the pattern of continual dependence upon a patron can be found in areas where the rewards for the worker attaching himself to an *oyabun* are
great. The term is used primarily among management personnel and union leaders where the chance for advancement is
greatly increased by being attached to a powerful or potentially powerful individual. It is thus understandable that factions play their greatest role among management and union
leaders.

Among blue-collar workers, in both the diecast and auto
parts company, the term *oyabun-kobun* was seldom used and
vertical factions did not reach very deeply into blue-collar
ranks. Even when the term was used by blue-collar workers
in the diecast plant, it had an attenuated meaning roughly
corresponding to teacher-protégé. Workers used the term in
an informal, joking way among themselves and never used
it in the presence of the superior to whom they were referring. The patron-client relation has become associated in the
public mind with the boss-follower ties of urban gangsters;
in return for loyalty the patron takes care of his client, par-

26. See Sidney Lens, *The Crisis of American Labor* (New York: A. S.
Barnes, 1961), pp. 101–132. A dramatic account of the violence accompany-
ing longshoring work at Kobe harbor carefully documents the role of the
tehaishi (labor contractor). Mori Hidete, "The Longshoremen of Kobe
Harbor," in *The Japanese Image*, Maurice Schneps and Alvin Cox (eds.),
(Tokyo: Orient/West, 1965), pp. 89–99.

ticularly by protecting him against the police. Such images are symbolic of both the decline of patron-client relations and the disrepute into which the practice has fallen.

In modern industry, as represented by the diecast or auto parts firm, this pattern of continual dependency among blue-collar workers is increasingly absent. The labor contractor loses his function where a permanent labor force comes into being. The growing labor shortage further reduces the dependence of workers, especially young workers, on particular individuals as workers can pick and choose jobs more freely. Ties between foreman and worker seldom reach the intensity personified by the extreme case of the mining industry where the *naya-gashira* pattern of patron-client relations flourished.[27] This is because of the increasing separation of leisure from work, reduction in the element of danger with more rational work methods, and integration of training know-how within the formal organization of the firm. In the same way, master-apprentice relations in the craft skills decline under modern technology, which creates new jobs requiring shorter training time and more standardized training methods.

The payoff for a modern *oyabun* to have blue-collar followers is not very great in comparison to past rewards reaped by the labor contractor. The bureaucratization and standardization of large-scale industry particularly affect blue-collar workers, reducing dependency on any one person. Unions have contributed to a standardization of wages. The blue-collar worker can at most hope to be promoted to supervisor, so the rewards for attaching himself to an *oyabun* are not great. The modern foreman does not hold the absolute power over his subordinates that the labor contractor or master craftsman commonly held. But in the union and management hierarchies, the steps on the ladder of success are longer, the rewards potentially greater, and the criteria for evaluating personnel more vague. In these cases it may pay to be attached to the coattails of an *oyabun*.

The decline of the *oyabun-kobun* relation among blue-

27. The *naya-gashira* pattern is reported by Sumiya Mikio, *op. cit.*, pp. 48–49.

collar workers undoubtedly contributes to a democratization of industrial relations. The reduction in the continual dependency of blue-collar workers and a standardization of their rewards reduces the opportunities for superiors to manipulate interpersonal relationships in the context of *oyabun-kobun* relations.

We have suggested that the vertical social ties deriving from the recruitment process and the more general ties reflected in the patron-client relation are playing a smaller role in the modern factory. This agrees with the convergence hypothesis with its emphasis on the diminishing role of particularistic obligations in advanced industrial societies. Yet to draw such a conclusion would be too hasty. For the specific vertical ties discussed above are based on more diffuse social obligations that are deeply rooted in Japanese consciousness. One may examine these obligations as represented by *giri* relations and *on* to further clarify the role of particularistic orientations for the contemporary blue-collar worker. Of particular interest is the role of vertical social ties in guaranteeing a stable career pattern among workers with permanent employment.

GIRI RELATIONS IN THE FACTORY

Giri relations are of special interest because they have been viewed as the epitome of traditionalism surviving in modern Japan, a symbol of uniqueness in national character.[28] The usage here is a more modest one, consistent with that suggested by Ronald Dore.[29] Rather than viewing *giri* relations as a "curious category of moral obligation," he stresses the comparative aspects involved in all reciprocal relations. Denying that *giri* relations are unique to Japan, he sees the differences between Japan and England as follows:

1. That *giri* relations arise with greater frequency and have a greater importance for the individual's material well-being in Japan.

28. Ruth Benedict, *The Chrysanthemum and the Sword* (Boston: Houghton Mifflin, 1946), pp. 133–176.
29. Ronald Dore, *City Life in Japan* (Berkeley and Los Angeles: University of California Press, 1958), p. 258.

2. That the acts required in such relationships are more clearly formalized in Japan.

3. That the obligations to perform such actions are often given a higher place than other more universalistic obligations.[30]

The very existence of such explicit terms in Japanese as *giri*, *on*, *ongaeshi* and *ninjō*, which specify relevant obligations, is an indication of the formalization of these exchange relations.

Giri relations as a traditional practice presuppose the existence of a set of norms binding the parties. *Giri* relations are rational in terms of the values shared by the group. In a limited sense, they may be defined as mutual cooperation. We have already come across the way *giri* relations serve as the underpinnings of patron-client relations. The young auto worker, for instance, felt *giri* to his patron for helping him get his job. This sense of obligation manifested itself in an ongoing relationship in which the patron took care of his charge and the worker consulted with his patron and accepted his guidance on factory-related matters.

In general, *giri* relations arise from obligations incurred by the individual as a result of his group membership. Although we may specify *giri* relations as dyadic they become meaningful sanctions only in a group context. The emphasis is on obligation rather than human spontaneity. The Japanese speak of persons feeling *giri* or knowing *giri*; it does not refer to behavior itself, rather to feelings of obligations that lead to behavior. *Giri* relations may link persons of equal or unequal status. Primarily the latter will concern us in our examination of the factory. Ordinarily, in a relationship among persons of unequal status it is the subordinate who speaks of feeling *giri* and not the superior. Since there is a network of interlocking *giri* relations, however, it is possible that a person of lower status and position such as a worker may have an alternate line of connection to a still higher superior such as the company president (perhaps they are from the same village). In this case the foreman may feel *giri* to the worker as part of his *giri* obligations to his own superior, the president. It is not uncommon for workers to

30. *Ibid.*

use the term *giri* in designating horizontal and vertical ties to others in the factory. Insofar as the term is used here as an analytic category, however, the concern is with the whole interchange of favors and obligations regardless of whether such behavior is labeled by the participants as *giri* or *on*.

Seeking to discover the differences and similarities between *giri* relations as practiced in the West and the traditional meaning they are said to have in Japan, we will focus on the various theories of exchange, proposed by sociologists in recent years.[31] Peter Blau's work is representative. His definition of social exchange excludes the kind of *giri* relations referred to above. He specifically defines social exchange as "voluntary actions of individuals that are motivated by the returns they are expected to bring and typically do bring from others." [32] Action that arises from conformity with internalized standards does not fall under his definition of exchange. Similarly, behavior oriented toward more ultimate values or questions of conscience rather than toward immediate rewards also does not fall under his conception of exchange. While Blau is concerned lest his framework be viewed as culture-bound, he is forced to admit that his framework is biased in favor of experiences in American culture.[33] His analysis is primarily concerned with the instrumental function of social exchange rather than situations where behavior occurs in conformity with internalized standards. In the latter, people do things because they are defined as right not because they serve some instrumental function. This distinction between instrumentally oriented behavior and behavior based on internalized standards points to a significant difference in the nature of social relations in the Japanese and American societies.[34]

Yet, it would leave the matter incomplete to emphasize

31. See Peter Blau, *Exchange and Power in Social Life* (New York: John Wiley, 1964); George Homans, *Social Behavior: Its Elementary Forms* (New York: Harcourt, Brace and World, 1961) and John Thibaut and H. Kelly, *The Social Psychology of Groups* (New York: John Wiley, 1959).

32. Blau, *op. cit.*, p. 91.

33. *Ibid.*, pp. 6–7.

34. Harumi Befu comes to a similar conclusion from a somewhat different route. Harumi Befu, "Gift-Giving and Social Reciprocity in Japan," *France-Asia/Asia*, No. 188 (Winter 1966–67).

only the differences between Western and Japanese social relations. Despite the tendency to label *giri* relations as a static traditional behavioral pattern, it has undergone considerable change and development before and during the emergence of industrial society. One must not ignore its continual evolution throughout Japanese history.[35] Moreover, *giri* relations have different meanings for different sub-cultures within Japanese society. Our concern here is a very limited one: the meaning of *giri* relations for contemporary blue-collar workers. Among these workers, we suggest, the instrumental function emphasized by Peter Blau is coming to play a vital role.

It is hard to write precisely about what is essentially a diffuse relationship that has various meanings for different sub-cultures; in seeking to crystallize its meaning, one tends to distort its content. The scientist's effort to bring order to all he observes is not always fruitful.

In general, *on* refers to a sense of indebtedness by a subordinate for favors bestowed by a superior. It is above all a power relationship involving superior and subordinate statuses. *On* may result from a specific favor or it may be a collective description of the relationship established with the superior. Given the structured role sets of superior-subordinate statuses in the factory, feelings of *on* are likely to reflect a continuing collective description of role relations. The subordinate in the factory is obliged to repay (*ongaeshi*) by hard work and loyalty the benefits received and he does so out of *giri* feelings. That is, the subordinate repays *on* because he feels *giri*. But the subordinate can never fully repay given his subordinate status. He is thus left in a continuing state of dependence. The responsibilities of group membership and the threat of group sanctions obligate the subordinate to conform to established norms of repayment. Therefore, *on* and *ongaeshi* must be understood in the context of *giri* relations.

As with *giri* relations, *on* should not be seen as a con-

35. A historical account of these changes appears in: "Giri," *Sekai Dai Hyakka Jiten* (World Encyclopedia). Vol. 8, Heibonsha, 1956, pp. 25–26.

figuration unique to Japan. Rather, we suggest that in any society that has a strong persisting hierarchical order, there must always be some form of *on, ongaeshi,* and *giri;* that is, a functional equivalent designed to institutionalize inequality. If a sharply hierarchical social structure is to persist beyond a coercive level, those with subordinate status must accept as legitimate the authority of those above them. *On, ongaeshi* and *giri* are merely the Japanese ways of representing these relationships.[36] Such relationships are not unknown in the West, where the lord and follower relation maintained an important position in the Middle Ages. Such particularistic loyalties declined, however, in favor of other more universalistic values in the late feudal and early modern period. Robert Bellah, in speculating why this did not occur in Japan, emphasizes the influence of Confucianism and Buddhism in generalizing the Japanese warrior ethic to an entire people.[37] But we may explain the need for such an ethic by the persisting hierarchical social order throughout Japanese industrialization. We would expect that as the hierarchical social order declines in contemporary Japan, so does the relative importance of such formalized obligations as *on ongaeshi,* and *giri.* Though the existence of such an ethic itself may slow up and even put a check on the weakening of this hierarchical order.

The Japanese commonly speak of *giri ninjō.* The distinction is made that *giri* relations are formal and contractual as opposed to *ninjō,* which is private and subordinate to *giri* relations.[38] *Ninjō,* defined as human kindness or compassion refers to what the individual would like to do as a response to his personal emotion. In the factory, the foreman would like not to report a subordinate's rule violation that is cause

36. Conversations with Tominaga Ken'ichi of Tokyo University, Ann Arbor, November 5, 1968.

37. Bellah, *op. cit.,* pp. 181–183.

38. In the context of the formal criteria for distributing rewards and the formal authority structure of the factory, however, *giri* relations do not appear and therefore may be viewed as part of the structure of informal relations. See Sugi Masataka, "The Concept of Ninjō," *Paternalism in the Japanese Economy,* John Bennett and Ishino Iwao (Minneapolis: University of Minnesota Press, 1963).

for discharge. He may be able to stretch the rules to report a minor rule violation which is not cause for discharge. This would be one way of expressing *ninjō*. If his *giri* responsibilities to his own superiors compel the foreman to report the exact rule violation, however, he may still find a way of expressing *ninjō* by helping the worker find a new job. Moreover, employment through his superior becomes an *on* for the worker which he cannot fully repay. Thus *ninjō* arises in the articulation of the *giri* relation, and it is something which workers expect of superiors to whom they feel *giri*.

Reciprocal relations implied by *giri* relations and the associated concepts of *on*, *ongaeshi* and *ninjō* are not necessarily symmetrical. To say that the foreman becomes a successful leader by bestowing his benefits in return for which workers display loyalty and cooperation in the shop does not imply symmetry. It is true that *giri* relations, a belief in the feudal concept that rank imposes obligation, and *ninjō* militate toward advantages for the blue-collar worker exactly because he is the subordinate in the relationship. Yet, one party may gain much more from the reciprocal relation than the other. Power relationships in Japanese society have been strongly weighted in favor of management as the superior party to the relationship throughout the course of industrialization. On the aggregate level of national political power, as already noted, the workers consistently have been on the short end. This lack of power on the aggregate level is linked to the asymmetry in interpersonal relations on the shop floor.[39]

THE INSTRUMENTAL USE OF GIRI

In a traditional sense, when a worker receives a favor from a superior and it is defined by the parties and social group as calling for *giri*, the subordinate does not fulfill *giri* relations as a favor to the superior or out of self-interest but as an obligation to serve. It is in this same sense that Peter

39. For a discussion of symmetry and asymmetry in reciprocal relations see Alvin Gouldner, "Reciprocity and Autonomy in Functional Theory," in *Symposium on Sociological Theory*, Llewellyn Gross (ed.), (New York: Harper and Row, 1959), pp. 241–270.

Blau interprets Bronislaw Malinowski's treatment of the Kula.[40] We may rephrase Blau's discussion of the commoner's relation to the chief to build an ideal type of the traditional Japanese subordinate's relation to his superior in the factory. The services and deference the subordinate furnishes to the superior are not considered favors that obligate the superior but are returns for obligations owed the superior. The underlying function is that the superior's leadership provides important benefits to the factory community. The subordinate's tribute to the superior both in the form of services, deference, and loyalty is a repayment of his continuous indebtedness. Institutionalized power commands services a superior can use to provide benefits to subordinates that fortify his power. This power makes the services of subordinates insufficient for establishing equality with the superior.[41] Such ties achieve particular intensity in the vertical dyadic relations of patron-client roles that are based on these generalized *giri* obligations. To what extent does such behavior and its underlying assumptions still exist among present-day blue-collar workers and their superiors? Workers were specifically asked to explain what *giri* relationships meant to them and to provide concrete examples.[42]

Workers were extremely conscious of the economic benefits to be derived from fulfilling *giri* to a benefactor. Their examples of *giri* relations were often to the effect that Mr. X loaned me money when I was in a jam so that I have an obligation to support him or help him out whenever I can. This consciousness of the material benefits to be derived from fulfilling *giri* led them to take an instrumental view toward it. As one worker put it, "I fulfill *giri* when it's in my interest to do so." This way of thinking was most pronounced in the Tokyo diecast plant. There, *giri* relations, particularly with superiors, were severely weakened under the stress of the management-union confrontation and the threatened closing

40. Peter Blau, *Exchange and Power in Social Life,* p. 110.
41. *Ibid.*
42. The Japanese used in the initial exchange was: *Kaisha de tsukiatte iru hito ni taishite giri o hatashimasu ka* (Among the people with whom you associate in the company, do you fulfill *giri*?).

of the Tokyo plant. In particular, the entrance of the new managers had broken the web of mutual obligations that had been built up. With the future of the company looking dim, it was not in the interest of workers to maintain and fulfill *giri* relations. One worker explained,

> I have the feeling that they are superiors and they may or may not be helpful to me in the future. Because of such things I give gifts to them at the time of the Buddhist summer festival and at the end of the year, and I think this comes under the heading of *giri*. Lately, however, I haven't had much trust in the superiors, so I don't do this anymore.

A twenty-nine year old worker preparing to quit said the subsection chief had taken care of him in the past, and this made quitting very hard. In recent months he had been turning down various favors from the sub-section chief so that in the near future he would feel more free to quit. These statements indicate that workers did regard favors from superiors as creating an obligation to serve on their part. This made them all the more cautious in entering into such relations; they consciously assessed the various costs and payoffs resulting from their being implicated in *giri* relations.

The situation at the diecast plant shows, in bold relief, the role of *giri* relations that could be expected in a stable or growing firm. In such firms, employees are more willing to have superiors take an interest in their personal affairs and to look after them at work because the rewards to be distributed are greater (particularly promotion) and the future is bright; they are more willing to incur *giri* obligations. In a firm with a dim future such as Takei these obligations only bind the worker to an insecure future. More evidence for this view is the unwillingness of the Tokyo diecast workers to ask their superiors' advice when marrying or have them act as their *nakōdo* (go-between), as is common in many Japanese companies. The *nakōdo* guarantees the marriage and the married couple can turn to him for advice and help in time of need. A strategically placed *nakōdo* in the company is under an obligation to see that his charge is treated well by the company especially when it comes to promotion. But workers in the

Tokyo diecast plant believed it would be better to pick someone outside the firm who might be of more help in the future. From the preceding we may deduce that the function of *giri* relations is one of guaranteeing a stable career pattern among workers. Where this is impossible, as in the case of the Tokyo diecast plant, *giri* is turned off. In either case, the instrumental character of *giri* relations is apparent. There is a conscious calculation among workers of the various costs and payoffs incurred by *giri* ties.

In both firms, young workers tended to reject *giri* relations. They often pointed out that older workers feel such obligations but that nowadays things are different, and young people no longer feel bound by these practices. After the war *giri* relations became associated in the public mind with the prewar values they conveyed. As a result, these relations were discredited somewhat and viewed as inconsistent with democratic practices. The young workers feel uneasy fulfilling *giri*. The ultimate view was expressed by a twenty-three-year-old maintenance man, who said that fulfilling *giri* to superiors was equivalent to "brown-nosing." There could be no more devasting rejection of traditional values. Most workers, however, did not take as extreme a view, but many believed that fulfilling *giri* to superiors was suspect as a cunning way to insure one's promotion. Almost all of the young workers made the point that excessive involvement in *giri* relations meant favoritism and behind-the-scene deals. Many took the position that *giri* relations were troublesome, because if they were not fulfilled, people would be critical. Their solution was that one should try to avoid *giri* relations. Some young workers in the diecast plant added that they avoided *giri* relations because they preferred to forget the company once work was over and *giri* obligations had a way of following one home.

One difficulty of interpreting these statements is that the young workers may change their views and behavior as they become older. Are the differences between old and young workers simply a function of the age cycle? Certainly, as length of service increases, workers can be expected to become more involved in the web of mutual obligations. Sev-

eral bits of evidence suggest that this is not the entire explanation. At the auto parts firm, management reported that
young workers would often quit without notice by simply
announcing, "Today I am quitting." Sometimes this would
be the day after the semi-annual bonuses were paid. Older
auto workers, however, would consult well in advance with
their superiors and discuss possible successors to their job. To
quit just after the bonus would violate their sense of duty to
the company. Some older workers even made it a point of
quitting just *before* the semi-annual bonus was paid. Management indicated that the behavior of young workers was a
new phenomenon. A fifty-year-old auto-parts worker outlined
the changes in *giri* relations in this way:

> In my youth we all inquired after a fellow worker when he
> was ill, and it was common sense for him to give something
> in return for his thanks when he recovered. But now they
> don't do such things. All they do is say "thank you" for such
> inquiry and for marriage or congratulatory presents and
> sometimes they don't even do that. They don't give a gift in
> return, because the times are different. Once such customs
> were dominant because there was a master-pupil relation-
> ship. There was a craftsman's spirit in the company that is
> not to be found now. When I entered the parent company
> thirty years ago, the workers rushed to wash the work clothes
> of the foreman though it was buttering him up in a sense.
> No worker would begin to eat until the foreman did. We
> did so because we thought highly of him. This is not to be
> found nowadays.

Not only do these statements point to the changes that
have taken place, notwithstanding some nostalgic embroidery,
but they show that technological change in leveling skills and
destroying the master-pupil relationship undermined one of
the important bases of *giri* relations. An advanced industrial
economy requires the routinization and institutionalization
of job training and hiring within the firm. This leads to a
reduction of the scope in which *giri* can operate. Workers
often said they did not feel *giri* obligations to the person who
taught them their job because the other party acted out of
his job responsibilities and no favor was involved. Older

workers reported that the situation was quite different in their youth where a strong obligation was created toward the person teaching you the job.

Aside from these changes, *giri* relations as a basis for distributing rewards do not automatically conflict with rational decision-making. Favors are not lightly dispensed by the foreman. He will be far more willing to help a young able worker who has a promising future than he will a lazy incompetent. In one case at the Tokyo diecast plant, the sub-section chief arranged for a hard-working diecaster to participate in the company experiments at conducting time studies. This gave the worker a break from the routine of his job and a chance to show his ability for possible promotion. As a result, he felt *giri* toward the sub-section chief. This sub-section chief did not pick just anyone; he selected a worker who could be an asset to him in the future. In this case, then, *giri* relations supplemented skill and performance as criteria for distributing rewards.

If *giri* relationships are contracted with an eye to economic advantage and can be turned off and on according to self-interest, these relationships cannot be seen as reflecting a static tradition. Instead, they appear functionally useful in this advanced industrial society as a secondary base for distributing rewards and securing loyalty and hard work from subordinates. Indeed, Japan's high level of industrialization hardly could have been achieved if such a basic social value as represented by *giri* relationships had not been put to instrumental use. One tactic for insuring that *giri* relations do not interfere with rational decision-making is to apply certain universalistic standards before allowing these particularistic considerations to come into play. In the hiring of friends and relatives, companies will commonly require that such applicants pass objective tests along with other applicants. Only then will the particularistic obligations be allowed to operate. Once the applicants for a particular job or position meet minimum standards of performance, the distribution of rewards on the basis of favors and obligations poses no insurmountable threat to economic rationality.

These processes show both similarities to and differences

from the American pattern. Melville Dalton studied the promotion pattern of American employees through managerial
hierarchies.[43] He found that informal factors such as religion,
associational memberships, and ethnic origin were important
in determining the likelihood of promotion. Yet prior to the
operation of these informal factors were the objective requirements for the various occupational levels. In short, given
several individuals with nearly equal objective qualifications,
informal factors will then come into play in the final selection.

This comparison between American and Japanese data,
notwithstanding the different populations, suggests that the
scope allowed for informal considerations is indeed reduced
in advanced industrial societies. Such informal relations, however, continue to play a strong secondary role, and their content strongly reflects the unique historical traditions of the
respective societies. Just as being a Mason may help American workers increase their chances of getting promoted,
establishing and fulfilling *giri* obligations may help insure
Japanese workers a stable career pattern.

The informal factors operating in Japanese factories
are historically unique. But in an analytical sense they are a
functional equivalent to those informal practices in other
advanced societies which facilitate career patterns of favored
individuals. It is oversimplification to say that pre-industrial
societies move from ascription and particularism to achievement and universalism as a criteria for decision-making during the course of industrialization. Far more subtle combina-
tions and shifts are possible.

GIRI: CITY AND COUNTRY COMPARED

It is highly doubtful that self-interest was absent in *giri*
relations of past centuries. It undoubtedly has always been a
strong element. Ronald Dore suggests the difference in the
modern usage of *giri* relation lies in the removal of the moral
element and in the increasingly business-like nature of *giri* re-

43. Melville Dalton, "Informal Factors in Career Achievement,"
American Journal of Sociology, Vol. 56 (March 1951).

lations typified by the "contact man." [44] In our terms, the fulfillment of *giri* obligations is no longer viewed as an agreed upon standard that is internalized as right. Tracing the background for this change, we can clearly see a weakening in the effectiveness of group sanctions which in turn permits the expression of self-interest. The mystique of group values and sanctions provides the moral element. In the closely integrated prewar village where cooperation on such things as irrigation was crucial to survival, possible exclusion from village cooperation was sufficient to keep individuals from turning *giri* relations off and on to suit their own interests. The rewards of cooperation and respect for the norms of the social group far outweighed any advantages in being a renegade. Respect for group values meant economic security. The ultimate sanction of exclusion could be fatal to the economic livelihood of the affected individual. In this atmosphere it is not surprising that the fulfillment of *giri* was viewed as a moral imperative. To question its fulfillment was to question the moral solidarity of the community and thus the very meaning of one's own existence. There is, then, an ideology of solidarity implicit in such relationships, which binds together members of the community.

In the city with a growing industrial economy the rewards for conformity are less evident and the chance for gain greater for those who chose not to conform. Social relations in the city are more impersonal and fractionalized. Dependency on any one social group is greatly reduced and the ability of the social group to impose sanctions on the individual is lessened. Hence, *giri* relations can be turned off and on more easily in accordance with self-interest. In the city the worker has greater economic opportunities from the variety of occupations practiced there. Since the alternatives for securing a livelihood are greater, the sanction of group disapproval means less. In the village one's neighbors are also those with whom one works, but in the city neighbors and

---

44. Ronald Dore, *op. cit.*, pp. 259–260. See also Ronald Dore, "Mobility: Equality, and Individuation in Modern Japan," *Aspects of Social Change in Modern Japan*, Ronald Dore (ed.), (Princeton University Press, 1967).

co-workers are two separate groups and so the intensity of
social relationships decreases.[45] The practice of mutual aid
that was so strong in Japanese villages is less important
among workers as the company and, increasingly, government
programs meet such needs. Giri relations imply a willingness
of the subordinate to sacrifice his self-interest to a superior.
Since the group pressures in the city and at the factory are
weaker than in the communal village, workers are less willing
to endure this sacrifice and, indeed, it is less necessary to do
so. At the same time, workers are freer to enter into giri relations of their own choice that will suit their self-interest.
With the moral content weakened, management also engages
in a more callous manipulation of the ideology of solidarity
for its own advantage.

Several workers from rural backgrounds were asked
about the differences between giri in the factory and giri in
the country.[46] A common statement was:

> The form of giri in the company and in the country is much
> different. In the country it is enormous. Even in very trivial
> things they fulfill giri. If I am treated by you today, I keep

45. The exception is, of course, where workers live in company dormitories.

46. One hypothesis in the research relating to giri was that the workers at the auto parts plant would be more intensely involved with giri relations and that these would be less instrumental than those of the Tokyo
diecast workers. This was expected because the auto parts workers were
primarily rural recruits who were closer to village values in time and space
than the Tokyo workers. Furthermore, as the auto parts workers were employed in a rapidly growing firm, it was expected that they would have more
to gain from becoming involved in strong giri relations.

Unfortunately, no conclusive determination on this hypothesis was
possible. The auto parts workers had a great deal of difficulty in speaking
on the meaning of giri in the factory. Because of their youth and short
seniority, they had not been able to accumulate the mutual obligations that
grow over time even if they were so inclined. Ronald Dore, in a private
communication, has suggested that the specific form of the initial question
may have prevented reaching a conclusive determination of our hypothesis.

The responses of the Tokyo diecast workers to questions on giri differed sharply with those of the auto workers. The diecast workers were generally quite articulate on the subject. That their higher educational level and
greater sophistication enabled them to handle complex concepts was no
doubt a factor. Also, because of the dim future of the Tokyo diecast plant,
giri relations were disintegrating and thus exposed for all to see.

fulfilling *giri* toward you long after. But if you live in Tokyo, you drink or eat together with your friends without worrying about it. Supposing it was his treat, you don't pay much attention to that or you don't think much about it. You just think of it to the extent that you will treat him next time because it's his treat now. In the country, it is not so. They think more deeply and take such things more seriously.

The substance of this statement is expressed well by Richard Beardsley who writes:

> *Giri* works well in a society of lifelong neighbors and associates. It is measured not from a single incident or transaction but from its coloring of an association that is expected to extend indefinitely through time.[47]

In this sense permanent employment in the factory, where it exists, is an extension or, more appropriately, a reversion to a situation which permits *giri* relations to insure stable career patterns. Nevertheless, the diecast workers were unanimous in their opinion that it was better to live in the city, where one was less bound by the restrictive obligations symbolized by *giri*.

MANAGEMENT SUCCESSION

Discussion in this chapter mainly focused on the nature of informal relations between management and workers. In particular, we delineated traditional relationships and analyzed present-day pressures, which undermine these relationships. An additional way to deal with this question is to consider the relation between bureaucratic work rules and informal social organization. In American factories, one approach has been to examine this relationship in the context of management succession.[48] Changes at the Tokyo diecast plant before and during the research provided an excellent opportunity to pursue the issue in comparative perspective.

47. John Hall and Richard Beardsley, *Twelve Doors to Japan* (New York: McGraw-Hill, 1965), p. 95.
48. Alvin Gouldner, *Patterns of Industrial Bureaucracy*; Robert Guest, "Managerial Succession in Complex Organizations," *American Journal of Sociology*, Vol. 68 (1962–63), pp. 47–54.

Specifically, the Takei family was expelled from the firm and replaced with managers sent in by the parent machine manufacturer.

The situation faced by the new managers studied by Alvin Gouldner and Robert Guest has much in common with that faced by Yamagishi-san, the new manager sent in by the machine manufacturer. All three were outsiders to their plant organizations and thus unhampered by previous personal commitments. Hence, their major commitments were not to their new subordinates but to their superiors outside the plant. They knew their future progress in the company depended on their ability to solve the problems plaguing their respective plants. These problems centered around poor performance and high costs; their mandate was to raise production and meet competitive market conditions. All were told they could make strategic replacements in management personnel.

At this point the similarity ends. Yamagishi-san's method of solving his problems had far more in common with Gouldner's Peele than with Guest's Cooley. Both Yamagishi-san and Peele entered plants where an "indulgency pattern" prevailed. Rule enforcement was lax; there was a reliance on close informal ties as a means of dealing with ongoing daily problems. In both cases, managerial authority had been based on personal loyalty rather than loyalty to and respect for the office of manager. In particular, the new managers had to deal with the lack of enthusiasm for their new plans by the existing managerial staffs. One of the high-ranking managers brought in by Yamagishi-san explained:

> We could not rely on those middle- and lower-level management personnel whose loyalties were to the old managers and to the workers. We would have liked to have kept the old section chiefs but could not, given their way of thinking and their past loyalties. This made it hard for them to go along with our plans for modernizing the firm and sabotaged many of our efforts to change things. When we entered the firm, the section chiefs and supervisors drew still closer to the workers and this made it difficult for us to carry out our policies.

Yamagishi-san quickly set about creating new posts and either brought in new people or promoted those whose loyalty would be to him. The job duties of the old section chiefs and supervisors were often lifted and given to others or they were promoted to powerless positions. As a consequence, one by one they quit.

With the ouster of the old middle and lower management personnel, the new diecast managers suddenly found themselves confronting the workers and the union. The old web of human relations broke with lower management personnel no longer able to manipulate vertical loyalties to mediate the conflict between management and workers. Consequently, the new managers, unfamiliar in their new surroundings and cut off from the normal flow of social relations, turned more and more to impersonal rules to implement their policies.

The pattern described here is strikingly similar to that described by Gouldner as a move from the indulgency pattern to a punishment-centered bureaucracy. Both managers saw the indulgency patterns at their plants as having to be uprooted if increased production was to be achieved. In Peele's case, the informal ties were so firmly bound up with the indulgency pattern and low productivity that he saw no alternative but to move toward a reliance on impersonal rules.[49] The new Japanese managers' desire to do away with the indulgency pattern must be understood in the context of their conception of modernization. While they appreciated the role of informal personal relations in managing and motivating workers, their conception of modernization meant that they were determined to establish formal standards for running the plant. They wanted to abolish the excesses associated with operating the plant on a more informal basis. This, in turn, was mixed with their plans to break the union's ability to resist their authority.

Through a kaleidoscope of worker observations on how the plant changed once the new managers came in, one may understand more exactly what the new managers meant by modernizing traditional practices and rationalizing operations:

49. Alvin Gouldner, *op. cit.*, p. 84.

Before the new managers came in, there was a family-like atmosphere. It seems like the managers were all related somehow. I think there was a lot of waste because the relatives weren't too efficient. Also there were lots of bad things going on like juggling the accounts, graft, and stealing of materials. Because of this, there were times when it made things pretty easy and relaxed for us. For example, in small matters, the superiors were more likely to shut their eyes to the breaking of rules and things like that. For the managers, this was probably a loss, but for us working guys, it somehow became an incentive for making us work with a good feeling. Without us thinking about what the hell the future of the company would be, we just concentrated on our work. Of course, because the company was pretty profitable in the old days, it also made it easier to do lots of things. For example, there were outings run by the company like going to the theater and so on. In this sense, it wasn't only working at the company; there were other things like having us relax at parties and trips. But now it's only work and after work you're on your own. In the old days management was personal and policies were put into practice with a warm feeling or human touch, like giving us a bonus on the commemoration day of the company. It seems to me there was a feeling of harmony (*wa*) between management and labor and between people. We knew what we could expect, and a man could get ahead according to his length of service. Nowadays, in a single word, everything has become more severe. The new labor management policies are rigid and cold. There are no longer so many workers who are related to superiors. Most of these people have been turned out of the company. The new managers have a different way of thinking and are determined to be successful because if they win a reputation here they will get ahead by being promoted to a higher position in some other company affiliated to the parent company. There are a lot more disagreeable things nowadays, and they try to force us unreasonably to do lots of things. Since they regard themselves as rivals to the union, they have adopted a tough line toward it. The workers and management have each gone their own separate ways. Still I have to admit that production has gone way up and things are done more scientifically, but I don't work with the same feeling nowadays; it's colder somehow.

Here, pieced together, are the basic sentiments expressed by workers in describing the changes from the family ownership to the new corporate managers. They retained a nostalgia for the old sure cozy way of doing things and a dislike for the "cold" rules of the new managers. This certainly involves an idealization of the past or what Gouldner refers to as the "Rebecca Myth." By romanticizing the past, the workers legitimate their own continued resistance to the new management.[50] At the same time, it is apparent from these comments that the workers also had a grudging respect for the new management for rooting out much of the excesses and corruption of the past and for raising production.

A major source of continued tension at Takei was related to the temporary duration of the outside managers in the plant. Workers and supervisors resented the unwillingness of the new managers to identify with the Takei firm. For the managers it was a matter of making good at Takei so they could return to the parent firm or spend the rest of their careers being shifted from one subcontract firm to another. Such a situation appears to cause unusual strain in Japan. Young and able supervisors in the suburban diecast plant, who owed their promotion to the new managers, reported great tension around this matter in 1969—some seven years after the entrance of the original outside managers. The basis of tension seems to lie in the ideology of the firm as a semi-closed corporate group. A steady stream of pronouncements from management stressed how workers should sacrifice for the sake of the company's survival. It becomes hard for employees to accept this when management officials themselves do not appear devoted to the company, but instead are aiming at outside promotion prospects. Moreover, tension is intensified among the middle-ranking supervisory staff who realize that they cannot be promoted to the top positions, which are monopolized by outsiders. Unlike the outside managers, promising members of the supervisory staff cannot

50. Alvin Gouldner, "The Problem of Succession and Bureaucracy," *Studies in Leadership: Leadership and Democratic Action*, Alvin Gouldner (ed.) (New York: Harper and Row, 1950), pp. 644–659.

hope to be promoted to the parent firm or one of its major affiliates.

The grudging respect workers expressed for the new management is critical for grasping the other basic difference that emerges from the actions taken by Peele and Yamagishi-san. The Gouldner analysis reveals an association between the rise of the punishment-centered bureaucracy and an increase in inter-personal tensions and an implied failure to increase production levels. In the case of Takei Diecast, the rise in inter-personal tensions is also quite noticeable, but the failure to raise production standards is temporary. Within a relatively short time, the Tokyo plant was showing sufficiently large profits so that management shelved its plans to shut it. The raised production level as an outcome of managerial succession is one that Guest associated with the representative mode of administration. Guest's Cooley relied on the existing managerial staff and sought rather successfully to involve them in solving production bottlenecks. Guest convincingly argues that the different course of action taken by Cooley in mobilizing existing informal relations stemmed from the different set of constraints under which he perceived himself to be operating.

The task is how to account for the fact that in the Tokyo diecast plant the punishment-centered bureaucracy became associated both with increased organizational tensions *and* raised productivity. Key to an understanding of this phenomenon seems to be the identification of the diecast workers with their firm's future. Those who did not quit, by the act of staying, indicated their lack of alternative prospects. Hence, it was in the interest of most to see the firm survive and prosper; this meant that production had to rise and the firm had to make a profit. This interest operated despite the increasing reliance on bureaucratic rules, the "cold impersonal atmosphere" which settled over the plant, and the specific confrontation between the union and the management. This suggests that worker response to management succession in terms of production levels often may depend on more factors than simply the management choice between the punishment and representative mode of bureaucracy.

This matter may be further pursued by examining some of the new practices instituted by the diecast managers. In a recent innovation they instructed foremen to act as intermediaries in worker requests and interaction. This go-through-the-foreman approach is designed for non-routine worker interaction. In these non-routine cases, workers are expected to make their requests to their foreman, and, if approved, the foreman will pass it on to the other worker as an order. An official of the parent machine manufacturing firm instituted this new procedure. He visited the Takei company once a month and gave lectures to all foremen and supervisors on modern management techniques. This is one way the parent company attempts to infuse modern values and procedures into its smaller affiliates like Takei. Many of the Tokyo diecast workers were skilled, so they found it unnecessary to rely on their foremen for advice and orders. In addition, the old Takei management had been lax and the workers had won considerable control over work decisions. Using the new instructions, management sought to win back this control over shop organization and behavior patterns.

One of the main sources of on-the-job worker satisfaction in the Tokyo plant was the spontaneity and mutual help among the workers.[51] This was especially true among the skilled workers, and the firm had a strong traditional craftsman spirit in its two main departments, the die making and casting sections. If successful, the new approach would mean a great loss in the spontaneity and mutual help that characterized the Tokyo plant and made work pleasant. It would mean a reduction in the worker's sphere of independence and responsibility, which seemed to be highly regarded by them.

51. Strong evidence for this contention is found among Tokyo workers who were transferred to the new suburban plant. One of the most common complaints of these workers was the lack of worker consultation and discussion on work problems. They particularly disliked the intensive work pace, which allowed little time for the leisurely association to which they were accustomed.

Undoubtedly, the company had and will continue to have some success in introducing its new approach and winning back its lost authority in the shop. There has been an increase in formal rules for personnel interactions. There has also been a decline in the worker satisfaction that comes from close worker-to-worker consultation in solving work problems. But there are obviously built-in limits to the go-through-the-foreman approach if production is not to bog down in a morass of rules. Even some foremen showed a reluctance to carry out the new policy. One explained:

> This new system would mean a lot more work for foremen, so it's not likely to be pushed too hard by them. Also in many sections there are skilled workers who often know more about the work than the foreman, so it wouldn't make sense to pass requests through him.

This attitude suggests management will have a hard time fully implementing its proposals. The workers were adept at putting up a stubborn rear-guard action. Still, some foremen were receptive to the new orders, for they saw a chance to increase their own personal power and authority.

In the new suburban plant, the introduction of the go-through-the-foreman approach presented no problem. The company, from the plant's opening, wielded its authority with a strong hand to prevent workers from gaining the kind of control that existed in the Tokyo plant. The young inexperienced workers recruited for the new plant could not turn to each other for advice, so they found it necessary to rely on their experienced foreman.

As part of the modernization of social relations in the company, the new management also instituted their version of the "human relations" approach. This was a clear attempt to avoid relying on a punishment-centered bureaucracy and, instead, to move toward a representative mode of administration. This included a program to educate foremen not to issue direct orders but to suggest a certain course of action after hearing worker views. Although the union leaders believed it was good that workers were now consulted more and that orders were not given just on the basis of the fore-

man's authority, they saw it essentially as a management attempt to weaken the union, manipulate the workers, and
draw them more tightly into the company orbit—a new way
to accomplish an old management policy.[52] Worker reaction
was divided. While some appreciated being consulted by the
foreman, others complained of the indirectness and dilly-
dallying of the new approach and preferred "a man-to-man
directness," with the foreman issuing unequivocal orders. Still
others were apathetic to the whole development.

Another part of the company's human relations program was the establishment in 1963 of monthly section meetings, designed to air worker grievances. Reaction to the meetings varied with different sections and between the Tokyo
and suburban diecast plants. The section meetings of the
Tokyo press and press maintenance section were lively affairs with workers raising numerous grievances and the supervisor defending himself as best he could. Discussions often
became heated. At one meeting a press maintenance worker
raised the issue of requisitioning supplies. He complained it
was a waste of time to have to walk over to get the supervisor's signature four or five times in a short period of time
when there was only a slight change in measurements. The supervisor said that this was a company rule and it had best
be followed. Other maintenance workers joined in the discussion and tempers flared as the argument went back and
forth for forty-five minutes. Finally, the supervisor closed the
discussion saying that it was his responsibility in the eyes of
the company so the workers had better get his signature. "A
rule is a rule and there is a good reason for it." The press
workers reacted critically to the section meetings. The ideal
section meeting from the majority point of view was one in
which a proposal is made, all discuss it, and then reach a
common agreement. If the proposal is accepted, the supervisor passes it on to management. The workers expect the
supervisor to be on their side, representing them vis-à-vis
management. But the press workers complained that their

52. The union reaction appears similar to that of some American
unions like the UAW to the human relations approach.

supervisor just gave answers to each proposal or said the company would think about it.

The meeting of the Tokyo machine maintenance section was closer to the ideal suggested by the press workers. Significantly, the supervisor of the machine maintenance section was a young man of thirty-one years who identified more closely with the workers and with whom they felt rapport. When the issue of signing requisitions came up in this section, the supervisor told workers to get his signature later or sign his name if he was not around. In general, the machine maintenance workers believed they had a supervisor who would stand up for their interests toward management. A still different situation existed in the diecast section of the Tokyo plant; the section meeting often was used by the union to pursue its demands when it suited union strategy. In 1965, union leaders convinced the diecast section workers to boycott the section meetings. In all sections, there were some workers who saw the meetings as a way to get two hours overtime without working while drinking tea and eating cookies. Others complained of formal red tape that lowered production such as the time wasted on section meetings.

In the suburban plant, the section meetings totally lost their meaning as a forum for airing grievances. One day before the meeting, the supervisor passed the word for workers to think of questions and issues for the meeting in great contrast to the sharp-tongued Tokyo workers, who needed no one to tell them to think of questions. At the meeting itself, the supervisors most of the time lectured on production. They constantly referred to the preceding month's production figures, to ways productivity could be raised, and asked for worker suggestions on raising production. The workers usually sat silently for two hours with only a couple venturing to make short comments as the meeting closed. The inexperience of the workers at the suburban diecast plant and management's attempt to turn section meetings into an appeal for raising production all but destroyed their original intent.

Management explained the purpose of the section meeting as an outlet for workers to get things off their chest and express their frustrations. It was an attempt to get workers to participate in and identify with their company. In most cases, the meetings did not operate at all as intended. In the press section, it did not work because the workers had expectations of getting results. When they were put off, it increased their frustration and anger. In the diecast section, the union sabotaged the meetings; in the suburban plant, management appeals for higher production dominated. In short, management's attempt to temper the rule-oriented mode of administration with moves toward a representative mode failed. Under these conditions, the punishment aspects of the bureaucratic rules became more pronounced.

I am not suggesting that the prevalence of the punishment-centered bureaucracy is typical of the solutions reached by Japanese management in its search for modernization. Common to both companies was the increasing role of impersonal bureaucratic standards to govern the work behavior of blue-collar employees. One consequence was a decrease in work spontaneity and a formalization of social relations.

It is unlikely that the growing emphasis on rules is an isolated phenomenon. More and more Japanese blue-collar workers are employed in big, growing firms that are recipients of modern ideas of management, which stress the role of bureaucratic rules. Nor is the initiation of the new rules to be understood only as a response to the spread of modern ideas: they are also a response to economic pressures. Increasing competition, expanding product markets, expanding production, introduction of modern technology, growing labor shortages, and rising wages require the introduction of more rational forms of organization based on impersonal standards to meet the demands inherent in such developments.

While the introduction of such rules is combined with an adaptation of them to existing social practices, the thrust is nevertheless in the direction of a modification of traditional forms of social control and social organization. However, no *a priori* basis exists for equating new thrusts with eventual overall dominance or for equating modification with eventual disappearance.

In the past, the scope of informal relationships in the factory was wide. Informal relationships played a key role in worker motivation and labor control. Such relationships are now subject to increasing attack. The move is toward a reduction in the scope of informal relationships; impersonal bureaucratic standards play an increasingly larger role. Combined with the changing labor market situation, it means a weakening of blue-collar worker dependence on the company and specific management personnel. Informal organization, however, does not disappear but is used in a more economically instrumental fashion. Workers often use *giri* relationships to insure themselves a stable career pattern. Management seeks to combine the use of such relationships with selection of promising young workers and development of work motivation and labor control. These usages by management and workers may be conflicting or complementary.

It is unlikely that these developments will be reversed. Temporary reversions to a buyer's market may take place, that would increase worker dependence on the firm. The reduced birth rate and the expanding economy, however, are not likely to produce the permanent large reserve of unemployed and underemployed that existed in the past. With almost all members of society now integrated into the market economy, they become susceptible not only to market fluctuations but to modern fiscal and monetary methods that control rates of economic growth and limit unemployment. The urbanization of the population makes it less possible for the unemployed to return to the farm as in the past. At the same time, this urbanization combined with rising educational levels leads to increased political sophistication, and political pressures make large-scale unemployment or underemployment intolerable.

CHAPTER VII

THE WORKER AND THE UNION:
AUTONOMY AND IDEOLOGY

His military map, on which enemy and friendly forces were
supposed to be clearly defined, was blurred with unknowns
of intermediate colors like indeterminate blobs of ink.

Abé Kobo—*The Woman in the Dunes*

The postwar unions, though not without links to the
prewar unions, are so different it is no exaggeration to say
their history is only some twenty odd years. In the postwar
period, the initial spurt and continued growth of unions gave
Japan over 10,000,000 union members. The peculiar conditions by which the labor unions were installed from above by
the Occupation Forces left its mark, though in diluted form.
There have been subtle blendings with past Japanese labor
practices, often with consequences totally unanticipated by
the initiators of the labor reforms.

The organizational form taken by most Japanese unions
is the so-called enterprise union, composed of the members
of a given company or plant.[1] In 1959, 88 percent of all unions were classified as enterprise unions with the remainder
divided primarily among craft organizations (6.6 percent)
and industrial organizations (3.1 percent). The enterprise

---

1. Principal sources for this background on enterprise unionism in-
clude: Solomon B. Levine, *Industrial Relations in Postwar Japan* (Urbana:
University of Illinois Press, 1958), pp. 89–107; Alice H. Cook, *Japanese
Trade Unionism* (Ithaca: Cornell University Press, 1966), pp. 28–83.

union commonly includes all plants in a company even
though they may have different production lines or fall into
different industries. Each plant, if there is more than one,
will be considered a branch in a larger enterprise-wide organization. These larger enterprise-wide organizations range from
centralized federations, which are the most common, to loose
confederations of almost autonomous branch unions. About
74 percent of enterprise unions are affiliated with a parent
body outside the enterprise, the majority being loosely-feder-
ated national industrial unions. The enterprise union is not
simply the administrative unit as it would be in a strong industrial union such as the United Auto Workers in the U.S.,
but tends to be a self-contained autonomous unit. Most
union functions such as collective negotiations and conclusion of agreements, striking, and grievance handling are performed in the enterprise union by union leaders who are employees of the firm. The enterprise union is financially self-
supporting, elects its own officers, collects its own dues, and
determines its own activities.

Generally, at the level of the national federations such
as Sōhyō and Dōmei, the union is a political organization
committed to national programs involving workers as citizens
rather than as employees or union members.[2] The national
unions offer few direct benefit services to the enterprise union
and its members; their appeals to the rank and file are made
on the basis of class consciousness. The annual spring offensive (shuntō) begun in 1955 under the leadership of Sōhyō
appears to be a relatively successful attempt to involve the
national centers more deeply in wage matters. Wage and related demands are set by Sōhyō in consultation with its affiliates and members of the Federation of Independent Unions
(Chūritsurōren). Pattern-setting unions are selected whose
settlements are expected to establish the pattern for weaker
unions. Enterprise unions do the actual bargaining, but they
are expected to fix their demands and schedule their tactics
according to the agreed pattern.

2. Bernard Karsh and Solomon B. Levine, "Present Dilemmas of the
Japanese Labor Movement," Proceedings, Industrial Relations Research Association, Spring, 1962.

Enterprise unions are often combined unions including both blue- and white-collar employees. A 1967 Ministry of Labor survey reports that 47 percent of the unions are combined organizations, 21 percent being exclusively blue-collar and 32 percent being exclusively white-collar.[3] Many of the exclusively white-collar unions are in "pure" white-collar industries. White-collar workers tend to supply a very high proportion of union leadership in the combined unions.

This unusual organizational form arose in the economic confusion after World War II and was encouraged by the Occupation's call for immediate formation of labor unions. The easiest and quickest way of forming unions was to organize workers at the enterprise. The large number of unemployed and underemployed workers forced employees to concentrate on protecting their own jobs; this was best done by enterprise unions. The economic instability of the period also increased diffusion of the nenkō wage and permanent employment system, which further strengthened the functional reasons for the emergence of enterprise unionism. Enterprise unionism may also have been an outgrowth of the wartime labor front Sangyō Hōkokukai. Popularly known as Sanpo, this patriotic organization was designed by the government to ensure the cooperation of management and labor in all companies. Sanpo was based on the traditional family system, taking as its slogan "jigyo ikka" (enterprise family). Management, as the father of the family, and the employees as the children, were all expected to work together in harmony to achieve higher productivity and victory in the war.[4] The cultural legacy of the corporate group provided the additional backing necessary to see the establishment and maintenance of enterprise unions.

From the union point of view, there are a number of strengths and weaknesses associated with enterprise unionism. First, union-company relations tend to develop according to the realities of the enterprise. The participation of white-

3. Japan Institute of Labour, "Collective Agreements at the Enterprise Level," Japan Labor Bulletin, Vol. 8, No. 11 (November 1969).
4. Ayusawa Iwao, A History of Labor in Modern Japan (Honolulu: East-West Center Press, 1966), pp. 229–230.

collar employees in particular increases union knowledge about the actual financial situation of the firm. The probability is thereby increased that there will be cooperation between union and company based on mutual trust. It may also lead to greater union bargaining power. Second, the very *raison d'etre* of the enterprise union lies in maintaining its members as employees in the company. It is possible to mobilize strong employee resistance to work force reduction, and this contributes to guaranteeing the employment security of union members. Third, because union leaders commonly come from within the firm, it is possible to develop strong bonds between leaders and the rank and file. Finally, enterprise unionism is based on the enterprise consciousness of employees and not on loyalty to employer or management alone. This makes it possible for enterprise unions to guarantee and extend employee rights within the enterprise.

A number of weaknesses are also associated with the enterprise union. Its members tend to become over dependent on the fortunes of their company. This strong identification with the interests of the company makes union members susceptible to company manipulation under such slogans as: "productivity increase movement" (*seisansei kōjō*), "protect the enterprise" (*kigyō bōei*), or "higher wages will bankrupt the firm." Under these circumstances, it becomes difficult for the union to represent effectively the interests of its members, as distinct from the interests of the company. One reflection of this is the tendency for paired struggles in which company and union cooperate to better the company's competitive position vis à vis other companies. The difficulties this creates for establishing strong industrial unions are obvious.

The presence of both white- and blue-collar workers in the same union often creates severe internal union conflicts. Like foremen, white-collar workers sometimes can be easily manipulated into supporting company interests.[5] The enterprise union often lacks interest in problems outside the enterprise based on national needs or social responsibilities; it is

5. White-collar workers are often active in forming second unions sympathetic to management interests. Fujita Wakao, *Dai Ni Kumiai* (The Second Union), revised edition (Tokyo: Nihon Hyōron Shinsha, 1960).

usually indifferent to the organization of unorganized workers outside the company. Indeed, because the union tends to identify with the interests of its company, it usually is opposed to the organization of the temporary workers in the firm. These are some of the strengths and weaknesses of the enterprise union as an organizational form. Within this scope we will describe and analyze the role of the labor union and relation between workers, unions, and companies.

UNION ACTIVITY IN THE SHOP

Japanese unions play a relatively limited role in the day-to-day shop activities of most firms. The diecast and auto parts firms were no exceptions; although there was a difference between them: The Tokyo diecast union had built its power in the shop in its first ten years and was viewed by the workers as being more active in trying to defend worker rights than was the case in the auto parts union. The Tokyo diecast union by its resistance to management made its presence felt on the shop floor on a variety of matters. The auto parts union by taking a posture of cooperation with management on shop problems was less able to make its presence felt among the workers. This difference, however, should not be overestimated because it was more apparent than real. The actions of the Tokyo union in resisting the company and trying to protect worker rights were more often futile than effective, particularly with the advent of the new management in 1962. Its actions were symbolic and expressive of worker desires but in effect not very different in outcome from those in the auto parts company. This kind of situation has prompted some observers to point out that Sōhyō federation unions with their Marxist philosophy and Dōmei federation unions with their more conciliatory views are not so very different in terms of what they achieve for workers in the shop.

Some of the reasons for this lack of shop activity have already been noted. The long-standing close relations between foreman and worker and the generally high value placed on interpersonal negotiation make resistance difficult. The unions, encouraged from above by the Occupation, had

no tradition of gradually building up worker rights. Historically, the many benefits that came about from employer
benevolence diminished worker initiative to oppose management. Worker identification with company production goals
make opposition in the shop still harder. The absence of an
explicit pay-by-work or performance system as a central feature of wage payment like that of the U.S. takes away one
of the strong incentives for union activity in the shop. In
both companies, union activities in the shop tended to be
ad hoc rather than being focused on job control with a formalized, often-used grievance procedure, as in the U.S. A
1967 Japanese labor ministry study reported that only 37 percent of the surveyed unions had formalized grievance machinery.[6] Individual workers seldom become identified with
specific grievances being processed by the union. Workers in
both firms showed a lack of consciousness of their rights and
a reluctance to exercise them; this was especially notable
among the young, inexperienced auto workers. The historic
subordination of workers to management authority, although
shaken and weakened by the Occupation and subsequent developments, has not been dislodged and remains a persistent
force.

When the auto parts union leaders were asked what
were their greatest problems with management, they mentioned wages, shortening of work hours, and the raising of
the retirement age but seldom mentioned shop problems.
The diecast union leaders, on the other hand, listed wages,
retirement allowances, and often mentioned shop grievances.
These included: intensified work loads, job transfers, overtime, shift work, safety hazards, company disciplinary action,
discrimination against union members, and welfare and recreation facilities. The diecast union also tried to control the
amount of company subcontracting so that work was not
taken away from union members. However, like many Japanese unions, the diecast union was not successful.[7]

6. *Japan Labor Bulletin*, Vol. 8, No. 12 (December 1969).
7. For results of a survey of management subcontracting and union
response see Margaret K. Chandler, "Management Rights: Made in Japan,"
Columbia Journal of World Business (Winter 1966).

In the auto parts plant, the workers presented most grievances in terms of, "work is hard to do because of," "certain obstacles are preventing good work," and "there are dangerous objects obstructing work." In short, most grievances were presented by workers in the context of production being held down because of this and that reason. The auto parts workers, recognizing that the union took a production-first policy, only presented those grievances to the union that related to obstacles to higher production or could be phrased that way. The union received no worker grievances on line speed, staffing, or difficulty of work. For these, workers turned to discussions and negotiations with their foremen. The clutch assembly foreman reported that he often received worker grievances on line speed and staffing matters.

In both companies, union grievance procedure was extremely informal. There were no papers to be filled out by the griever and there was no specified person to whom he was to direct his grievance. Sometimes it was the shop steward, at other times the chief steward, and at still other times some member of the union executive board. There were no union personnel whose sole function was to handle grievances. One example of the low institutionalization of grievance procedure was: Whether an issue became a union concern in the diecast plant often depended on the presence in the section of a union activist who would act as a catalyst. The absence of formal grievance procedures reflects the absence of a tradition of shop activity in Japanese unions. Workers did not expect these procedures and they were not established.[8]

As may be expected where union activity on worker grievances is limited, the shop stewards in both companies saw themselves primarily as transmitters of worker sentiment to the union executive board and in turn disseminators of union information to the workers. At most they gave an on-

8. The difference between American and Japanese practice, while significant, is not as great as it may seem. American unionists are also reported to commonly bypass the formal grievance machinery for more informal procedures. Many American unionists are also reluctant to press grievances for fear of being labeled troublemakers in the company. Leonard Sayles and George Strauss, *The Local Union: Its Place in the Industrial Plant* (New York: Harper, 1953), pp. 27–33.

the-spot report to the union if a dispute erupted in their section, but they did not view themselves as having a key role in handling or eliciting worker grievances. In the diecast firm, a rotation system was used by workers to fill the chief steward and sub-steward positions. With the exception of union activists, most workers regarded the post as a nuisance but something that had to be done. The auto parts firm had no such system; the same workers often were re-elected to the post every year. The post was seen more as a step up the company ladder for some bright young man.

In considering the content of union shop activities, we will examine the direct results arising from auto parts union leaders visiting the U.S. Many of the leaders of the federation to which the auto parts union belongs had been to the U.S.; two of the key figures at the Gujo firm had also been there as members of labor teams.

Several union leaders interviewed on this matter listed a number of changes, which they attributed to their American visit. In particular, the Japanese unionists spoke of how the visit had strengthened their view that priority must be given to "economic unionism" rather than the "political unionism" of the Marxist unions. By this they meant strong emphasis on wage increases. They neglected to mention, however, what many consider the cornerstone of economic unionism in America, a militant shop organization focused on job control and job consciousness. Instead, they preferred to speak of how their visit contributed to the modernization of labor relations, with their union now accepting and even pushing management to replace jobs requiring hard physical labor with labor-saving machines. Workers were exhorted to: "work hard, raise production, and your share will increase." This is a view of modernization many American union leaders would surely find suspect. No doubt these Japanese unionists saw what they wanted to see. It is a commonplace observation that short-term cultural exchanges often only reinforce preconceptions and stereotypes.[9]

Union involvement in the workshop is not static but

9. Bernard Karsh has pointed to the way in which American unionists and visiting Japanese unionists talk past each other as a result of different definitions of such basic terms as union, strike, and technology. Bernard

changes and fluctuates in response to the conditions of
the day and long-term underlying changes. There is some
evidence that Japanese union involvement in the shop has
increased recently and will continue to do so with rapid technological and organizational change. Apart from the firms
studied, evidence for this contention comes from a study of
rapidly growing firms where increasing rationalization led to
a greater possibility of union organization and more formal
handling of grievances in the shop.[10] Union action programs
also indicate a growing concern with workshop problems and
so does the development of workshop tactics by the unions.

In the two firms, one source of increased union activity
in the shop was in response to management attempts to
streamline production. This left less time for the spontaneous
worker interaction and consultation characteristic of the older
Tokyo diecast plant. In the suburban diecast plant and the
auto parts company, the work pace was intense, breaks more
systematized and fewer, and workers subject to more direct
regulation in doing their work. The latter conditions would
seem to be part of a trend of Japanese management seeking
a more effective use of their labor forces. It suggests that in
the future workers will find less satisfaction in shop social
relations, which may lead to worker pressure for union protection of their interests in the shop. Yet, the whole tradition
of shop relations is such that it would be naive to expect a
model of job-conscious unionism to emerge. Indeed, it would
be parochial to assume that effective representation of worker
interests is compatible only with a militant shop organization
based on job consciousness and job control. An alternative
approach can be seen in the emergence of the workshop
struggle tactic as used by Japanese unions.

The development of the workshop struggle tactic falls
into two stages. Right after World War II and closely allied
with the Communist strategy of dominating the unions, the

Karsh, "The Exportability of Trade Union Movements: The Japan-U.S.
Trade Union 'Cultural Exchange Program,' " *The Changing Patterns of Industrial Relations* (Tokyo: The Japan Institute of Labor, 1965), pp. 55–68.

10. Okamoto Hideaki and Matsumoto Shizō, "Seichō Sangyō ni okeru
Nijū Kōzō to Rōdō Kanri," (Dual Structure and Labor Administration in
Growing Industry) in *Nijū Kōzō no Bunseki* (Analysis of the Dual Struc-
ture), Tamanoi Yoshirō (ed.), (Tokyo: Tōyō Keizai, 1964).

unions used the tactic of workshop struggle to gain recognition for themselves, occupy plants, take over production, and "democratize" the firm. They demanded that autocratic managers and foremen, particularly those identified with the war effort, be forced to resign.

A second phase began in 1952 in the coal mining industry and spread to other industries especially after 1955. The development was weakened in 1960 with the crushing of the militant coalminers' union, *Tanrō*, but it continues in various forms. While it is as yet difficult to assess the meaning of this second phase, some features stand out. Workshop struggle may involve: workshop meetings on company time or after work, short work stoppages, slowdowns and refusal of overtime. At the same time, various demands are made upon management. Workshop struggle, based on the participation of all workers in a given production unit, is designed to put pressure on management to deal with shop grievances. It is a functional equivalent to formal grievance procedure as it is understood in the West. Depending on the plant, however, it has other meanings as well. It is still often tied to the strategy of local Communist leaders who try to "bore from within" to capture control of the unions from higher ranking socialist leaders and to "revolutionize from below." Workshop struggle is also a strategy of enterprise union leaders to mobilize support of the workers as is apparent from its popularity prior to union elections. Sometimes it is a mechanism of company control used by management to mobilize workers to support a second union. While all these meanings may be involved at various times and to varying degrees, the role of workshop struggle in calling attention to worker grievances in the shop and establishing worker control over shop rules is apparent.[11]

INTERNAL UNION DEMOCRACY

For those interested in grasping the impact of postwar democracy in Japan, one approach is through an examination

11. Ōkochi Kazuo, *et al.*, *Rōdō Kumiai no Kōzō to Kino* (The Structure and Functions of Labor Unions), (Tokyo: Tokyo University Publishing Association, 1959).

of internal union democracy. What are the conditions of internal union democracy? How do we evaluate the presence or absence of union democracy? What conclusions can be drawn about union democracy and leaders?

There is much dispute over the extent and meaning of democracy in American unions, not to speak of Japanese unions. To avoid unsubstantiated statements, comparisons with American unions will be held to a minimum. Rather the focus will be on comparisons between the diecast company and the auto plant. It may be argued that it is unacceptable to apply the concept of democracy to the union movement of another society. Because the extent and scope of democracy is a response to unique historical conditions, we cannot apply culture-bound concepts such as democracy to other societies. For the Soviet the term democracy may mean egalitarianism in an economic sense; for the American it may mean political liberty under a two-party system.

The procedure here is to assume a cultural relativist position and still use the concept of democracy as an analytic tool. At a minimum, we may evaluate the extent to which societies meet their own professed ideals of democracy. One may point out that America failed its black population by denying it political liberty, or that Soviet Russia in the name of egalitarianism created a new privileged class. The purpose is not to label behavior as democratic or undemocratic; it is to point to the tensions for change that are created where there is a gap between professed ideals and the existing social situation. An alternative approach would be to eliminate the use of the term democracy because it carries such heavy value connotations. One could be content to speak of the mechanisms for selection of leaders and the degree of control exercised by workers in the selection. Yet democracy as ideology is demonstrably present in contemporary Japan, and as such is part of the social situation. To ignore its presence is to ignore an element in the social situation that influences outcomes.

Though the Tokyo diecast union was militantly Marxist, few workers questioned its status as a democratically constituted union. Union elections were conducted with secret ballots, and, at least until the withdrawal of foremen before the formation of the second union, there were opposing candidates (required by union constitution) with meaningfully different positions. The head of the right-wing socialist faction, who was to be active in forming the new union, agreed that the affairs of the union were conducted in a proper manner representing the views of the majority of the workers. He did believe, however, that many of the workers were misguided in their views because of the propaganda of the extreme left faction. He also thought that it was hard to express opposition viewpoints because of the well-organized Communist faction represented by their youth group, Minseidō. There was, however, no direct criticism of the union as undemocratic. The Communists, at the time of the formation of the second union, still controlled only three of ten positions on the union executive board. In the Tokyo plant, during union meetings held at this time, opposition to the union leadership was still being expressed. Vocal opposition had been even stronger in the past before the foremen and other members of the right-wing socialist faction began to withdraw from the union. In the suburban diecast plant, which accounted for five of the ten union executive board seats, the case for internal union democracy was less clear. The opposition to the mainstream faction had chosen not to join or had withdrawn from the union, so that at the time of the formation of the second union, two-thirds of the plant's workers were non-union. In the leaflets distributed during the formation of the second union, this point was used to argue that the existing union did not reflect the will of the majority of workers at the plant and was thus undemocratic. Although union democracy did play a role in the propaganda of the new union, it had little to do with the reasons which workers gave for joining. Most workers said they joined so that there would be one union to which everyone belonged that would insure peaceful relations with management and among workers. In fact, many workers joined the new union because the leaders of their clique set the tone for their decisions.

In looking at both cases, the most important condition for guaranteeing internal union democracy would seem to be the presence of a well-organized opposition to the leadership.

In the Tokyo diecast plant, from the union's inception in 1953 until 1965, there had been a well-organized opposition roughly according to political stance. Opposing the majority left-socialist faction were the right socialists and the Communists. Both oppositions commanded large followings and until 1965 it had been common that members of the three factions served together on the union executive board. The existence of the two opposition factions and their holding union executive board positions above all guaranteed a democratic infrastructure in the union.[12] It was the growing absence of such opposition through withdrawals from union membership that weakened the content of this democracy. Because of management's hard line, the Socialists found that for the union to survive they increasingly had to cooperate with the Communists. By 1966, workers who opposed both management and the Communists were reluctant to run for election, fearing that being a candidate would endanger their future in the company. The Communists, mostly young men without family responsibilities, were the only ones willing to stand up to management's hard line. Management's position was that even with only three Communists on the union executive board, the Communists ran the union through "remote control." Management pressures to get workers to withdraw from the union and management's active support of the formation of the second union suggests a self-fulfilling prophecy. Acting on their conviction that the union was Communist-dominated from the beginning, they proceeded in such a way that the Tokyo union was finally left to the Communists by default. This points to the W. I. Thomas theorem, "if men define situations as real they are real in their consequences."[13]

12. Lipset, Trow, and Coleman have made this point in their study of the International Typographers Union. They maintain that the union's tradition of democracy arose to a great extent from the existence of an institutionalized opposition faction ever alert to point out the failings of the faction in power. See Seymour Lipset, Martin Trow, and James Coleman, *Union Democracy* (Glencoe: Free Press, 1956).

13. For a discussion of the self-fulfilling prophecy in the context of the W. I. Thomas theorem and sociological theory, see Robert K. Merton, *Social Theory and Social Structure* (Glencoe: Free Press, revised ed., 1957), pp. 421–436.

The cycle, however, does not end at this point. With
the successful formation of the second union at the suburban
diecast plant in 1966, management sought to reap the advantages of its having provided the major impetus and support for its initiation. The new union leaders, under heavy
obligation to the company and subject to strong pressures by
management, committed the union to modest wage demands
and active efforts to support the company's economic reconstruction plan. The basis for this policy was the continuation
of the stabilization contract.

Under these conditions, autonomous union activity was
all but impossible, and the union became little more than
an administrative arm of the company. Management, however, in seeking to take maximum advantage of its power
position once again created a potential for change. Worker
dissatisfaction began to grow over low wages and the failure
of the union leaders to represent their interests effectively.
As time passed, it became more difficult to legitimate union
policies in terms of anti-Communist activities. Late in 1968,
the slate of union officers sympathetic to the company were
defeated in a union election. The new slate pledged itself to
a militant wage policy while continuing to support cooperation with the company's production goals. The emphasis,
however, had clearly shifted from the latter to the former.
With the expiration of the stabilization contract in 1969, the
company called for its renewal, while some of the more militant members of the union executive board called for its
abolition. The new contract represented a compromise. Based
on the company's growing profits, the union won much improved wage increases in line with recent wage packages
agreed upon in the manufacturing sector. But the union
agreed to these wage increases in the framework of a new
three-year stabilization contract; thus committing itself to
three more years of relative inactivity. One aspect of the
union's increased militancy was reflected in their new policy
to reopen discussions with their formerly despised opposition
at the Tokyo plant. Quite clearly, opposition factions had
once again appeared in the suburban diecast plant union.

Certain sociological principles are expressed in these developments. Predominant institutionalization of one alternative does not dispel or dismiss its counterpart.[14] No sociostructural pattern is fully institutionalized, and any attempt by one group to fully exploit its advantages sets up the possibility of countervailing powers initiated by dissatisfied elements. Union democracy, like societal democracy, ebbs and flows in response to the pull of internal dynamics and environmental effects.

A further glimpse into the meaning and operation of internal union democracy can be had by examining elections at the auto parts union. Elections are, of course, only one aspect of internal union democracy; in a broader sense we are interested in the degree to which the union is responsive to the majority viewpoint held by workers. This can often be difficult to measure, however, and in this sense the way elections are conducted can be a revealing indicator of the quality of internal union democracy.

Union elections at the auto parts company are conducted once a year by secret ballot. The union executive board recommends a slate of sixteen to fill the sixteen positions. An election committee certifies the candidates; as a matter of policy, members stated that certification was open to all employees. In most elections, however, there are no other candidates besides those recommended by the union executive board. That is, there were only sixteen candidates for the sixteen offices for the last several years, and they were supported by 99 percent of the workers.

A number of workers critical of union policy were asked, "Why don't you replace the present leaders with those more to your liking?" They generally answered, "It's not easy, for one thing, the executive board controls who gets nominated." One worker explained:

> Before the union election, the candidates are selected by the (union) superiors without consulting us. We can be a candidate without such a recommendation, but then we

14. See Wilbert Moore, "A Reconsideration of Theories of Social Change," *American Sociological Review*, Vol. 25 (December 1960). Pitirim Sorokin suggests a similar view with his "principle of limits." Pitirim Sorokin, *Social and Cultural Dynamics* (Boston: Porter Sargent, 1957), p. 522.

would be called in by the union and persuaded not to run.[15]
If we would dare to be candidates we would be watched by
the authorities.[16]

The union claim that anyone could become a candidate was
apparently not very meaningful to the workers. Moreover,
the union and the company were so closely intertwined that
to declare one's candidacy in opposition to the executive
board slate was, in effect, to declare one's opposition to company management. This would be a dangerous business only
a brave or perhaps foolhardy individual would attempt. The
general view among workers was that the elections were decided in a somewhat mysterious way by higher-ups and opposition was useless.

Union leaders defended their election practices with
the following statements:

1. One candidate for each office can be democratic.
Since 99 percent of the workers support the slate in elections,
it obviously represents the will of almost all employees. There
is no sense in turning the election into a popularity contest
if there are no real differences among the workers.

2. To have too many candidates will result in those who
are defeated going back to the shop with feelings of ill will
and animosity against the victors. This leads to factions and
possible splits in the union. So selection must be made be-
forehand.

3. The Communists and their youth organization are
active in this region, and it is a matter of self-preservation to
see that they do not get control. Even if some of the young
militants who criticize the union wage policy do not seem
like Communists on the surface, if you dig deep enough it
is the Communists who are really responsible.

4. It would not make sense for the union to recommend
for their slate opposition workers or to encourage opposition
candidates; such young people have no understanding of the
function and operation of union organization. Union officials

15. *Ue kara shizen ni kimatchau bokura ni sōdan naku rikkōho
dekiru sureba kumiai ni yobarete settoku sareru no de wa nai ka.*
16. It is not clear whether he is referring to union or company authorities or both.

have the responsibility to recommend the best man to pass
on the union intact and see that its basic policies will be
carried out in the future. We cannot jeopardize the basic
philosophy of the union by handing it over to young incompetents.

5. A certain gap between leadership and rank and file
is unavoidable, because leaders know more and understand
the weak economic foundation of the company and learn
that they must compromise.

This defense is remarkably frank and provides some in-
sight into the union leadership's understanding of internal
union democracy. Its claim that the 99 percent worker support of the election slate is proof of union democracy is a
shallow one. It recalls a critique of totalitarian regimes made
by Walter Lippman. Referring to these 99 percent election
turnouts, he suggested that whenever there is such a superficial appearance of unanimity and conformity there will
always be at least a minority, perhaps a majority, who, although silenced by various means, will remain unconverted
and unconvinced.[17] The leaders' unwillingness to accept factions and their consequences reflects a basic unwillingness
to accept democratic procedure; it is institutionalized factions
such as existed in the diecast plant that provide a key basis
for union democracy. This is not to say that factions cannot
be disruptive and threatening, especially if factional loyalties
are carried to the extreme, as is often the case in Japan. But
the existence of factions may be the price one must pay if
democratic interplay within the organization is desired. The
reference to the role of Communists among young dissidents
is an admission that an opposition did, in fact, exist. At the
same time, this waving of the red flag is a common ploy of
those who seek to discredit their opposition without inquiring
into the merit of their position.

In referring to the responsibility of the executive board
to pass on the union and its basic policies intact to their successors, the union leaders come closest to explaining the election set-up in functional terms, namely, the election set-up

17. Walter Lippman, "On the Importance of Being Free," *Encounter*,
Vol. 143 (August 1965), pp. 88–90.

served to control access to union office and as a consequence perpetuated the oligopolistic control of the ruling clique. This ruling clique consisted primarily of supervisory personnel who adopted a production first/cooperative policy with management. The predominance of youthful rural recruits with little industrial experience left the union to this ruling clique by default. The makeup of the eight full-time member executive board of the union at the time of the research is indicative of the break between rank-and-file members and union leaders. The average age of the executive board was thirty-two as compared to twenty-four for the entire company. Of the eight members, five were supervisors, two were foremen, and only one was a worker. We have already pointed to the difficulties of building an autonomous union when supervisory staff and members of the personnel section play a leading role in the union. In their capacity as agents of the company, they can be too easily imposed upon by the company. It is understandable that Fujita Wakao and others see this particular age composition as the time most conducive to the formation of a company union.[18]

Their analysis interprets labor union militancy in large-scale industry in terms of a three-phase cycle, each phase taking seven years. In the first phase most workers have a very short length of service; the older workers, who are a minority, cooperate closely with management so the union is a *de facto* company union. In the second phase the union leaders become senior workers who have been promoted to foremen positions. When they fail to effectively represent the workers a conflict emerges, with the young workers struggling against management and their own leaders. These young workers become the senior members in the third phase, but as not all can be promoted, a severe competition emerges. The union may become militant as the majority in this group, who can not be promoted to the limited number of positions, take over leadership in the union. As a consequence, the union

18. Fujita Wakao, Ujihara Shojirō, and Funahashi Naomichi, *Nihongata Rōdō Kumiai to Nenkō Seido* (Japanese-Style Labor Unions and the Age-Seniority System), (Tokyo: Shinbunsha, 1963).

undergoes a crisis, often resulting in a split with the emergence of a second union and a return to phase one.

The pattern of preselecting union candidates often with only one candidate standing for election is not an uncommon practice among Japanese unions. This is true in both Marxist and non-Marxist unions as at the auto parts firm. The practice is not necessarily undemocratic. A key determinant is how the candidates are selected. In many companies, the union executive board recommendation is based on workshop discussions among workers in which one candidate is pushed forward, it being understood that the election itself is only a formality. This, though not in accord with democratic behavior as understood in the U.S., does contain, in essence, the meaning of democracy in that the rank and file determine who their representatives will be. In some firms, however, even workshop meetings may be manipulated by the union; therefore, whether a democratic procedure obtains is a matter of empirical investigation. Such procedures may also be seen in the context of Japanese social behavior in which there is an attempt to settle matters informally by consensus and mutual understanding. In yet another sense recommendation of candidates by incumbent union officers is not necessarily undemocratic because these recommendations are subject to a worker vote of confidence in many plants. This procedure is often necessary because of the lack of interest of workers in becoming union officers. In this situation, whatever undemocratic element exists, arises from lack of worker interest and participation rather than from conscious design of incumbent union officials.

THE REVOLUTION THAT FIZZLED

Union democracy is to be understood not only by election practices but also by the responsiveness of union officers to the demands of members. One approach is to examine attitudes and behavior of the membership. Do workers feel free to express their dissatisfaction and do they actually do so? Do union policies reflect the views of the rank and file?

The following account presents and analyzes how a union processed a wage demand, tried to win over the workers, and the worker response. The specific wage demand is the auto parts union demand for the year-end bonus.

The workers had their first hint of the amount of the union wage demand on November 8 when they received a union handout. It stated that all member unions of the federation had agreed to strive to secure at least 1.5 months' wages as the year-end temporary payment. The dominating theme of this document was that economic conditions are poor, so the union should not make excessive demands. The importance of protecting worker livelihoods was mentioned, but primarily in terms of maintaining their long-term livelihood by strengthening the individual enterprises. It argued that Japan is experiencing a serious depression and that the planned international trade liberalization poses many problems for the auto industry.

Although it is difficult to assess the legitimacy of the union federation claims, some statement is possible. There is no doubt that in Japanese terms, 1965 was a "recession" year with profits declining in a wide range of industries. The auto industry, however, as one of the most rapidly growing Japanese industries, did not suffer to any great extent. The Bank of Japan reported that in the manufacturing sector for the first half of 1965 only the petroleum and automobile industries did not show a decline in their profits.[19] Moreover, the parent firm of the Gujo Auto Parts Company ranked among the top industrial earners in the April to September period, according to the Bank of Japan. As a key and rapidly-growing subcontractor in which modern technology had been invested, there is no question that Gujo Auto Parts had a firm foundation and a bright future. Published figures released in 1966 by the company showed that its profits in the period from February 1965 to August 1965 were the highest for any six-month period in company history.

The above is not unequivocal evidence that the union federation overestimated the company difficulties. The truth

19. *The Japan Times* (Tokyo), February 4, 1966.

of the matter seems to lie more in understanding that the large auto makers have put great pressure on their parts makers to cut production costs to make possible a large-scale export drive as well as to gain a greater share of the growing domestic market.[20] The union wage demand statement reflects the kind of strong identification with the individual firm that arises from worker consciousness and enterprise unionism.

Though Japanese collective bargaining is generally decentralized with the union of each company determining its own bargaining position, this is not exactly true in the auto industry. Unions in the large number of affiliated and subcontract firms take their bargaining cues from the union of the parent firm. This practice, however, should not be equated with industry-wide bargaining, since the scope is limited to member unions of the national federation, which, in effect, includes only the union of the parent firm and its affiliates and subcontractors. The justification for this subordination of smaller firms to the parent firm is that workers in affiliates and subcontractors can secure their livelihood only if the parent firm survives and prospers.[21]

The November 8 union handout was the subject of lunchtime workshop meetings throughout the auto parts company that day. Workers were asked to raise questions on points they did not understand. In the clutch department, one meeting was held for all 190 workers. The handout was read in entirety and a general discussion followed. Some workers complained that they had already read the bulletin so that it was a waste of time to read it again; several workers raised questions on points they did not understand; and two

20. It is estimated that almost 70 percent of all Japanese auto parts are made by subcontractors. In 1969, a scandal erupted over public disclosure of large numbers of defective Japanese cars. Informed observers attributed these defects in part to the subcontractors who sought to meet the demands of the major auto firms for reduced costs. This was accomplished by lowering the quality of the product in a way which could not easily be detected.

21. Sumiya Mikio, "Jidōsha Kōgyō," (Automobile Industry), in *Sangyō betsu Chingin Kettei no Kikō* (The Structure of Wage Determination by Industry), Ōkochi Kazuo, (ed.), (Tokyo: Japan Institute of Labour, 1964).

workers asked that the union take rising prices more into consideration before formulating wage demands.

The next word the workers received of the union demands came on November 16, when another handout was distributed containing the bonus demand of the Gujo auto parts union. It was set at the equivalent of 2.3 months of the standard wage payment, or .8 above the suggested minimum of the auto union federation. Setting the demand higher than the union federation demand had the effect of making the enterprise union seem more militant. In fact, year-end bonuses in the auto industry in 1965 ranged between 2.3 and 3.4 months' pay, so that the original auto federation proposal of 1.5 was not a very realistic one. In effect, this 2.3 months' standard wage averaged to 41,257 yen per person.

In the second handout of the union, eight considerations were stated as having been decisive in formulating the Gujo union demand. Of the eight points only one (consumer prices have continued to rise) can be seen as a clear argument for advancing a higher wage demand. The rest of the points, for the most part, are explanations designed to get workers to accept a lower wage demand. Most are framed by the argument that only with the long-run development of the firm can there be stability in living standards. The poor prospects of the auto industry, the parts makers, and Gujo Auto Parts in particular, are emphasized along with the need to grasp the "real state of the enterprise" in formulating union demands.

On the same day that the handout was distributed, workshop meetings were held to present the demands. The night shift workshop meeting opened with the union representative giving the workers a fifteen-minute run-down on the economic problems besetting the country and the auto industry.[22] He used the remaining fifteen minutes to present the union demand for an equivalent of 2.3 standard monthly wages. The meeting closed with the speaker calling for worker response at the workshop meeting to be held the following day. The workers applauded at the end of the meeting.[23]

22. I was working the night shift that week.
23. The Tokyo diecast workers never applauded at the end of union

After the workshop meeting, as the clutch assembly and machine workers returned to the shop, there was occasional grumbling concerning the low wage demands. At the 5 A.M. break, a spontaneous denunciation of the low union wage demand broke out among the fifteen workers taking their break; bitter, sarcastic, sometimes humorous comments streamed forth.[24] The criticisms ranged from a disbelief in the poor financial position of the company, a lament that workers were not in a position to know if the company was telling the truth, complaints that every year there was always some excuse for holding down the wage demands, and a denunciation of the union as weak and ineffectual. Even the most company-oriented of the work crew said, "I don't have any respect for the union, because I value money and they aren't doing anything for me." The outburst included a discussion of how the group could make known their unified views. This whole line of thinking was lost, however, in the enthusiasm of the moment, and the break ended with no agreement being reached on how to handle their dissent.

The following day, workshop meetings were again held to get the workers' response to the union wage demands. The night shift meeting began with a union representative reading the union bulletin distributed the day before. The floor was then thrown open for the workers to raise points they did not understand and to present their views. First, a couple of workers raised questions about issues they did not understand; this gave the union representative a chance to defend the 2.3 demand by pointing to declining profits of the company during the year. Next, a worker gave a five-minute speech in support of the union demand. The union official called for more opinions but few were forthcoming. There was supposed to be another meeting the next night, he said, but since no opposing opinions were offered, perhaps the present meeting was sufficient. At this point, he looked to his

workshop meetings. Perhaps this was symbolic that they did not hold the union leaders in official awe and respect as the young inexperienced auto workers did.

24. As noted earlier, no foremen were on the night shift to inhibit criticisms of the company or union.

audience for confirmation, and received scattered cries of "okay, okay." He called for an open vote on the union demand. All of the 300 workers present raised their hands in favor of the union demand. The meeting closed with applause. Despite the researcher's expectation that the indignant workers of the night before might raise severe criticisms of the union demand, not one voice was heard in dissent.

Immediately after the meeting, the clutch assembly and machine workers had a quick smoke before starting work. The workers play-acted what it would have been like if they had raised their hands in opposition to the union demand. One worker provoked laughter as he lifted up his leg indicating that he had his leg raised up in opposition during the vote, it was just that nobody saw it. This playing out of mock resistance gave vent to the frustrations the workers felt at not being able to make their voices heard.

Later in the morning, the clutch assembly and machine workers each were asked what had happened to their defiance of the night before.[25] The union representative had certainly given them every opportunity to express their views at the workshop meeting. The majority of those questioned said that they were still opposed to the 2.3 demand. A sample of different worker statements was:

A. "Well, the matter was already decided and it would not have made much difference if we had expressed our opposition. Besides, the union is weak." —Still opposed.

B. "When the workers heard that the profits of the company had been reduced, their will to resist disappeared." —Still opposed.

C. "My former company went broke because we had a leftist union that was always out to get what it could. I understand our union's position." —No longer opposed.

D. "If the guys had listened to my suggestion last night, formed a unified opinion, and then handed it over to the shop steward for delivery at the meeting, this wouldn't have happened. It's hard for an individual to get up and voice his

25. Many of the workers were embarrassed by my pointing to the contradiction between their bold statements of the night before and their failure to speak up at the workshop meeting.

opinion against the union. There is pressure from the union for workers not to express opposition." —Still opposed.[26]

E. "There is suppression of the workers' views by the union leaders—not a formal suppression, rather it's understood that one shouldn't express opposition to union policies." —Still opposed.

There was an element of sham in the way the whole wage issue developed. The union federation's recommendation was carefully staged so that it was superseded by the higher demand made by the enterprise union. At the workshop meeting, which everyone attended, the union representative announced, "We have sympathy for the company position but to defend the livelihood of workers we will submit our demand of 2.3 months. Let us all struggle together to achieve this." Applause followed.

While the workers played along with the script, they were not necessarily taken in by it. Most said that because a union demand had never been rejected, the issue was for all practical purposes decided when the union announced its demand. One company-oriented worker explained:

> Of course, the union will get the 2.3 demand from the company. The matter is already decided, though the union and company will go through the pretense of a formal process of bargaining for several sessions. It wouldn't look right if they didn't, but it doesn't mean a damn.

Some workers said they thought the union wage demands were made with prior consultation with management. The general view of workers was that the success of the union in achieving its demands over the years was a sign of weakness, not strength.[27]

If workers did not accept the union line, why did they participate in the staged performance symbolized so aptly by their applause at the end of workshop meetings and silence

26. When questioned the following evening, this worker had changed his bitter opposition to resignation and said, "I guess I don't understand these things so well. I'm young and haven't been here long."

27. A management official, asked how it was that the union had always had its demands met, answered that the union evidently did a good research job and understood the importance of company ability to pay.

during the meetings? The auto parts union leaders dismissed this entire series of incidents as reflecting the universal tendency of workers to be dissatisfied with union wage policy. They believed it in no way reflected criticism of the union. No doubt some aspects of the workers' behavior and views can be attributed to this. It does not explain, however, the workers' inability to act on their displeasure. What is apparent in worker behavior and statements is that many were opposed to the union demand. But as a result of their youthful inexperience, unwillingness to act as individuals, inability to speak publicly, poor organizational abilities and perceived pressures from the union and company, they were unable to make their opposition known at the union meeting. The union leaders were not viewed as representatives of workers but as men of superior position, age, experience, and status who must be respected. There was a feeling of powerlessness among the workers. This was compounded by a union so administratively entwined with the company that the authority of the company rubbed off on union leaders. Workers participated in the staged performance because, with the union being so closely entwined with the company, it was viewed as part of their job just as punching the time card and pushing the button to start their machines. This occurs in the context of a society that places great emphasis on consensus and internal group solidarity. By participating in the staged performance, workers were buying a harmonious relationship with the company. The auto parts workers often commented that opposition to the union would mean conflict, which should be avoided if possible.

It should be remembered that even in the Tokyo diecast plant union those outside the ruling faction complained of the difficulty in expressing opposition to the left-socialist leadership. While the extent to which this occurred was not comparable to the auto parts union, it indicates that ideology is not the only consideration. The nature of the firm as a semi-closed corporate group still further reinforced by enterprise unionism insures a strong in-group solidarity that makes it difficult to raise dissenting voices, whether it be a Communist union, a left-socialist union, or a union committed to management cooperation. Internal union democracy is obviously hard to develop under such circumstances.

Despite the strong words used by many auto parts workers to object to the union wage policy, most responded that without the union wages would be lower. If union democracy is defined in terms of effectiveness, there was a belief among workers that the union, however weak, did operate in their interests.

In assessing possible changes in the future which would increase the control of the rank and file over the leadership and thus increase internal union democracy, the auto parts union's own rhetoric may well play a role. The union leaders consistently spoke of the need to educate the workers in democratic unionism. When they adopted their demands, they appealed to the workers with such slogans as "fighting for the workers' interests" and "defending the workers' livelihood." This use of democratic rhetoric is understandable in a society where democracy has come to be identified with everything that is good and pure. One stands a greater chance of success if the audience can be convinced that the label applies to whatever item is being sold. In the context of the Sōhyō-Dōmei labor federations' competition, the term democracy is used by both to refer to their own organization, while the opposition is attacked for lacking this purifying quality. It is unlikely that the auto parts leaders could cast off the rhetoric in the future, if only because it would be a potential weapon in the hands of any opposition. Besides, it is quite likely that they were sincere in their beliefs on the meaning of democracy.

In seeking to coopt the mantle of democratic unionism as most Japanese unions do, however, there is a certain risk; that is, if the reality of union actions does not match the rhetoric, the potential for social change increases. The auto parts workers' behavior and views on restriction of production, the wage demand issue, and the election set-up clearly showed they were skeptical of union claims. The explanation for their docility, as already shown, lies elsewhere.

There are signs that the auto parts workers may use their understanding of the gap between rhetoric and practice to turn the rhetoric into reality in the future. Official ideologies, as exemplified in the democratic rhetoric of the auto parts union leaders, function as a two-edged sword. They render the workers subject to the will of the union leaders, but they also render the leaders vulnerable to the wishes and desires of the union members.[28] On the one hand, the democratic ideology brings legitimacy to the actions of the union leaders; its source of strength for the auto parts union leaders is no different from its appeal to Americans or Russians. By denying that the leaders rule by virtue of birth, education, or ability, it claims that they rule in the name of the people, which, in effect, denies the existence of a ruling class; in denying the existence of a ruling class, opponents find it harder to identify, attack, and replace their leaders. On the other hand, no ideology or its advocates can survive if there is no substance to back up claims. This, then, is the dilemma the auto parts union leaders face. They will be confronted by an increasingly sophisticated membership in the future and a slowdown in the remarkable growth of the auto industry in the coming decades. The unions have taken the responsibility for mobilizing the new rural recruits in urban forms of organization. As is often the case, however, mobilization to suit the interests of one set of leaders can be turned to other purposes. The mobilized workers will develop the sophistication that permits them to apply their organizational experience to other ends. Under these circumstances, the union leaders must be prepared either to deliver on the promises implied in their ideology or face ouster by an aroused membership. This was what the management and second union leaders at the suburban diecast plant discovered—much to their dismay.

When it was suggested to company officials that they might have to face a more militant union in the future, there was one dominant reaction. They jumped to the conclusion that the reference was to a Marxist union which would follow a policy of confrontation with the company. This way of thinking was noted among the diecast management, too. It

28. This is an adaptation of a theme developed by Gerhard Lenski. See Gerhard Lenski, *Power and Privilege* (New York: McGraw-Hill, 1966), pp. 180–181.

was difficult for them to conceive of a militant union taking a strong position on wages and working conditions without linking such a union to Marxist strategy. They could not conceive of a middle ground divorced from political ideology where the union would pursue a vigorous defense of workers' interests for better working conditions and higher wages. They held this viewpoint in spite of the fact that a number of the young dissidents who were questioned were not talking in terms of political ideology but in terms of a stronger union that concentrated on higher wages. In part, the auto parts managers were prisoners of their own company history, which had seen the replacement of an active left-wing union with a second union that followed a policy of cooperation with management. These were the options management saw open.[29] There is a truth to the company position, however, which, as we shall see, transcends its own experience.

The auto parts management believed, as did a number of union officials, that in the future the possibility of these younger workers putting pressure on the present union leadership for a more militant union could be avoided. Both parties saw the means to do this in terms of an increased emphasis on union education designed to get the workers to understand such matters as the importance of company ability to pay. A leading management official explained,

> The experienced mature labor union leaders, who are far advanced in understanding the proper role of the labor union, will be able to absorb any pressures by the young inexperienced workers.

Of course, any labor union exercises leadership and in some way tries to educate its members, but the extent to which this view seems imbedded in the auto parts union and the company raises some questions about its democratic content. At what point does education change into indoctrination? The management view that union officers were far advanced of the membership and had a responsibility to lead the mem-

29. There are no statistics on the precise number of present-day unions that had their origin as second unions, but by all accounts the number is considerable.

bership has parallels to the Marxist notion of the vanguard elite, which, as history shows, is not bound by accepted democratic procedures.

UNION AUTONOMY AND THE COMPANY

One of the key variables determining the content and meaning of internal union democracy as well as union effectiveness in representing workers, is the degree of union autonomy from the company. Autonomy, defined as independence from external control, is a particularly useful concept because it is a continuous variable.[30] We assume that a low level of union autonomy results in reduced union strength vis-à-vis the company and a low level of internal union democracy. Although there are a number of other possible intervening variables, it is likely that increased union autonomy will increase the possibilities for developing internal union democracy and effectiveness.[31]

The nature of enterprise unionism reflects strong employee identification with the company. It is difficult, therefore, for union autonomy to develop in Japanese firms. This difficulty is symbolized by the slogan "mutual understanding" (sōgo rikai) as it was used by the auto parts firm management to describe labor relations. The term was given concrete meaning on various levels. At the highest level was the joint labor-management deliberation committee (rōshikyōgikai). Significantly, this committee was an old idea which had been rejected by the company until the new second union was formed in the early nineteen fifties.

These committees or councils, designed to secure cooperation and harmony between management and labor, ideally are concerned with seeking ways of increasing profits and the source of profits, in contrast to collective bargaining, which is negotiation over the distribution of profits. In practice, how-

30. A general treatment of autonomy in organizations appears in Fred Katz, *Autonomy and Organization* (New York: Random House, 1968).
31. An increase in union autonomy if carried to an extreme can lead to a reduced effectiveness and to a reduced degree of internal democracy. This may be the case where the only relation between union and management is confrontation and struggle.

ever, the distinction is not always easy to make. Approximately 40 percent of all Japanese enterprise unions have such councils. Their spread, in recent years, is attributed in part to rapid technological change and attempts to deal with its dislocating effects in the shop. In the most extensive survey yet undertaken, the Japan Productivity Center found that 60 to 65 percent of all councils surveyed dealt with standards for job transfers, introduction of new technology, vocational training plans, and working conditions. Sixty-five to 70 percent dealt with improvement of the supervisory system and grievance procedure. The same survey showed that on the subject of working conditions, 58 percent of the councils had joint determinative power; 33.5 percent were consultative; and 4.6 percent were informative (3.5 percent were classified as others). With their strong emphasis on increasing production and developing the enterprise, these committees often work against the emergence of an autonomous union devoted to the protection of worker rights and interests.[32]

The auto parts company also held monthly liaison meetings which were designed to develop mutual understanding between union and company, and in which such items as accident prevention, monthly production figures, production bottlenecks, defective parts, job transfers, staffing, and overtime were discussed. It is difficult to ascertain the significance of these meetings. Undoubtedly, management was willing to agree to union requests within the scope of their cooperation policy. For example, the union requested rescheduling of work days by the company so that all holidays would be on the weekend to allow two consecutive days of vacation. However, quite likely the union demands were made within the framework of its commitment to a production-first policy. In contrast, the diecast management, confronted with a militant union, sought to restrict company-union negotiations to those areas required by law, convention, or earlier contract agreements.

32. On the subject of joint councils see: Mitsufuji Tadashi, "The Impact of Joint Councils on Collective Bargaining in Japan," in *Social and Economic Aspects of Japan*, Uchida Naosaku and Ikeda Kotarō (eds.), (Tokyo: Economic Institute of Seijo University, 1967), pp. 183–200.

A better understanding of how the policy of mutual understanding is implemented may be gained by examining job transfers. The 1967 labor ministry survey found among the 66 percent of unions which concluded collective agreements the following conditions regarding job transfers: union consent was required in 8 percent, consultation in 26 percent, the submission of union opinion in 11 percent, prior notice in 17 percent, notification after the event in 7 percent, and "no concern of the union" in 31 percent of the cases.[33]

At the diecast company, workers often refused job transfers and had strong fixed ideas about the relative merits of different jobs and sections. The union strongly defended the right to refuse. In the new suburban plant and the auto parts firm, job transfers were seldom refused by the workers. Their youth, inexperience, lack of knowledge, and inability to differentiate between jobs in the factory contributed to a willingness to accept management judgment. The dominant role of management in providing training for workers and especially the auto parts company's secure future strengthened this willingness.

The difference between the Tokyo diecast plant union and the new diecast plant union on job transfers was seen quite clearly during the formation of the new union. The new union passed out leaflets to workers attacking the Tokyo union on the matter of job transfers. It maintained that workers should, if possible, accept job transfers in the interest of building a bigger, stronger company rather than "selfishly reject job transfers as encouraged by the Tokyo union." As with overtime, what the Tokyo workers viewed as the protection of worker rights was translated as selfishness by the new union.

In the auto parts company, the official procedure for job transfers calls for a representative designated by the company's personnel section to make a job transfer suggestion to a representative of the union executive board. The union is expected to respond within one week. During this time the union representative discusses the company proposal first with the shop stewards in the sections concerned and then

33. *Japan Labor Bulletin*, Vol. 8, No. 11 (November 1969).

with the individuals in question. According to this procedure, the company representative is not to raise the matter directly with the individual worker but to leave it to union officials. A formal order for job transfer is not issued until the individual has agreed to the transfer.

The auto parts union officials said, if the worker could show that he was unable to do the new job, that the new job would reduce his chances for promotion, or that such a shift would not increase production, they would support his refusal. In such cases, the union seeks a substitute acceptable to the company. But if the company can show that the worker is indispensable to raising production, the union officials admitted they would accede to the company request. The auto parts union officers talked constantly about the effect on production as a basic criterion for union decisions.

One way of interpreting the above is that the auto parts union is powerful enough to have forced the firm to channel all job transfer requests through the union, thus making the company give up an important managerial prerogative. From the views and statements of workers, however, this interpretation seems incorrect. It is more likely the company usually counts on union support in such matters, especially if it can justify the transfer in terms of its beneficial effect on production. It uses the union to make it harder for workers to refuse job transfer requests. Expressed in another way, the union is part of the administrative apparatus of the company on the matter of job transfers. A number of factors suggest this interpretation to be correct. First, most workers who had any knowledge of the union regarded the union as weak. The union was built in the early nineteen fifties as a second union with the strong encouragement of management. It is difficult to view the union as a powerful organization that won control from management, or at least a veto power over job transfers, and unlikely that management simply handed over prerogatives to the union without assurance that the union would act in accord with company interests. Second, when workers were asked about the union's role in job transfers they often were unaware of any important role played by the union. Despite the agreement between company and

union, the company often did not go through the agreed
channel but approached workers directly. Generally, the union entered the picture when workers showed reluctance to
accept the job transfer. On one occasion, it was announced
at a workship meeting that the union had persuaded three
workers to accept job transfers. Afterwards, a member of the
union executive board explained,

> Nobody likes to change sections when he has become well
> established, but the union explains the wider purposes and
> common interests that will be served if the individual trans-
> fers. Without putting direct pressure on the individual we
> also say, "Now aren't you misjudging the situation, isn't it
> in your own interest to move, won't this change increase
> your promotion chances since you would be moving from a
> section where everyone has eight years seniority like your-
> self to a section where most guys have only two years
> seniority?"

The absence of a high degree of union autonomy is also
reflected in the views of union leaders toward their job.
Union leaders were asked, "Do you see your union work as
a line of career advancement?" In both companies, almost
without exception, the union leaders found the question difficult to understand. The nature of the enterprise union, as
it is bound to the company, made it hard for them to see
it as a separate entity from the company. The practice in
both companies of promoting union leaders to company supervisory positions or even section chiefs reflected the mesh
between the enterprise union and the company. It militated
against leaders thinking of their union job as a career.

Besides viewing his job as a link in a union career line, a
second characteristic of a Western professional union leader
is mobility. It makes no difference to him for which union he
works. But in Japan, companies and the very nature of enterprise unions discourage outsiders (non-employees of the firm)
from working in the firm's union or even participating in
negotiations.[34] These factors reduce professional union lead-

34. In the public sector unions were not allowed to have non-
employees as bargaining representatives. The refusal of companies to accept
non-employees in their enterprise unions was made formally illegal with

ership at the enterprise level. The absence of professional leadership, in turn, reduces union autonomy and increases dependence upon the firm.

The policy of mutual understanding was based on mutual trust (sōgo shinrai). It was another slogan used by the auto parts company. Management emphasized that it gave confidential information to the workers and the union to build this mutual trust. On a personal level, the relations between union leaders and management personnel were carefully cultivated. The union leaders had free access to the hotel the company management used for entertainment purposes. The union was also brought into the formal operation of the company's recreation program. On all levels there was an attempt to integrate the union with the company's administrative structure for the control of workers; this made it difficult to develop union autonomy to any great degree. Rather than union autonomy, company cooptation seems to have been the dominating characteristic of this case. Mutual understanding based on mutual trust works in the interests of workers and democracy only if the power between management and labor is fairly evenly balanced. When the company holds a commanding edge, as is so often the case in Japan, mutual understanding is little more than a front for company domination.[35]

Union leaders explained that worker criticism of the policy of mutual understanding meant that additional education was required. Besides the question of elitist control, this explanation poses yet another issue. George Orwell made

the 1966 ratification of International Labor Organization Convention 87. I.L.O. 87 specifies that workers have the right to designate their own bargaining representatives irrespective of the employee status of the representative. It is too early to know what changes will result, but the structure of enterprise unionism, the weight of accepted practice, and the conventional views of management and workers, suggest radical changes are unlikely.

35. In Sweden extensive labor-management cooperation to raise production has not led to charges that worker interests are sacrificed. The strength of the Swedish unions and the absence of an excessive identification of workers with their company are probably key factors for this difference. See K. Faxen and E. Pattersson, "Labour-Management Co-operation at the Level of the Undertaking in Sweden," International Labour Review, Vol. 96, No. 2 (August 1967), pp. 194–203.

the following observation in *Gulliver's Travels*: "When they (human beings) are supposedly governed by 'love or reason,' he (the individual) is under continuous pressure to . . . behave and think in exactly the same way as everyone else." [36] The workers at Gujo Auto Parts are ostensibly governed by a view in which mutual understanding is the only reasonable course; all other approaches are officially absent. The official line is that higher production will in the long run insure higher wages and so eradicate any incipient problems. To voice other views is to endanger one's job security or promotion prospects. The totalitarian tendency is inherent when workers, though not compelled to do anything, are "exhorted," "advised," and "educated." Industrial democracy, however, means recognition of different roles and interests for the managers and the managed and cooperation where interests and roles overlap. Such a situation permits expression and regulation of conflict. The attempt to wipe out lines of conflict by instituting an ideology of harmony and unity may increase rather than decrease the potential for violent conflict. Particularly intense conflicts, which are not susceptible to the ideology of harmony and unity, are likely to explode violently, for they lack legitimate channels for their expression. This may be a factor in the nature of Japanese strikes; though most are usually short, some are extremely long, intense, and violent.

The situation at the auto parts firm is not representative of all Japanese unions. But the meaning that mutual understanding, union democracy, and union autonomy took on there reflects a crystallization of tendencies which is present in most Japanese firms. This is true of unions that explicitly assert a policy of mutual cooperation as well as those that purport to follow a leftist ideology. The common characteristics of Japanese unions are excessive identification with the interests of the firm, a desire to avoid conflict, enterprise unionism, and subordination to the authority of management —all rooted in worker and management consciousness.

36. Parentheses added. George Orwell, "Politics vs. Literature: An Examination of Gulliver's Travels," *The Orwell Reader* (New York: Harcourt, Brace, 1956), p. 293.

The dual meaning of the policy of mutual cooperation was best symbolized by worker reference to the union as a gear in the company. This implied a strong criticism of a weak union that lacked autonomy. However, the workers also said that they drew advantages from the union being a gear in the company. They believed the union had a say in many more matters than would be the case if it adopted a more militant posture.

The union, by virtue of its acceptance by management, had access to inside happenings, which provided workers with an all-important predictability. They had a degree of security and knowledge of future developments. This does not necessarily mean workers influenced developments except in a passive sense by relying on management to do the right thing. Above all, the mutual cooperation approach to labor-management relations was a path that minimized conflict and maximized harmony, an all-important consideration in the semi-closed corporate world of the Japanese firm.

The success of this approach in the long run hinges on an economic bargain between union and company. The union gives over to management control in the shop, including even the right to fire under extreme circumstances. In return the union is promised that its members will share in the economic benefits that will result. The nature of the bargain and whether it is kept by the company depends on such factors as market conditions, size of the enterprise, amount of labor mobility, growth rate of firm and industry, and the good will of the company and strength of the union. However, union strength tends to be compromised because it becomes a victim of its call for mutual cooperation. The ultimate weapon, the strike, is inconsistent with the avowed policy of mutual understanding.

The good will of the company in keeping its end of the bargain does not arise from intrinsic kindness but from enlightened self-interest. Japanese companies learned much from the history of the postwar period with its legacy of militant left-wing unions. By keeping their bargain, they buy insurance that present unions will not be replaced by more militant ones. The unions making this economic bargain de-

262 JAPANESE BLUE COLLAR

pend for their existence on the threat created by more militant unions that might replace them.

While workers may sacrifice their rights in the shop,
they may still view this bargain as highly rewarding. The notion that bread, not democracy, is more important is a powerful argument no less among Japanese workers than among
American unionists as seen in the popular image of Jimmy
Hoffa and the Teamsters. If bread can be had without conflict, that is all the better, and makes it consistent with deep-
rooted values in the society. Compared to prewar Japan, this
economic bargain, for all its limitations, is a democratic advance over a time when such bargains were less likely and
employee representation organizations under management
domination more common. It is a democratic advance because it involves a recognition of the workers' right to a
progressively higher standard of living.

SOME EXAMPLES OF VOTING BEHAVIOR

The Tokyo diecast plant was characterized by class-
conscious Socialist party supporters and a well-organized
minority of Communist party supporters. These hardened
urban types differed greatly from the inexperienced, youthful
rural recruits in the auto parts company who showed little
interest in politics.

The differences were reflected in worker voting behavior
at the time of this study. Tokyo municipal elections were
scheduled for the summer of 1965. The diecast plant union,
at a lunchtime meeting the day before the election, recommended three local candidates. Two were Socialists, one a
Communist. The union also announced a company suggestion that the workers not work overtime on election day, but
leave at 4 P.M. to reach the polls before they closed at
6 P.M. This company proposal was backed by a company
announcement that workers would be docked an hour's wages
if, as in the past, they were more than fifteen minutes late
on election day morning. Worker reaction to this set of statements was strong. The union recommended that everyone
come in late next morning as a show of defiance to the new
company policy.

The next morning only three workers of the fourteen-member press sections started work at 8 A.M. Two lived outside Tokyo and were not eligible to vote, and the third believed all politicians to be a bunch of crooks so he never voted in any election. The response of the press workers was duplicated in most sections of the plant. One non-union worker who chose to come in late expressed the views of most workers:

> The managers support the Liberal-Democratic Party, and they know most workers support the progressive revolutionary parties. The company statements are designed to cut down voting among workers in support of the Socialists or Communists. They know many workers need the overtime and might choose to work overtime rather than vote.

In response to the challenge, the majority of workers chose to be late and asserted what they believed to be their legitimate voting rights. They believed management had harassed them and reacted accordingly.

The class-conscious action in assertion of what the workers believed to be their democratic rights was quite unlike the behavior of the Gujo auto parts workers. Many auto parts workers explained that they supported the Democratic Socialist Party (DSP) because of a company-union recommendation to do so.[37] One worker recounted how he came to support the DSP as follows:

> When I became twenty years old, the company people told me many things like asking me to support the DSP, so I vote for them. At election time in an all-employee meeting they ask us, "Please support the DSP." One or two men in the higher management of the company, I guess they are heads of divisions, attend the meeting. First, the union speaker talks and then the man from the company. Or if no one comes from the company, the union man asks us to support the DSP.

Worker discussion of this is matter-of-fact, which indicates many workers saw nothing unusual about the company and union making such joint requests. They are not recounting

37. The Gujo union, as a member of the union federation affiliated with Dōmei, officially supports the Democratic Socialist Party.

a secret, but merely describing the way things are done.[38]
Workers generally followed the recommendation because, as
one worker put it, it is a company policy and "what's in the
company interest is in our interest." [39] Those workers who
supported the Socialist party admitted it only in private for
fear of pressure from union or company.[40] Union officials
denied they stood on the same platform with management
officials, and together with them advised workers to vote for
the DSP, as had been reported by a number of workers. They
pointed out that many young workers could not really distinguish between union and company personnel. Even if the
union was correct and the workers were mistaken, this again
shows how closely meshed union and company were in the
eyes of the workers. It is also easy to see why workers believed criticism of the union involved criticism of the company.[41] The overall docile acceptance of the exhortation to
vote for the DSP or fear of revealing if you actually voted for
the Socialist party should not be interpreted as indicating a
total absence of class-conscious behavior by the auto parts
workers. The very fact that company personnel did not urge
the workers to support the Liberal-Democratic party is, in
itself, a recognition by management that the workers would

38. If this seems strange and extreme, it should be noted that in
postwar elections numerous chairmen and presidents of large corporations
have run for political office. All employees of a firm are expected to support
the candidate and indeed be active in the campaign. Support of the candidate by employees is specifically predicated on the mobilization of enterprise
consciousness that can be seen from slogans like "Just right for the enterprise image of our company," and "On the honor of our company." See
Asahi Evening News, editorial, July 8, 1968.

39. Uchi no kaisha no baai, Minshatō. Kaisha no yuri no tame
(pause) yappari kaisha no purasu wareware no purasu. Dono ten ka wakaran
ga.

40. This contrasts with the Tokyo diecast plant where a number of
workers openly supported the DSP instead of the Socialist or Communist
Parties without fear of retaliation. It is not that the Socialists or Communists are somehow more tolerant of opposition than the Democratic Socialists. The difference does not lie in ideology but in such factors as age
composition and the rural-urban distribution of the labor force.

41. A union official countered that the inability of workers to distinguish union leaders from management officials stemmed from the shallow
history of the labor movement in Japan and the absence of a confrontation
between union and company such as developed in the United States.

not see it in their interests to vote for the LDP. The recommendation must, above all, be understood in the framework of the policy of mutual understanding between union and company.

THE APPEAL OF LEFT-WING IDEOLOGY

Blue-collar workers' attachment to the Marxist parties is founded in the historical development of Japan and present-day realities. Of particular importance are: the repressive conditions in prewar society, the surrender, the sudden burst of freedom decreed by the Occupation, the disorganization of the immediate postwar period, the rapid growth of industry, the authoritarian tendencies of employers and the ruling LDP and Japan's envelopment in the cold war. These are some key factors in the polarization of Japanese politics with blue-collar workers in particular tending to adhere to the Marxist parties. Recent surveys have examined the appeal of socialism to Japanese employees in large firms. Generally, the percentage supporting socialism rises when preferences are solicited and declines sharply when realistic possibilities are probed. It appears somewhat over 40 percent of blue-collar workers in large unionized firms would like to see a socialist society established. For example, the Hitachi Corporation Union conducted a survey of almost all its 10,000 members at the Hitachi city plant in 1967. One question was: "Under capitalism workers are always unhappy, therefore a society based on socialism should be established." Almost 46 percent of middle school graduates (blue-collar) agreed with the statement but support declined markedly to 25.4 percent among high school graduates and to 15.5 percent among university graduates. The "no response" category also declined similarly so that opposition rose from 39 percent for middle school graduates to 64.6 percent among high school graduates and 78.8 percent for university graduates.[42]

Our task is to examine the appeal of left-wing union leaders in the shop and the nature and meaning of their ac-

42. Hitachi Corporation Union, *Ichiman Kumiaiin no Ishiki* (Attitudes of 10,000 Union Members) (Tokyo: The Union, 1969), pp. 125–126.

tivities. What functions are performed for the workers by left-wing leaders that are not fulfilled by alternative leaders?

Because the authority of the Japanese employer has been almost absolute throughout industrialization, even with postwar democratization it is extremely difficult for workers to assert their rights and oppose management in the shop. Worker will to resist is undermined by excessive employee identification with the fortunes of the firm. For the average worker to stand up and demand protection of his rights in the shop is still very hard. Union leaders who oppose management are able to do so by arming themselves with the political ideology of Marxism. Marxism gives them the moral armor to confront management and sustain them in their opposition. The ready availability of Marxist ideology, which permeates the Japanese intellectual class, is well suited for the potential union leader, searching for an anchor to hold him fast in his struggle with management. In this connection, workers, union leaders, management officials, and academicians were asked whether it was possible for them to conceive of militant opposition to management in contemporary enterprise unions without the union leader in question having a Marxist orientation. The answer by all parties was an unequivocal no. In this sense, then, management apprehensions in the two firms about a militant union being a Marxist union were justified.

As political ideology gives the union leader the strength to confront management in the shop, the political slogans and actions of the union leader become symbols for the worker. They symbolize a willingness to oppose management and stand up for the protection of worker's rights and achievement of their demands. While working at the diecast plant, I was at first puzzled why sophisticated and articulate non-Communist workers supported the Communist elements in the union leadership. The reason for this behavior becomes clear when one understands that the political slogans are seen by workers as symbols of a willingness to oppose management in the shop. The left-wing union leader is not elected for his political beliefs, but for the symbolic value of these political beliefs. They indicate that the leader will forcefully stand for workers' interests in the shop. Therefore, the election of such a leader is both an expressive and instrumental act. It is instrumental because it advances worker rights in the shop and expressive because it gives satisfying expression to a state of mind rather than an effort to achieve specific revolutionary objectives. The neglect of the expressive, seemingly irrational elements in man's behavior, often confounds commonsense understanding of political behavior. Such conventional wisdom is based on Western rational models that see men as exclusively making rational choices toward the achievement of instrumental goals.

To say that political ideology is adopted for its symbolic value does not mean that political ideology is neutral in its consequences. On the contrary, it may lead the union on a course of intense struggle either in the factory or in the streets (participating in national political demonstrations). This struggle can be interpreted by the worker as symbolic of a willingness to oppose management and the Government or as action designed to secure fixed political goals or both. Often, however, the workers will not be prepared for intense struggle resulting from notions of class conflict. In other words, workers are not class-conscious in the Marxian sense of recognizing their exploitation, identifying their oppressors as capitalists and taking collective action to build a new society. In this context the charge is sometimes justified that the political tactics of left-wing union leaders betray the interests of the workers. It is also this gap between symbols and commitment that is a factor in the common Japanese phenomenon of militant unions breaking up under the stress of intense struggle (strike) when the workers' livelihood is threatened, and the formation of a management-oriented second union is initiated.

An added element in the struggle against management authority is its entanglement with the conflict between age classes. It is apparent in the young age of the left-wing militants in the shop. Age or generational conflicts are increasing in all industrial societies. It has become commonplace to speak of the search for identity among youth in a rapidly changing society. The search, it is said, makes youth particularly susceptible to the appeals of ideology.[43] This analysis seems especially relevant to Japanese youth. In Japan the age-stratification of the factory, the youthfulness of employees in the rapidly expanding industries, the dislocating effects of a high economic growth rate, and the discrediting of the older generation and their values after the great war, all shape the conflict strikingly. They bring it into the shop, intensify it, and they bind it to the economic class struggle.

Political ideology in unions has multiple purposes and consequences quite different from ideology designed exclusively to secure fixed political goals. The political demonstration, a hallmark of the Japanese labor movement, must be understood primarily as an expressive act designed to call attention to worker discontent at being the "outs." Participation in these events often has the character of a "company outing"; the mobilization of workers commonly takes place through company based loyalties and obligations. Nevertheless, it is difficult in practice to make a determination of what purpose is served by union action; what are the "real" consequences; and how should one evaluate them. It is an area of biases and passions. For example, a common tactic and often a sincere belief of Japanese management, when the company is confronted by a militant union, is to label it Communist and appeal to the workers to reject it on the grounds that the union struggle ignores workers' real interests. Management maintains that the outcome can only be the destruction of the company, and consequently the destruction of worker livelihoods. Yet to label workers dupes misled by Marxist propaganda or as Marxists, fails to understand that workers are responding to political ideology as the symbol of protection of young peoples' and workers' rights and achievement of their demands in a society that has left them as the "outs," subject to the will of employers.

An attraction to Marxist political symbols and action is, of course, not the only possible response of the "outs." An alternative is turning towards nationalism and religion. The

43. For discussions of the generation conflict in industrial societies and the search for identity among youth see: Gerhard Lenski, *op. cit.*, pp. 426–428. Erik Erikson, *Identity: Youth and Crisis* (New York: W. W. Norton, 1968).

rapidly growing Sōka Gakkai movement has shown increasing interest in penetrating labor unions and workshops. It has particular success with miners and socially, politically, and economically marginal groups, especially petty entrepreneurs and workers employed in small-scale industry.[44]

The experience of Japanese Socialists has led them to believe that the main threat to the democratic left comes from a "reactionary government aligned with monopoly capitalists" and not from the totalitarian left. It is this position that sets them off from social democratic unionists in Western Europe. It also goes a long way toward explaining the ambivalent attitude toward the national and international Communist movement. Given the symbolic role of political ideology in the shop, it would be a mistake to take at face value union press releases and stated motivations and goals. These should be distinguished from the consequences of Sōhyō's existence. Sōhyō, for all its revolutionary rhetoric, posturing, and ideologically motivated leadership, arranges for the participation of workers in the industrial relations system; real disruption and revolt would be more likely without this organization.[45] By bargaining with employers over wage levels and staging "struggles" to achieve its objectives, the membership is assured that its interests are being protected and advanced. The position of existing union leadership is thereby strengthened and mutually acceptable conditions are set which make the work force needed by industry available. The union leadership, in turn, is obligated to the

44. The image of Sōka Gakkai appealing to the rootless was sustained in the Tokyo diecast factory where the handful of Sōka Gakkai members were identified by their fellows as introverted, having few social contacts, and having low participation rates in the union. A larger group of Sōka Gakkai members were employed in the suburban diecast plant, primarily the ex-miners who brought their religion with them. This may have been a factor in their rejection of the first union at the Tokyo plant, which they regarded as Communist. Non-Sōka Gakkai members in both plants showed no particular antagonism toward individual Sōka Gakkai members nor did management appear to discriminate against them; but many workers objected to Sōka Gakkai mixing religion with unions and politics.

45. This is an application of a theme elaborated by Prof. Murray Edelman of the Univ. of Wisconsin. Prof. Edelman was kind enough to make available a manuscript entitled "The Conservative Political Consequences of Labor Conflict." It will appear shortly in the book *Essays in Industrial Relations Theory*, Gerald Somers (ed.).

government and business leaders to provide the necessary framework of benefits and posturing which makes this all possible. Itō Mitsuharu points to the informal cooperation between top ranking labor leaders and management as a result of adopting the Spring Offensive tactic.[46] Others note the informal understandings reached by left-wing leaders and management at the enterprise level. This symbiotic exchange process is critical to understanding how Sōhyō or, for that matter the Communist C.G.I.L. union federation of Italy or the C.G.T. in France, can adopt a revolutionary rhetoric but in practice contribute to the strengthening of existing structural arrangements.

The assertion of Japanese workers' interests in the postwar period is inseparable from Marxist ideology. Rising living standards, higher educational levels, and an occupational structure shifting to white-collar employment, however, seem likely to weaken the potency of the Marxist appeal. The growing strength of the Dōmei federation in the private sector points in this direction. Yet those unions espousing mutual understanding and mutual trust between management and labor may also find their policies less viable in the face of a more urban, educated and militant labor force. The strength of Sōhyō's approach should not be underestimated. It has carried out reformist policies which have brought economic, social, political, and psychological benefits to members and non-members; it is the major mass organization which has been able to stand up to management and governmental authority. The growing role of the International Metalworkers Federation–Japan Council may help more unions develop sufficient autonomy to effectively represent worker interests. The emergence of a unified labor movement in the seventies is not as unlikely as it may have appeared just a few years ago. Of one thing we can be sure: with only some twenty-five years of history, the dynamism of Japan's modern labor movement promises great changes in the future.

46. Itō Mitsuharu, "A Structural Analysis of Conservative and Progressive Forces in Japan," *Journal of Social and Political Ideas in Japan*, Vol. 4, No. 2 (August 1966). Originally published in *Tenbō* (February 1965).

CHAPTER VIII

CHANGING CHARACTERISTICS OF
BLUE-COLLAR WORKERS

Throughout Japan's industrialization the web of reciprocal obligations has been a powerful control device committing workers to factory life and making them conform to
company discipline. Superior-subordinate relationships, in
particular, obligated the superior to paternalistic care of his
charge and the subordinate to repay with loyalty and hard
work. Economic insecurity in the city resulting from inadequate social welfare measures and vast underemployment in
the country reinforced and tightened the web. The mutual
interdependence in the factory, where individual will of
necessity was subordinated to group efforts for survival, fits
well the varying patterns of cooperation and stratification
that had been established over the centuries in innumerable
Japanese villages. Judging by the absence of strong revolutionary currents and the failure of workers to organize themselves as an effective social or political force, the structure of
authority as it rests on this web was remarkably absorbent
of successive shock waves emanating from the introduction
of modern technology. Concessions and compromises in interpersonal relations required by involvement in the web are
key elements in understanding the irrelevancy of Marxist expectations of revolutionary social change in the course of
Japanese industrialization.

From the Meiji period onwards the ruling class sought
to make Japan strong, first in the face of Western threats and

then to embark on its imperialist adventure. This required a
policy of rapid industrialization for which the ruling class
closely allied itself with major industrial enterprises. It is not
surprising that after the first great liberalizing reforms of the
Meiji reformation, the ruling class gradually put its stamp
of approval on traditional values and practices designed to
boost the authority of employers in the rapidly developing
industrial firms. This enabled production to continue unin-
terrupted by work stoppages and without the payment of
high wages which would have diverted capital from still
greater efforts at industrialization.

The crushing defeat suffered in World War II and
subsequent reforms by the Occupation caused a severe shock
to the whole prewar structure of authority in the workshop.
With the change in the Occupation policy from reform to
rehabilitation, the restoration of Japanese sovereignty, and
the recovery of confidence by management, the prewar authority relations were re-established, though hardly in the
same way and with the same potency. Too much had
changed. The democratic constitution, the encouragement
given to a free labor movement, a free press, a legalized Socialist opposition, the revolutionary land reform, and above
all the discrediting of traditional values and practices associated with the wartime disaster prevented a return to business
as usual. While the meaning of the democracy the Occupation sought to impose was vague for many Japanese, its
potency as a symbol of the world in which they want to live
is undeniable.

During Japan's rapid industrialization, new organizational forms and practices were legitimated and individual
performance was motivated by traditional values stressing internal harmony, loyalty, and paternalism. This ideology was
quite rational in the sense that it was consistent with generally accepted social values. It would have been irrational
and would have made industrial success problematic to have
ignored these internalized values. In present-day Japan, however, there is a marked change in social values. Management
increasingly is forced to defend traditional practices and to
motivate workers by more universalistic values that stress

ability, performance, and democracy. This creates tensions that become potential sources of further social change.

The research in the diecast and in the auto parts companies pinpointed a number of areas where changes are occurring. These changes are weakening the traditional structure of management authority and creating a more militant worker. In particular, we pointed to labor market changes, the demographic transition, urbanization, higher educational levels, rapid economic growth, rising standards of living, and shifts to capital intensive machine technology located in large-scale firms.

We can expect an intensification of these pressures in the future. But other factors also condition the extent to which authority relations will be eroded. Most important perhaps will be whether Japan can maintain the growth rate of the last decade. Any flattening of the growth curve over a long period will have enormous consequences for management authority in the shop, worker behavior, and the political involvement of labor unions. The actual effect of trade liberalization, with its influx of foreign capital and goods into Japan, will also have an important impact. The auto parts firm used trade liberalization to justify holding down wages. Its management appealed to workers to work together to raise productivity in order to insure the survival of the firm. There is ample evidence that Japanese employers increasingly are using such appeals, and that, to some extent, they are meeting with success. Not surprisingly, the trade liberalization issue is provoking a new sense of nationalism with managers playing the role of defenders of the national interest. That workers see themselves as part of a team combatting the foreign threat was clearly demonstrated in the auto parts firm. During a company athletic meet, the workers put on a skit of an auto race in which a Volkswagen disintegrated when confronted with the Japanese entry. However, trade liberalization also leads toward a consolidation of firms and unions in the auto industry. As a result, unions become accustomed to think in terms of industry-wide problems and more conscious of international standards for wages and work conditions; this serves to reduce enterprise consciousness.

These pressures do not mean the resilient web of tradition has suddenly gone slack. Despite reduced management authority in the shop and a greater democratization of industrial relations, it is a gradual change consistent with Japan's historical legacy. Our findings such as changes in the wage structure and the meaning of *giri*, show that social change is consistently hedged by a firm grip on the past. Sometimes past form was maintained, other times past content. Management shows great ingenuity in improvising, streamlining, and adapting traditional values and practices to meet modern requirments. What distinguishes conservative societies like Japan from other more tradition-free societies is the degree to which their actors are skillful and under compulsion to link present experiences with past values and practices.

One striking way many ongoing changes are incorporated in the web of tradition is the persisting role of the corporate world of the factory as a containing framework. While numerous indicators reveal an increased egalitarianism in the firm, there are far fewer signs that the exclusive view of the factory is breaking down. The collectivist frame of action, while not unchanging, is persistent.

In the West, universalistic egalitarian principles expressed in class loyalties and the union movement, and the individualistic conception of merit have been competitive values that divided worker loyalties and diluted work motivation. In Japan, the collective conception of merit and an egalitarian spirit limited to a given firm are supportive of high work motivation. Though a successful formula for raising production, it is not without tensions. It often leads to subordination of individual employee interests to a collective good as defined by management. Present mass consumption based values and the changing labor market, however, permit workers to be more able and willing to reject management definitions and substitute their own individual solutions for collective ones they judge inadequate.

Growing similarities between factories in Japan and in advanced western nations are apparent. The increasing direct reward of achievement, the growing role of impersonal rules, the weakening of interpersonal loyalties in a traditional sense, and a rising inter-firm mobility are but a few clear convergences. How can we resolve the contradiction between the evidence for continuity and the evidence for the convergence hypothesis? We suggest the convergence hypothesis and the opposing position that cultural differences will be preserved are essentially responses to wrong questions. To say industrial societies are becoming more similar than dissimilar, although seemingly true with respect to Japan and the advanced countries of the West, is after all not a very profound observation. Classifications using the tradition versus modernity oppositions are poor descriptions of empirical complexities and obscure more interesting questions. What is the relationship between universal tendencies of industrialization, and unique cultural and sociostructural identities? What is the importance of the historical timing of industrialization? The interactions of these factors and the changes and accommodations that flow from them are likely to produce societies whose national identities are distinct. Of course, the solution is not simply to emphasize national differences. We found the concept of functional equivalents a useful alternative in ordering our data.

Present changes in the direction of convergence cannot be projected to assume the disappearance of distinct Japanese practices. Human actors are imbued with historical values and socially defined needs. We cannot confine ourselves to speak of organizational requirements based on given levels of industrial technology. Clark Kerr and his associates who argue for the convergence hypothesis speak of industrial man as a new kind of person. They see industrial man as a creature of technological history only; but industrial man is also a creature of political and cultural history. E. P. Thompson caught this sense well in his discussion of the making of the English working class:

> The making of the working class . . . was not the spontaneous generation of the factory-system. Nor should we think of an external force—the "industrial revolution"— working upon some nondescript undifferentiated raw material of humanity, and turning it out at the other end as a

"fresh race of beings." The changing productive relations and working conditions of the Industrial Revolution were imposed, not upon raw material, but upon the free-born Englishman—and the free-born Englishman as Paine had left him or as the Methodists had moulded him. The factory hand or stockinger was also the inheritor of Bunyan, of remembered village rights, of notions of equality before the law, of craft traditions. He was the object of massive religious indoctrination and the creator of new political traditions. The working class made itself as much as it was made.[1]

Alexander Gerschenkron notes that, in principle, every historical event changes the course of all subsequent events. While there is growing convergence among industrial nations when using aggregate measures of education and consumption, the convergence appears to be asymptotic. Detailed explanations of behavior will continue to require, though in declining importance, a knowledge of historical identities.

This has implications for those who see the case of Japan as a middle road experiment to industrialization between the extremes of the Soviet Russian and Western European experience. This viewpoint implies that Japan may serve as a model for the contemporary technologically underdeveloped countries. The notion of Japan as a middle road experiment is at best a figure of speech and a misleading one at that. G. C. Allen, in a paraphrasing of Schumpeter, has suggested "every case of economic development is a 'historical individual' and had better be treated as such." While the industrial revolution certainly introduces common imperatives to industrializing nations, their combination with the unique historical experiences of each country denies the simple applicability of one country's experience to another. Even China, which purports to follow the Marxist-Leninist model as developed in Soviet Russia, has found it necessary to originate its own variety of rapid industrialization. Although each successive level of industrialization may open common options and close others, the actual choices made by a people

1. E. P. Thompson, *The Making of the English Working Class* (New York: Random House, 1963), p. 194.

are in terms of the subtle interactions between the common options and its specific social, political, and cultural history. This also applies to the critical role of blue-collar workers in the industrial process. It should be quite clear that the kinds of specific interpersonal and authority relationships at the shop level that have contributed to the rapid industrialization of Japan would be almost impossible to duplicate in today's technologically underdeveloped countries, and most likely they would be viewed as highly undesirable as well.

To return to one of the questions posed in this research: May contemporary blue-collar workers be viewed as tradition bound, or is the term tradition bound inappropriate? The cynicism and skepticism of the urban, high-school educated, and mobile Tokyo diecast workers, their willingness to exercise civil rights, their willingness to oppose management, their "consumption fever," their competitiveness, and their instrumental use of traditional relationships are characteristics that can hardly be described as tradition bound and they are increasingly common. This profile of the Tokyo diecast workers does not easily fit any image of the Japanese put forth by such scholars as Ruth Benedict and James Abegglen. It suggests there has been rapid social change in the postwar period. It also casts doubt on the strength and extent of the alleged Japanese tradition, with its "holy trinity" of subordination, group loyalties, and non-competition. The above characteristics point to a great deal of conflict. It seems likely the stereotype of the submissive, loyal, and non-competitive Japanese worker has been exaggerated.

According to this "holy trinity," the strength of traditional values and practices is the key factor accounting for the weakness of Marxist ideology in Japan. While undoubtedly true, this generalization ignores the symbiotic relationship that exists between tradition and the revolutionary appeal of Marxism. The stability flowing from traditional authority relationships, in dialectic fashion, helps create the conflict that is expressed in terms of Marxist ideology. This is relevant to the assessment of the future appeal of Marxism to Japanese workers. The symbolism of Marxism will continue to appeal to Japanese workers as long as management continues to assert its authority in traditional terms. Should such ideology diminish in its appeal in the future, it will not be simply because of rising standards of living and educational levels, but because workers no longer fear retaliation in their efforts to stand up to management's authority in the shop.

However strong tradition was, it is clear there has also been a loosening of the web and the ties of belonging with successive stages of industrialization and war. The search for a lost security may be a common element of traditionalism in Japan and in the Western countries. Increasingly Japanese workers face a growing freedom and material abundance combined with a loss of the sense of belonging to and identification with nature, clan, and religion. The worker, by virtue of the changes taking place, will become freer to develop and control his individual existence. At the same time, it is questionable that the business firm of the future can sustain the predictability, security, and control established in past sociostructural forms. With increasing independence and a release from group ties, how will workers use their new independence? Will they become more alienated with a consequent decline in their "will to work"? Will they seek to reintegrate their lives in a way consistent with democratic values or will they seek submission to some new authority? Eric Fromm has observed that modern man seeks to escape from the responsibilities of freedom. These issues are hardly unique to the Japanese.

SELECTED BIBLIOGRAPHY

ENGLISH LANGUAGE MATERIALS ON JAPAN [1]

Abegglen, James. *The Japanese Factory*. Glencoe: Free Press, 1958.
———. "Subordination and Autonomy Attitudes of Japanese Workers," *American Journal of Sociology*, Vol. 63, No. 1 (September, 1957).
Ayusawa, Iwao. *A History of Labor in Modern Japan*. Honolulu: East-West Center Press, 1966.
Azumi, Koya. "Length of Work Life of Japanese Men," *Monthly Labor Review*, Vol. 81 (December, 1958).
———. "Modernization and Particularism: The Case of Japanese Employment." Paper presented at the 1966 meeting of the American Sociological Association.
Ballon, Robert. *Japan's Life-Time Salary System*. Bulletin No. 11, Tokyo: Sophia University Socio-Economic Institute, 1966.
———. (ed.). *Doing Business in Japan*. Rutland and Tokyo: Charles E. Tuttle, rev. ed., 1968.
———. (ed.). *The Japanese Employee*. Rutland and Tokyo: Charles E. Tuttle, 1969.
Befu, Harumi. "Gift-Giving and Social Reciprocity in Japan," *France-Asia/Asia*, No. 188 (Winter, 1966–67).
Bellah, Robert. *Tokugawa Religion: The Values of Pre-Industrial Japan*. Glencoe: Free Press, 1957.
———. "Reflections on the Protestant Ethic Analogy in Asia," *Journal of Social Issues*, Vol. 14 (January, 1963).
Bendix, Reinhard. "A Case Study in Cultural and Educational Mobility: Japan and the Protestant Ethic," in *Social Structure and Mobility in Economic Development*, Neil Smelser and Seymour Lipset (eds.), Chicago: Aldine Publishing Company, 1966.
Benedict, Ruth. *The Chrysanthemum and the Sword*. Boston: Houghton-Mifflin, 1946.
Bennett, John. "Tradition, Modernity and Communalism in Japan's

---

1. This list includes Japanese statistical compilations published with English headings.

Modernization," *Journal of Social Issues*, Vol. 24, No. 4 (October, 1968).

————. and Ishino, Iwao. *Paternalism in the Japanese Economy.* Minneapolis: University of Minnesota Press, 1963.

Broadbridge, Seymour. *Industrial Dualism in Japan.* Chicago: Aldine Publishing Company, 1966.

The Center for Japanese Social and Political Studies. *The Japan Interpreter*, formerly *Journal of Social and Political Ideas in Japan.* Tokyo: The Center. The Center was established in April, 1962 and the Journal is designed to transmit to foreign readers ideas currently being expressed by Japanese intellectuals.

Chandler, Margaret K. "Management Rights: Made in Japan," *Columba Journal of World Business* (Winter, 1966).

Cole, Allen B. *Political Tendencies of Japanese in Small Enterprises.* New York: Institute of Pacific Relations, 1959.

————. et al. *Socialist Parties in Postwar Japan.* New Haven: Yale University Press, 1966.

Cole, Robert E. "Japanese Workers, Unions, and the Marxist Appeal," *The Japan Interpreter*, Vol. 6, No. 2 (Summer, 1970).

————. "The Theory of Institutionalization: Permanent Employment and Tradition in Japan," *Economic Development and Cultural Change*, forthcoming.

Cook, Alice H. *Japanese Trade Unionism.* Ithaca: Cornell University Press, 1966.

Dator, James A. "The 'Protestant Ethic' in Japan," *The Journal of Developing Areas*, Vol. 1, No. 1 (October, 1966).

Dore, Ronald (ed.). *Aspects of Social Change in Modern Japan.* Princeton: Princeton University Press, 1967.

————. *City Life in Japan.* Berkeley: University of California Press, 1963.

East-West Center. *The Role of the "Second Union" in Labor Management Relations in Japan*, Occasional Papers of Research Translations, Institute of Advanced Projects, Translation Series No. 3, Honolulu, 1964.

Fujita, Yoshitaka. *Wages and Labor Situation in Today's Japan.* Tokyo: Japan Federation of Employers' Associations, 1965.

Fukutake, Tadashi. *Man and Society in Japan.* Tokyo: Tokyo University Press, 1962.

Gibney, Frank. *Five Gentlemen of Japan.* Rutland: Charles E. Tuttle Company, 1953.

Gotō, Motō. "Political Awareness Among the Japanese, On the Asahi Shinbun Public Opinion Survey," *Japan Quarterly*, Vol. 14, No. 2 (April–June, 1967).

Hagen, Everett. "Some Implications of Personality Theory for the Theory of Industrial Relations," *Industrial and Labor Relations Review*, Vol. 18, No. 3 (April, 1965).

Hall, John. "Feudalism in Japan—A Reassessment," *Comparative Studies in Society and History*. Vol. 5, No. 1 (October, 1962).

———, and Beardsley, Richard. *Twelve Doors to Japan*. New York: McGraw-Hill, 1965.

Hepler, Chester W. "Labor Boss System in Japan," *Monthly Labor Review*, Vol. 68, No. 1 (January, 1949).

Ishino, Iwao. "Motivational Factors in a Japanese Labor Supply Organization," *Human Organization*, Vol. 15, No. 2 (Summer, 1956).

———. "The Oyabun-Kobun: A Japanese Ritual Kinship Institution." *American Anthropologist*, Vol. 55, No. 5 (1953).

Itō, Takkichi. "The High Growth of the Japanese Economy and the Problems of Small Enterprises," *The Developing Economies*, Vol. 1, No. 2 (July–December, 1963).

Jansen, Marius B. (ed.). *Changing Japanese Attitudes Toward Modernization*. Princeton: Princeton University Press, 1965.

———. "Three Slogans of Modernization in Japan." Paper presented to International Conference on the Problems of Modernization in Asia, University of Korea, 1965.

Japan Ammonium Sulphate Industry Association. *Impact of Technological Change on Labor in Chemical Industry*. Wage and Hour Study Team, Tokyo: The Association, 1966.

Japan Federation of Employers' Associations, *JFEA News*. Tokyo: The Federation.

Japan Institute of Labour. *Japan's Labor Statistics*. Tokyo: The Institute, 1967.

———. *Japan Labor Bulletin*. Tokyo: The Institute, published monthly from 1962 to present. Prior to 1962 the Japan Labor Bulletin was published as an organ of the Ministry of Labor.

Japan Institute of Labour. *The Changing Patterns of Industrial Relations*. Tokyo: The Institute, 1965.

Japan International Social Security Association. *Study of Social Insurance Schemes in Japan*. Tokyo: The Association, 1965.

Japanese Government. Economic Planning Agency. *Economc Survey of Japan*. Tokyo: The Japan Times, published annually.

———. Ministry of Health and Welfare. *Social Welfare Services in Japan*. Tokyo: The Ministry, 1965.

———. Ministry of Labor. *Japan Labour Legislation 1968*. Tokyo: Institute of Labor Policy, 1968.

———. ———. *Year Book of Labor Statistics*. Tokyo: The Ministry, published annually from 1949.

———. ———. Women's and Minor's Bureau. *Status of Women in Japan*. Tokyo: The Ministry, 1962.

———. ———. Women's and Minor's Bureau. *Women Workers in Japan, 1964*. Tokyo: The Ministry, 1964.

———. Office of the Prime Minister. *Annual Report of the Family Income and Expenditure Survey*. Tokyo: The Office, 1966.

Japanese Government. Social Insurance Agency. *Outline of Social Insurance in Japan*. Tokyo: The Agency, 1966.

Joint Wage Research Center. *Statistical Report on Wages in Japan, 1955–1964.* Tokyo: The Center, 1966.

Kaji, T. "Conditions of Life Among Japanese Miners," *International Trade Union Movement*, Vol. 3 (November–December, 1923).

Karsh, Bernard and Solomon B. Levine. "Present Dilemmas of the Japanese Labor Movement," Industrial Relations Research Association, Proceedings (Spring, 1962).

Kinai, Senji. "The Slums of Kamagasaki," in *The Japanese Image*, Maurice Schneps and Alvin Cox (eds.). Tokyo: Orient/West, 1965.

Kirkup, James. *Japan Industrial*. Vols. I and II, Tokyo: Perfect English Publicity, 1964.

Komai, Hiroshi. *Changing Pattern of Japanese Attitudes Toward Work: A Consequence of Recent High Economic Growth*. Tokyo: Institute of Population Problems, 1969.

Komiya, Ryūtarō (ed.). *Postwar Economc Growth in Japan*. Berkeley: University of California Press, 1966.

Kublin, Hyman. *Asian Revolutionary: The Life of Sen Katayama*. Princeton: Princeton University Press, 1964.

Levine, Solomon B. "Unionization of White Collar Employees in Japan," in *White Collar Trade Unions*, Adolf Sturmthal (ed.). Urbana: University of Illinois Press, 1964.

———. *Industrial Relations in Postwar Japan*. Urbana: University of Illinois Press, 1958.

———. "Labor Markets and Collective Bargaining in Japan," in *The State and Economic Enterprise in Japan*, William W. Lockwood (ed.). Princeton: Princeton University Press, 1965.

Lockwood, William W. *The Economic Development of Japan*. Princeton: Princeton University Press, 1954.

———, (ed.). *The State and Economic Enterprise in Japan*. Princeton: Princeton University Press, 1965.

Martin, Samuel. "Speech Levels in Japan and Korea," in *Language in Culture and Society*, Dell Hymes (ed.). New York: Harper and Row, 1964.

Minobe, Ryokichi. "People's Living After Economic Growth," *Contemporary Japan*, Vol. 28, No. 3 (May, 1966).

Misawa, Jun. "Political Consciousness of Organized Labor," *Japan Socialist Review*, No. 24 (October 15, 1962).

Mitsufuji, Tadashi. "The Impact of Joint Councils on Collective Bargaining in Japan," in *Social and Economic Aspects of Japan*, Uchida, Naosaku and Ikeda Kotarō (eds.). Tokyo: Economic Institute of Seijo University, 1967.

Miyamoto, Yoshiharu Scott. "Contemporary Japan: The Individual and the Group," *Transactions of the American Philosophical Society*, New Series, Vol. 50 (Part I, 1960).

Mori, Hidete. "The Longshoremen of Kobe Harbor," in *The Japanese Image*, Maurice Schneps and Alvin Cox (eds.). Tokyo: Orient/West, 1965.

Nakane, Chie. "Towards a Theory of Japanese Social Structure: An Unilateral Society," *The Economic Weekly* (Bombay), Vol. 17 (February, 1965).

————. *Kinship and Economic Organization in Rural Japan*. New York: Humanities Press, 1967.

Odaka, Kunio. "An Iron Workers' Community in Japan: A Study in the Sociology of Industrial Groups," *American Sociological Review*, Vol. 15 (April, 1950).

————. "Industrial Workers' Identification with Union and Management in Postwar Japan," *American Journal of Sociology* (Spring, 1954).

————. "Work and Leisure; As Viewed by Japanese Industrial Workers." Paper presented at the Sixth World Congress of Sociology, Evian, 1966.

————, and Nishihara, Shigeki. "Social Mobility in Japan: A Report on the 1955 Survey of Social Stratification and Social Mobility in Japan," *East Asian Cultural Studies*, Vol. 4, No. 14 (March, 1965).

Ōkochi, Kazuo. *Labor in Modern Japan*. Tokyo: Science Council of Japan, 1958.

Olson, Lawrence. *Dimensions of Japan*. New York: American Universities Field Staff, 1963.

Oshima, H. T. "Veblen on Japan," *Social Research*, Vol. 10, No. 4 (November, 1943).

Plath, David W. *The After Hours: Modern Japan and the Search for Enjoyment*. Berkeley: University of California Press, 1964.

Riichi, Yokomitsu. "Machine," trans. E. Seidensticker, *Modern Japanese Authors*, Vol. 10. Tokyo: Hara Shobo, 1965.

Scalapino, Robert. *The Japanese Communist Movement, 1920–1966*. Berkeley: University of California Press, 1967.

————, and Junnosuke, Masumi. *Parties and Politics in Contemporary Japan*. Berkeley: University of California Press, 1962.

Shindo, Takejiro. *Labor in the Japanese Cotton Industry*. Tokyo: Japan Society for the Promotion of Science, 1961.

Shirai, Taishirō. "The Impact of Rapid Economic Growth on the Employment Structure in Japan." Paper presented to Conference on Problems of Employment in Economic Development, Geneva, 1963.

Soukup, James R. "Labor and Politics in Japan: A Study of Interest Group Attitudes and Activities," *The Journal of Politics*, Vol. 22 (1960).

Sumiya, Mikio. *Social Impact of Industrialization in Japan.* Tokyo: Japanese National Commission for UNESCO, 1963.
Taira, Koji. "Characteristics of Japanese Labor Markets," *Economic Development and Cultural Change,* Vol. 10 (January, 1962).
————. "The Labor Market in Japanese Development," *British Journal of Industrial Relations,* Vol. 2, No. 2 (July, 1964).
Takiji, Kobayashi. "The Cannery Boat," trans. anonymously, *Modern Japanese Literature.* Rutland: Charles E. Tuttle Company, 1956.
Tominaga, Ken'ichi. "Occupational Mobility in Japanese Society: Analysis of Labor Market in Japan," *Journal of Economic Behavior* (Tokyo), Vol. 2, No. 1 (April, 1962).
————. "Some Sociological Comments on Observations of Japanese Society by Western Social Scientists." Paper presented at the University of Michigan, Center for Japanese Studies, Ann Arbor, 1968.
Totten, George. *The Social Democratic Movement in Prewar Japan.* New Haven: Yale University Press, 1966.
Tsuda, Masumi. *The Basic Structure of Japanese Labor Relations.* Tokyo: The Society for the Social Sciences, Musashi University, 1965.
Umemura, M. "An Analysis of Employment Structure in Japan," *Hitotsubashi Journal of Economics,* Vol. 2, No. 2 (1962).
Veblen, Thorstein. "The Opportunity of Japan," *The Journal of Race Development,* Vol. 6 (July, 1915).
Vogel, Ezra. *Japan's New Middle Class.* Berkeley: University of California Press, 1963.
Whitehill, Jr. Arthur and Takezawa, Shin'ichi. *The Other Worker.* Honolulu: East-West Center Press, 1968.
Wilkinson, Thomas O. *The Urbanization of Japanese Labor 1868–1955.* Amherst: University of Massachusetts Press, 1965.
Yamanaka, Tokutaro (ed.). *Small Business in Japan.* Tokyo: Japan Times, no date.
Yoshino, M. Y. *Japan's Managerial System.* Cambridge: MIT Press, 1968.

GENERAL ENGLISH LANGUAGE MATERIALS

Axelrod, Morris. "Urban Structure and Social Participation," *American Sociological Review,* 21 (February, 1956).
Bendix, Reinhard. "Concepts and Generalizations in Comparative Sociological Studies," *American Sociological Review,* Vol. 28, No. 4 (August, 1963).
————. "Tradition and Modernity Reconsidered," *Comparative Studies in Society and History,* Vol. 9, No. 3 (April, 1967).
Blau, Peter. *Exchange and Power in Social Life.* New York: John Wiley, 1959.

Blauner, Robert. *Alienation and Freedom: The Factory Worker and His Industry.* Chicago: University of Chicago Press, 1964.

Chinoy, Ely. *Automobile Workers and the American Dream.* Garden City: Doubleday, 1955.

Dalton, Melville. "Informal Factors in Career Achievement," *American Journal of Sociology*, Vol. 56 (March, 1951).

Department of Research, AFL–CIO. "Seniority-Fair Play on the Job," *AFL-CIO American Federationist* (September, 1961).

Dubin, Robert. *The World of Work.* Englewood Cliffs: Prentice-Hall, 1958.

———. "Industrial Workers' Worlds: A Study of the 'Central Life Interests' of Industrial Workers," *Social Problems*, Vol. 3, No. 3 (January, 1956).

Dunlop, John. *Industrial Relations Systems.* New York: Henry Holt, 1958.

Edelman, Murray. *The Symbolic Uses of Politics.* Urbana: University of Illinois Press, 1964.

Eisenstadt, S. N. *From Generation to Generation.* New York: Free Press, 1956.

———. *Essays in Comparative Institutions.* New York: John Wiley, 1965.

Erikson, Erik. *Identity: Youth and Crisis.* New York: W. W. Norton, 1968.

Faunce, William (ed.). *Readings in Industrial Sociology.* New York: Appleton-Century-Crofts, 1967.

Faxen, K. and E. Pettersson. "Labour-Management Co-operation at the Level of the Undertaking in Sweden," *International Labour Review*, Vol. 96, No. 2 (August, 1967).

Friedman, Georges. *Industrial Society.* Glencoe: Free Press, 1955.

Geertz, Clifford. "Ideology as a Cultural System," in *Ideology and Discontent*, David Apter (ed.), New York: Free Press, 1964.

Gerschenkron, Alexander. *Economic Backwardness in Historical Perspective.* New York: Frederick Praeger, 1962.

Gerth, H. H. and C. Wright Mills. *Character and Social Structure: The Psychology of Social Institutions.* New York: Harcourt, Brace, 1953.

Glick, Paul. *American Families.* New York: John Wiley, 1957.

Goffman, Erving. "Cooling the Mark Out: Some Aspects of Adaptation to Failure," *Psychiatry*, Vol. 15 (November, 1952).

———. *Asylums.* New York: Doubleday and Company, 1961.

Gouldner, Alvin. *Patterns of Industrial Bureaucracy.* Glencoe: Free Press, 1954.

———. "Reciprocity and Autonomy in Functional Theory," in *Symposium on Sociological Theory*, Llewellyn Gross (ed.). New York: Harper and Row, 1959.

Gouldner, Alvin. "The Problems of Succession and Bureaucracy," in *Studies in Leadership: Leadership and Democratic Action*, Alvin Gouldner (ed.). New York: Harper and Row, 1950.

Guest, Robert. "Managerial Succession in Complex Organizations," *American Journal of Sociology*, Vol. 68 (1962–63).

Gusfield, Joseph. "Tradition and Modernity: Misplaced Polarities in the Study of Social Change," *The American Journal of Sociology*, Vol. 72, No. 4 (January, 1967).

Higgins, Benjamin. "The Dualistic Theory of Underdeveloped Areas," in *Leading Issues in Development Economics*, Gerald Meier (ed.). New York: Oxford University Press, 1964.

Hoselitz, Bert and Wilbert Moore (eds.). *Industrialization and Society*. The Hague: UNESCO-Mouton, 1966.

Hutton, J. H. *Caste in India: Its Nature, Function and Origin*. London: Oxford University Press, 1951.

Katz, Fred. *Autonomy and Organization*. New York: Random House, 1968.

Kerr, Clark, *et al*. *Industrialism and Industrial Man*. Cambridge: Harvard University Press, 1960.

Lens, Sidney. *The Crisis of American Labor*. New York: A. S. Barnes, 1961.

Lenski, Gerhard. *Power and Privilege*. New York: McGraw-Hill, 1966.

Lerner, Daniel. *The Passing of Traditional Society*. Glencoe: Free Press, 1962.

Lippman, Walter. "On the Importance of Being Free," *Encounter*, Vol. 143 (August, 1965).

Lipset, Seymour, *et al*. *Union Democracy*. Glencoe: Free Press, 1956.

Merton, Robert. *Social Theory and Social Structure*. Glencoe: Free Press, 1957.

Meyers, Frederic. *The Analytic Meaning of Seniority*. University of California, Institute of Industrial Relations. Reprinted from the 18th Annual Meeting Industrial Relations Research Association, 1965.

Moore, Wilbert. *Social Change*. Englewood Cliffs: Prentice-Hall, 1963.

———. "A Reconsideration of Theories of Social Change." *American Sociological Review*, Vol. 25 (December, 1960).

Nosow, Sigmund, and William Form (eds.). *Man, Work and Society*. New York: Basic Books, 1962.

Organization for Economic Development and Co-operation. *Wages and Labour Mobility*. Paris: OECD, 1965.

Orwell, George. "Politics vs. Literature: An Examination of 'Gulliver's Travels,'" *The Orwell Reader*. New York: Harcourt, Brace, 1956.

Parsons, Talcott. *The Social System*. Glencoe: Free Press, 1951.

Paukert, Felix. "Social Security and Income Redistribution: A Comparative Study," *International Labour Review*, Vol. 98, No. 5 (November, 1968).

Riesman, David and Warner Bloomberg Jr. "Work and Leisure: Fusion or Polarity," in *Research in Industrial and Human Relations*. C. M. Arensbert *et al.* (eds.). New York: Harper and Brothers, 1957.

Roy, Donald. "Quota Restriction and Goldbricking in a Machine Shop," *The American Journal of Sociology*, Vol. 57 (March, 1952).

Ryder, Norman. "The Cohort as a Concept in the Study of Social Change," *American Sociological Review*, Vol. 30, No. 6 (December, 1965).

Sayles, Leonard. *Behavior of Industrial Work Groups*. New York: John Wiley, 1958.

————, and George Strauss. *The Local Union: Its Place in the Industrial Plant*. New York: Harper and Brothers, 1953.

Simmel, Georg. "Notes on the Stranger," *The Sociology of Georg Simmel*, translated and edited by Kurt H. Wolff. Glencoe: Free Press, 1950.

Shostak, Arthur and William Gomberg (eds.). *Blue-Collar World*. Englewood Cliffs: Prentice-Hall, 1964.

Smith, Michael. "Pre-Industrial Stratification Systems," in *Social Structure and Mobility in Economic Development*, Neil Smelser and Seymour Lipset (eds.). Chicago: Aldine Publishing Company, 1966.

Sorokin, Pitirim. *Social and Cultural Dynamics*. Boston: Porter Sargent, 1957.

Taylor, George. "Seniority Concepts," *Arbitration Today*. Proceedings of the Eighth Annual Meeting of the National Academy of Arbitrators, Washington, Bureau of National Affairs, 1955.

Thompson, E. P. *The Making of the English Working Class*. New York: Random House, 1963.

Veblen, Thorstein. *The Theory of Business Enterprise*. New York: Scribner's, 1915.

Waisanen, Fred and Alfredo Mendez. "Some Correlates of Functional Literacy," Paper presented to the Inter-American Congress in Psychology, Miami, 1964.

Walker, Charles and Robert Guest. *The Man on the Assembly Line*. Cambridge: Harvard University Press, 1952.

Whyte, William Foote. *Money and Motivation*. New York: Harper and Brothers, 1955.

Wilensky, Harold. "Careers, Life Style, and Social Integration," *International Social Science Journal*, Vol. 12 (Fall, 1960).

Wray, Donald. "Marginal Men of Industry: The Foreman," *American Journal of Sociology*, 54 (January, 1949).

JAPANESE LANGUAGE MATERIALS

Fujita, Wakao. *Dai Ni Kumiai* (The Second Union). Tokyo: Nihon Hyōron Shinsha, 1960.

——, Ujihara Shōjirō, and Funahashi Naomichi. *Nihon-gata Rōdō Kumiai to Nenkō Seido* (Japanese-Style Labor Unions and the Age-Seniority System). Tokyo: Shinbunsha, 1963.

Hazama Hiroshi. *Nihon-teki Keiei no Keifu* (The Genealogy of Japanese-Style Management). Tokyo: Noritsu Kyokai, 1963.

——. *Nihon Rōmu Kanrishi Kenkyū* (Studies in the History of Japanese Labor and Management Relations). Tokyo: Diamond Co., 1964.

Inoue, Akira. "Shūgyō Kisoku no Jittai to Sono Mondaiten" (Actual Conditions of Work Rules and Problems), *Kikan Rōdōhō* (Labor Law Agency), No. 48, Vol. 13 (Summer, 1963).

Japan Federation of Employers' Associations. *Seishōnen no Rōmu-kanri* (Personnel Management of Youth). Tokyo: Federation, 1963.

JAPANESE GOVERNMENT

Ministry of Labor. *Sengo Rōdō Keizaishi* (Postwar Labor Economic History). Tokyo: Labor Laws Association, 1966.

——. *Sengo Rōdō Keizaishi: Kaisetsuhen* (Postwar Labor Economic History: Explanatory Volume). Tokyo: Labor Laws Association, 1968.

——. *Rōdō Idō, Sengo no Suii to Genjō* (Labor Mobility: Present Conditions and Changes in the Postwar Period). Tokyo: The Ministry, 1968.

——. *Shinki Chugakukō Sotsugyō Shūshokusha no Shūshoku Rishoku Jōkyō Chōsa* (Research on the Circumstances of Employment Separation of Recently Employed Middle School Graduates). Tokyo: The Ministry, 1969.

——. *Rōdō Hakusho* (Labor White Paper). Tokyo: The Ministry, published annually.

——. *Chingin Kōzō Kihon Chōsa* (Wage Structure Basic Survey). Tokyo: The Ministry, published annually.

Office of the Prime Minister. *Rōdōryoku Chōsa Hōkoku* (Report of the Labor Force Survey). Tokyo: The Office, published annually.

——. *Shūgyō Kōzō Kihon Chōsa Hōkoku* (Employment Status Survey), Tokyo: The Office, published every three years.

Kida, Minoru. *Nippon Buraku* (The Japanese Village). Tokyo: Iwanami New Series, 1957.

Kurozumi, Akira. *Teinensei Taishokukin Taishoku Nenkin* (Retirement System: Lump Sum Retirement Allowances and Retirement Pensions). Tokyo: Rōdō Junposha, 1966.

Morioka, Kiyomi. "Rōdōsha Kazoku ni okeru Jidō Yōikuhi no Kenkyū (I) -Kazoku Shūki kara Mita Seikatsu Kōzō o Chūshin ni-" (Study on the Child-Rearing Expenses of the Worker Family, Part I: Analysis of Life Organization in Terms of Family Cycle), *Kikan Shakai Hoshō Kenkyū* (Quarterly of Social Security Research), Vol. 2, No. 3 (December, 1966).

Nakane, Chie. "Nihon-teki Shakai Kōzō no Hakken: Tan'itsu Shakai no Riron" (An Approach to Social Structure of Japan-Theory of a Unitary Society), *Chūō Kōron* (Central Review), Vol. 79, No. 5 (May, 1964).

————. *Tate Shakai no Ningen Kankei: Tan'itsu Shakai no Riron* (Human Relations in a Vertical Society: A Theory on a Unitary Society). Tokyo: Kōdansha, 1967.

Odaka, Kunio. "Sangyō no Kindaika to Keiei no Minshuka," (Modernization of Industry and Democratization of Management), *Chūō Kōron* (Central Review) (July, 1961).

Okamoto, Hideaki. *Nihon no Genba Kantokusha* (Shop Floor Supervisors in Japan). Tokyo: Industrial Training Association, 1964.

————. *Kōgyōka to Genba Kantokusha* (Industrialization and Supervisors). Tokyo: Japan Institute of Labor, 1966.

————, and Matsumoto, Shizo. "Seichō Sangyō ni okeru Nijū Kōzō to Rōdō Kanri." (Dual Structure and Labor Administration in Growing Industry), in *Nijū Kōzō no Bunseki* (Analysis of the Dual Structure), Yoshiro Tamanoi (ed.). Tokyo: Tōyō Keizai, 1964.

Ōkochi, Kazuo. *Nihon Rōdō Kumiai Ron* (Discourse on Japanese Labor Unions). Tokyo: Yuhikaku, 1953.

————, et al. *Rōdō Kumiai no Kōzō to Kinō* (The Structure and Functions of Labor Unions). Tokyo: Tokyo University Publishing Association, 1959.

Sumiya, Mikio. "Jidosha Kōgyō" (Automobile Industry), *Sangyō betsu Chingin Kettei no Kikō* (The Structure of Wage Determination by Industry), Ōkochi Kazuo (ed.). Tokyo: Japan Institute of Labour, 1964.

————. *Nihon Shihon Shugi to Rōdō Mondai* (Japanese Capitalism and Labor Problems). Tokyo: Tokyo University Press, 1967.

————. *Nihon Rōdō Undōshi* (History of the Japanese Labor Movement). Tokyo: Yushindo, 1966.

Takahashi, Ko. *Nihon Rōshi Kankei Kenkyū* (Research on Japanese Type Labor-Management Relations). Tokyo: Miraisha, 1965.

Tokyo City Economic Bureau. *Tōkyō ni okeru Daikasuto Sangyō no Jittai Bunseki* (Analysis of the Actual Conditions of the Diecast Industry in Tokyo). Tokyo, The Bureau, 1960.

Tominaga, Ken'ichi. "Nihon Shakai to Rōdō Idō," (Japanese Society and Labor Mobility), in *Gijitsu Kakushin to Ningen no Mondai* (Technological Innovation and Human Problems), Odaka Kunio (ed.). Tokyo: Diamond Press, 1964.

Yokoyama, Gennosuke. *Nippon no Kasō Shakai* (Japan's Lower Class Society). Tokyo: Iwanami Shoten, 1948.

INDEX

JAPANESE BLUE COLLAR
The Changing Tradition

By Robert E. Cole

This study probes the interaction between the universal aspects of the industrialization process and the Japanese culture and social structure. Mr. Cole examines the role of tradition among contemporary Japanese blue-collar workers and compares Japanese and Western organizational patterns. His findings shed light on the "convergence" theory that industrial societies become more alike as successively higher stages of industrialization are reached and as national identities play an increasingly restricted role.

Mr. Cole lived for a year in a Tokyo factory neighborhood, becoming acquainted with Japanese workers and formally interviewing many of them. For more than four months he studied their behavior while employed as a blue-collar worker in a Tokyo diecast plant and in a rural auto-parts factory. His book therefore represents a rare application of the participation-observation method to the analysis of a foreign culture. To place his first-hand experience in a meaningful context, he studied existing research data